About Island Press

Island Press, a nonprofit organization, publishes, markets, and distributes the most advanced thinking on the conservation of our natural resources—books about soil, land, water, forests, wildlife, and hazardous and toxic wastes. These books are practical tools used by public officials, business and industry leaders, natural resource managers, and concerned citizens working to solve both local and global resource problems.

Founded in 1978, Island Press reorganized in 1984 to meet the increasing demand for substantive books on all resource-related issues. Island Press publishes and distributes under its own imprint and offers these services to other nonprofit organizations.

Support for Island Press is provided by The Geraldine R. Dodge Foundation, The Energy Foundation, The Charles Engelhard Foundation, The Ford Foundation, Glen Eagles Foundation, The George Gund Foundation, William and Flora Hewlett Foundation, The James Irvine Foundation, The John D. and Catherine T. MacArthur Foundation, The Andrew W. Mellon Foundation, The Joyce Mertz-Gilmore Foundation, The New-Land Foundation, The Pew Charitable Trusts, The Rockefeller Brothers Fund, The Tides Foundation, and individual donors.

About the Rails-to-Trails Conservancy

The mission of the Rails-to-Trails Conservancy (RTC) is to enhance America's communities and countrysides by converting thousands of miles of abandoned rail corridors, and connecting open space, into a nationwide network of public trails.

Established in 1985, the Rails-to-Trails Conservancy is a national nonprofit public charity with more than fifty thousand members. In addition to a staff of twenty based in Washington, D.C., RTC has six staffed chapter offices in Florida, Illinois, Michigan, Ohio, Pennsylvania, and Washington State.

The Rails-to-Trails Conservancy notifies trail advocates and local governments of upcoming railroad abandonments; assists public and private agencies in the legalities of trail corridor acquisition; provides technical assistance to private citizens as well as trail planners, designers, and managers on trail design, development, and protection; and publicizes rails-to-trails issues throughout the country.

For additional information or membership information, contact the Rails-to-Trails Conservancy at 1400 Sixteenth Street, N.W., Suite 300, Washington, D.C. 20036, or call (202) 797-5400.

TRAILS FOR THE TWENTY-FIRST CENTURY

TRAILS FOR THE TWENTY-FIRST CENTURY

Planning, Design, and Management Manual for Multi-Use Trails

Edited by Karen-Lee Ryan

Charles A. Flink, Peter Lagerwey, Diana Balmori, and Robert M. Searns

Rails-to-Trails Conservancy

Washington, D.C. ■ Covelo, California

This publication was developed in cooperation with the National Park Service.

Illustrations by Balmori Associates
Design: Robert Barkin and Carlos Alexandre

ISLAND PRESS is a trademark of The Center for Resource Economics.

Library of Congress Cataloging-in-Publication Data

Trails for the twenty-first century: planning, design, and management
     manual for multi-use trails / edited by Karen-Lee Ryan.
          p.   cm.
     Includes bibliographical references (p.) and index.
     ISBN 1-55963-237-2   — ISBN 1-55963-238-0 (pbk.)
     1. Trails — United States — Planning. 2. Trails — United States — Design.
I. Ryan, Karen-Lee.
GV 191.4.T73   1993
796.5'0973 — dc20   93-8433
                                                     CIP

Printed on recycled, acid-free paper

Manufactured in the United States of America
10 9 8 7 6 5 4 3 2

About the Authors

KAREN-LEE RYAN is Director of Publications for the Rails-to-Trails Conservancy. She oversees the development, production and marketing of more than a dozen trail-related publications and serves as editor of RTC's quarterly newsletter. She has conducted numerous presentations at conferences in the United States and Canada and coordinated a traveling seminar series for RTC. She has been on the Board of Directors of the Coalition for the Capital Crescent Trail since 1989, serving as Board Chair from 1991-1992. She received a degree in journalism from Indiana University.

CHARLES A. FLINK, President of Greenways Incorporated in Cary, N.C., is a registered landscape architect. He has personally planned or designed more than 300 miles of greenways in the eastern United States, and he has worked on international greenway projects in Toronto and Tokyo. He has also lectured on greenways at international conferences in Canada and Venezuela. He is co-author of *Greenways: A Practical Guide to Planning, Design and Management* (published by Island Press),

served three terms as Board Chair for American Trails, and is a member of the North Carolina Greenways Advisory Panel. He graduated with honors from North Carolina State University, where he now serves as an adjunct professor.

PETER LAGERWEY is the Bicycle and Pedestrian Coordinator for the City of Seattle. He also works as a consultant for state and local governments involved in the planning, development and promotion of bicycle/pedestrian projects and programs. This includes training planners and engineers, developing local bicycle/pedestrian plans, creating trail master plans and conducting research projects. He has served as Chair of the Transportation Research Board Committee on Bicycling. He received a master's in planning from the University of Michigan.

DIANA BALMORI is Principal for Design at Balmori Associates, Inc. and a Visiting Critic at the Yale University Schools of Architecture and Forestry. Her work on Connecticut's Farmington Canal Rail-Trail won the AIA/ASLA Public Space Award in

1990 and will be exhibited at the Museum of Contemporary Art in Los Angeles in 1994. She has been widely published and exhibited. Her latest works include *Transitory Gardens (the Gardens of the Homeless)* with photographer Margaret Morton, and *The American Lawn: A Search for Environmental Harmony,* co-authored with F. Herbert Bormann and Gordon Geballe.

ROBERT M. SEARNS, AICP, owns Urban Edges, Inc., a design/planning firm based in Denver that specializes in trails and greenways. He was Project Director of Denver's Platte River Greenway and developed the award-winning Arapahoe Greenway. Among his other projects, he created "10,000 Trees!"—a volunteer river corridor revegetation project—and developed a non-motorized transportation plan for Missoula, Montana. He has written articles for several publications including *Landscape Architecture Magazine* and has conducted workshops in the United States, Canada and Russia. He is co-author of *Greenways: A Practical Guide to Planning, Design and Management.*

Contents

Foreword

Imagine a vast network of trails across the nation connecting our city centers to the countryside and countless communities to one another . . . a network linking neighborhoods to workplaces and congested areas to open spaces . . . a system serving transportation needs and meeting the demand for close-to-home recreation.

This is not a fantasy. It is a vision of a future national trail system endorsed by the Rails-to-Trails Conservancy, the National Park Service, and other sponsors of *Trails for the Twenty-first Century.* Our common goal is the creation of a nation-wide network of multi-use trails—local, regional, and national systems—that allow walkers, bicyclists, people with disabilities, equestrians, runners, skiers, hikers, and others to enjoy the beauty of the American landscape.

What will this national trail system look like? Public and private trail advocates include the following characteristics in such a system:

- ▶ Trails within fifteen minutes of every household
- ▶ Trails for *everybody,* not a single user group, age group, or fitness group

- ▶ Federal, state, local, and private trails, all interconnected to form a continuous system
- ▶ Trails that become part of our nation's infrastructure—as important to community health as roads, streets, and utility corridors—and form the backbone of alternative transportation systems for both urban and rural America
- ▶ Trails built through *local* effort, yet tied together through regional and national coordination
- ▶ Trails that highlight and preserve the natural features and cultural heritage of America while providing access to some very special places, such as rivers and streams, historical structures, railroad and canal routes, and cultural institutions

But trails don't just happen. They take hard work. *Trails for the Twenty-first Century* is intended to help those planning, designing, and managing multi-use trails on the local, regional, or statewide level. It will guide you through a step-by-step process to maximize the potential of your trail or trail system. It provides advice on how to

work with landowners, other managing or funding agencies at several levels of government, citizen groups, architects, lawyers, engineers, historians, and naturalists—all the people you will need to develop your trail system. It also offers suggestions on how to obtain volunteer help and explains how to protect your trail from encroachment, development, and other outside threats after it is built.

Trails for the Twenty-first Century is long overdue; trail advocates and managers have been calling for such a guide for years. We salute all the authors of this book working under the direction of Karen-Lee Ryan for their valuable contributions and knowledge of multi-use trail development and management. The information in this book, combined with the deep commitment of trail volunteers and advocates, will help turn today's vision of a national trail system into a reality early in the twenty-first century.

David G. Burwell, President,
Rails-to-Trails Conservancy
William T. Spitzer, Chief, Recreation Resources Assistance Division,
National Park Service

TRAILS
FOR THE
TWENTY-FIRST
CENTURY

Multi-Use Trails as a New Kind of Space

A new kind of public space is making its appearance across the country. The time has come to announce its arrival and to begin its formal planning, design, and management.

As thousands of miles of abandoned railroad corridors, former canals, and other unused transportation routes are converted into multi-use trails nationwide, it is imperative to recognize their unique qualities. Multi-use trails are a modern public space unlike any other, and they must be designed in a way that takes full advantage of their unusual characteristics. The linear corridors from which multi-use trails are formed are generally flat and frequently run along rivers and streams. Because of the continuous, linear nature of these corridors, they link abundant resources to each other. In addition, the corridors played an important part in American history.

Railroads and canals, which at one time connected every small town and large city, stimulated industrial growth and rapid development throughout the nation. Unfortunately, new technology has forced a decline in the use of these systems, but recycling them into multi-use trails offers the ideal solution: Not only does it save an extensive and irreplaceable corridor system through diverse landscapes, but it also preserves a significant portion of this country's heritage. The "newness" of multi-use trails is in fact a reflection of the old, of history—and they should be designed with this in mind.

Without an awareness of what distinguishes these "linear parks" from other public spaces, there is a risk that they will be treated in a mechanical, uniform fashion. Plunking down an asphalt path with a few signs and dubbing the result a multi-use trail ignores the wealth of possibilities that each trail can offer. Unlike backcountry hiking trails or designated bike routes, multi-use trails invite various users—including walkers, joggers, bicyclists, people in wheelchairs, cross-country skiers, equestrians, and others—to share a trail corridor collectively. Planners, designers, and managers of multi-use trails need to take into account the assorted needs of these different users as well as the various communities and landscapes through which the trails pass.

One of the last, great public space innovations was the "American park" designed by Frederick Law Olmsted, who saw it as a vehicle for democracy. His vision called for a tranquil refuge from the crowded, concrete city, an urban park where rich and poor alike could escape the crush of people to an untouched nature. It is a testament to Olmsted's idea that after almost a century his parks, which include New York's Central Park, Boston's "Emerald Necklace," and the National Zoo in Washington, D.C., are still among the most popular public spaces in America.

Today, trail supporters can engender a renewed vision of what public space is and can be. The network of multi-use trails continues to grow exponentially because millions of people enjoy them so much. These trails owe their broad appeal to the diverse roles they play and the various needs they fill for different communities.

Recreation and Transportation

For many communities, a multi-use trail serves as a close-to-home recreational area that can accommodate a range of users including equestrians, walkers, bicyclists, joggers, cross-country skiers, roller and in-line skaters, people in wheelchairs, hikers, birdwatchers, parents with strollers, snow-mobilers, and anglers (figure I.1).

Coupled with these recreational uses is the functional role of virtually all multi-use trails. Whether used for a shortcut to a local library or for a 20-mile bicycle commute into a major metropolitan area, these trails serve an important transportation purpose. Because of their linear nature and previous uses, multi-use trails connect things together—neighborhoods to community and cultural resources (libraries, schools, businesses, museums, shops), small towns to metropolitan areas, and city centers to countrysides—intrinsically serving as transportation corridors. Urban pathways are often heralded as playing a key role in alternative transportation, but many short trails (even in rural areas) offer numerous transportation opportunities. In fact, many municipalities are realizing that the time has come to develop multi-use corridors that offer routes for nonpolluting methods of transportation, which can reduce congestion, promote energy conservation, and improve air quality. These factors, in tandem with a growing number of nearby recreational opportunities, can enhance the quality of life for local residents.

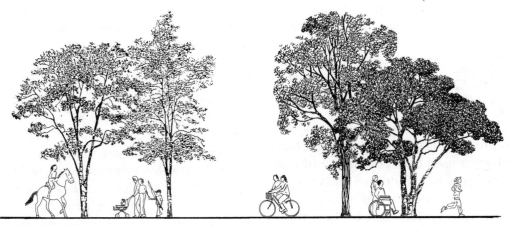

Figure I.1: Multi-use trail.

Open Space Preservation and Ecology

Trail corridors preserve open space. In some urban areas, a trail created from an abandoned rail corridor may be the *only* open space left to preserve (figure I.2). The linear nature of a trail may be one way to offer green parklike space to people who cannot gain easy access to traditional, faraway blocks of open space.

Preserving linear corridors also creates a refuge for wildlife and native plants. The multi-use trail's long and narrow form can be used as a corridor for wildlife species to move across the landscape. The use of hedgerows, a particularly appropriate planting for a linear park, can provide much-needed cover and protection for birds, small mammals, and other wildlife. Hedges and other plantings for wildlife food and shelter can also promote the growth of a broad range of plants near the trail by sheltering seeds in birds' droppings, by preserving humidity, and by protecting an area from wind.

Preserving open space for people to enjoy does not necessarily mean the loss of ecological health if sound environmental practices are employed. Some assume that native species can only thrive if a corridor is left "natural." However, few multi-use trails are truly "natural" because their environment has been severely disturbed by their previous uses. Invasive plants, such as poison ivy, usually thrive in such areas because they are capable of sustaining more abuse than many native species are. Typically, native species must be reintroduced if the area is to approximate its "natural" ecology.

Historic Preservation

Many multi-use trail corridors offer unexpected historical riches. Not only do artifacts representing a period of industrialization remain—water towers, switching signals, stations, bridges, and tunnels—but many multi-use trails traverse parts of cities and the countryside that reveal specific eras of industrialization, such as factories housed in brick buildings, and specific eras of agriculture, such as silos and grain elevators adjacent to farms. These structures, and the corridors they occupy, symbolize the history of American industry, engineering, and labor. The construction of railroads, canals, and roads was an enormous industrial feat. Many multi-use trails preserve these artifacts and recognize the achievements of their builders, thus educating users about the routes' histories. The structures, and the stories of those who built them, give the

Figure I.2: Urban trail use.

multi-use trail a "power of place," strengthening a user's understanding of, and connection to, the multi-use trail and its surrounding region.

Neighborhood Development

The current times are marked by human separateness—blacks from whites, rich from poor, urban dwellers from rural residents—creating a de

facto segregation in living zones. Multi-use trails, which typically cut through diverse areas, have the ability to begin stitching these groups together through a common goal of creating a neighborhood amenity. At the same time they can highlight the uniqueness of each community.

The form and location of multi-use trails are the cornerstones of their success. As yesterday's primary transportation corridors, these trails can reconnect residential and industrial areas, cities and farmland, and new immigrant neighborhoods to established ones. And, along the way, a trail can assume each area's individual character and meet specific local needs. In many ways, these multi-use trails become a community's "backyard," where people can get away from the hectic pace of everyday life to spend time with friends and neighbors and enjoy the outdoors in a refreshing environment.

How This Manual Can Help You

Hopefully you already own (or have at least identified) a future multi-use trail corridor. At this point, your goal should be to determine what roles it will play for the communities through which it passes. The trail's roles will be determined by the corridor and its surroundings, the trail's potential users and neighbors, and the capabilities and constraints of your agency or organization.

This manual will help you accomplish this goal and many others. The manual has been developed to guide you through a step-by-step process to plan, design, and manage your trail and to maximize its potential. The information provided here has been culled from the experiences of scores of trail managers and trail enthusiasts across the nation. However, you should remember that these are just *guidelines,* and they pertain only to trail corridors with a history of human use, such as a railroad or canal. Natural corridors—with no prior human use—are outside the scope of this book.

The guidelines presented in this manual should be extremely useful, but they do have limitations. You cannot set parameters for your trail without taking into account your corridor's individual setting. This manual strives to offer a range of possibilities and acceptable alternatives wherever possible. As you plan, design, and manage your multi-use trail, consider all the possibilities and work with local residents and trail neighbors to determine what will ultimately work best in your community.

1

Getting Started

PHYSICAL INVENTORY AND ASSESSMENT OF THE SITE

The first step in creating a multi-use trail is to conduct a physical assessment of the natural resources and constructed ("built") features within the corridor. This includes an accurate description and documentation of the landscape's native elements, the built features of the corridor, the corridor's location in relation to other major natural or developed facilities, and the route or layout of the corridor as it traverses your community, region, or state.

To conduct an assessment, you need to get out on your trail corridor and inventory what you see and how you feel as you move along it. Begin by obtaining large, accurate maps from your local planning agency or from the United States Geological Survey. Select maps that illustrate the known features within and surrounding the corridor (figure 1.1), and plan how to record your findings. Written descriptions, tape-recorded comments, photographs, and video are excellent ways to document your findings.

This assessment will help you understand how all the physical elements

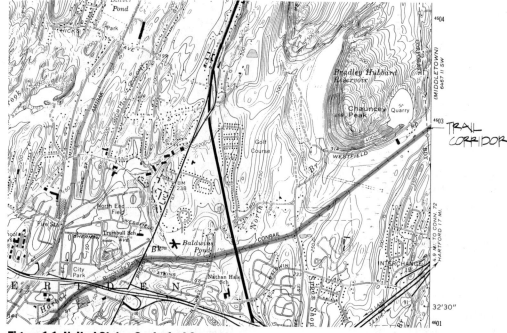

Figure 1.1: United States Geological Survey map.

fit together to shape your trail. As you examine the natural and built elements of the corridor, you will notice areas where trail development is compatible or in conflict with existing resources. Compatible areas require little change to accommodate a trail. Areas of conflict, however, will need creative design resolution, described later in this manual. In other words, you are looking for the physical "opportunities" and "constraints" within the corridor.

Assess the following elements in terms of what opportunities they present or what constraints they pose for development of a multi-use trail.

Natural Features of the Corridor

Begin the actual assessment with an examination of the natural features within and adjacent to the corridor. How might these natural features affect the development of your multi-

11

use trail? How can they be modified, without causing irreparable harm, so that trail development can be accomplished successfully?

■ Existing Vegetation

The more vegetation within the corridor, the more difficult it is to identify which species may pose a problem when you create a trail (figure 1.2). In evaluating the vegetation, define the various plant species (paying particular attention to any endangered or rare species) and record the median heights of trees and shrubs, the age of growth, the type of growth (predominantly deciduous or evergreen), and seasonal qualities—bloom period, fall color, winter foliage. This information will be used later to define landscape modifications and additions that should be made to your completed multi-use trail (see "Landscaping" in chapter 3).

A trail corridor contains two vegetative edges, the lengthwise sides of the trail. After clearing and trail development have occurred, it is often the aggressive, weedy species that initially grow back along these edges. This growth can affect a trail: The aggressive root systems often migrate into the trail's subsurface, with limbs and

Photo: Enid Hodes

Figure 1.2: Overgrown corridor.

leaves growing toward the corridor's open space, where air movement and sunlight are unobstructed. Therefore, you should determine the growth rate, water, sunlight, and temperature requirements for each major invasive plant group along your corridor.

Look for those plants that appear most invasive or dominant in the corridor. If you cannot identify a particular plant, collect samples of leaves and take them to a botanist or horticulturist for proper assessment. Determine whether the growth rates of weedy plants within the corridor will affect future trail use. If so, you will need to design the trail to avoid these plants or prescribe landscape management treat-

ments to ensure that the vegetation does not hamper safety along the trail.

Sometimes the existing vegetation along a former rail corridor is the only species capable of surviving. Investigate whether railroad companies or local transportation agencies sprayed growth retardants or poisons to reduce leaf mass or exterminate naturally occurring vegetation. If so, the vegetation that led to these practices may still be present. Will roots eventually come through the surface and damage the trail? Assess the overall health, growth habit, and long-term impact of these plants on your corridor.

■ Surrounding Topography

The corridor's surface reflects the dynamics of the local landscape and its geology. The composition of bedrock and soils provides the structure for the landform, be it mountainous, gently rolling, or flat. Grades and slopes can affect future trail development, so you will need to determine the slope, or gradient, within the corridor.

An accurate assessment of surrounding topography should be done to define the type of drainage controls needed to facilitate safe multi-use trail development. The surrounding topography or slopes affect the amount of surface water flowing into and through the corridor, so you need to know where off-site water collects and drains through the corridor. If necessary, employ the services of a hydrologist, engineer, landscape architect, or land surveyor to help you properly assess the drainage patterns through the corridor. Controlling surface water is the most important aspect of trail design and development.

■ Adjacent or Intersecting Streams
Streams and rivers present the most challenges to proper drainage within the corridor. The first step is to find out whether the corridor is within a flood-prone area. Where is it parallel to or intersected by water courses? Are they likely to damage the trail corridor when in flood? This helps to determine whether you should develop the trail on existing natural grade or whether you will need to build a bridge or boardwalk to cross a flood-prone area.

If you are dealing with a relatively undisturbed abandoned rail corridor, it is likely that the railroad developers handled most hydrological problems. However, if some of the culverts or drains were modified or became

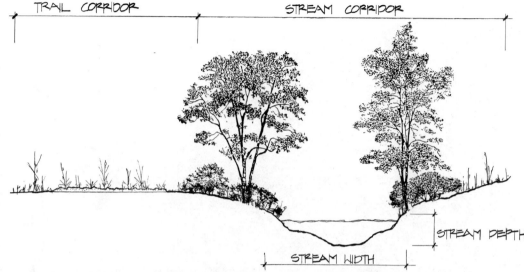

Figure 1.3: Stream running parallel to trail corridor.

plugged, or if the track area was severely modified, removed, or filled in, you may have some flooding problems.

If a corridor has no bridges and crosses a stream, your next step is to determine the stream's width from top of bank to top of bank. Also, measure the depth of the stream from top of bank to bottom of the channel, and locate the stream's origin. Find out the adjacent land uses upstream from the crossing to determine whether the stream is classified as urban or rural. This information will be used later

when you design the appropriate stream crossing for your trail.

Perform a similar analysis for adjacent streams (figure 1.3). You need to know if and when an adjacent stream may flood and how serious an impact a flood would have on the trail corridor. If possible, determine the velocity and volume of the stream. The U.S. Army Corps of Engineers and Federal Emergency Management Agency can provide you with information from section 404 of the Clean Water Act to help you evaluate stream crossings.

Photo: Mary Eads

Figure 1.4: A bridge over the Kansas River, formerly operated by Atchinson, Topeka and Santa Fe.

Built Features within the Corridor

Built features along the corridor are usually significant and largely utilitarian: a bridge across a river, a tunnel through a mountain, or a power substation. Other built structures, like abandoned railroad depots, whistle posts, and defunct mills, may no longer be used but are objects of cultural and historic interest.

To evaluate the integrity of these structures, employ a qualified structural engineer or architect with historic structure experience. Do not evaluate buildings yourself—the potential legal liability is enormous. To help assess the structures' historic significance, seek out a historian or registered architect.

Consider the following questions for each structure: What is its dominant characteristic? How old is it? Given its current condition, can it safely support future trail use? Is it accessible to people with disabilities? What modifications are needed so that the structure remains an asset for trail use? When you have answered these questions, you can decide which structures should be incorporated into the trail's development and which should be removed.

Stream access is another major issue to consider when conducting your assessment. Where are existing access points? Interesting views? Fishing and swimming spots? Canoe or boat launch and recovery? Where can new ones be placed? Can land- and water-based trail activities be integrated?

■ Significant Natural Features
Lakes and ponds, rock outcroppings, wetlands, or other natural features in your region are important attractions. In completing your evaluation, note the size, shape, location, and other aspects of these features. Are they accessible to the public? Will public use result in their deterioration? Your answers should define the value of these features to the overall character of your multi-use trail. Often, significant natural features are the highlights of a trail, but they also can be developmental constraints.

■ Bridges

Your corridor may have one bridge or several (figure 1.4). The structural engineer you employ to evaluate each bridge should inspect the footings or piers that support it, the bridge's superstructure, and its approaches. You should obtain a certified report from your engineer describing the bridge's current condition and what is needed to bring the bridge into compliance with local, state, and federal laws. Remind your structural engineer that the live load for future trail use will be substantially less than that which the bridge was built to support. Reducing the live-load rating can result in a different evaluation of the bridge's capacity and capability. This information will be important when you actually begin designing your bridges for trail use (see "Bridges for Multi-Use Trails" in chapter 3).

■ Tunnels

These are complicated and unique structures. Most were originally constructed to meet site-specific requirements. If possible, locate the tunnel's original engineering drawings. These will describe significant structural features of the tunnel that are not readily

Photo: Wilma Frey

Figure 1.5: A preserved canal lock along the Delaware and Raritan Canal State Park in New Jersey.

apparent from visual inspection. Again, as with bridges, obtain a certified report from a structural engineer describing the current condition of the tunnel. This information will help you make sure your tunnel can be successfully adapted for trail design (see "Tunnels" in chapter 3).

■ Canals

A variety of materials have been used to construct locks and canals. A canal's structural integrity is dependent on the material used in construction and on the settling or shifting of the earth that surrounds the structure. Core samples of the soil mass behind these structures are as important as the evaluation of the joints and mass of the walls, channel bottom, and locks (figure 1.5). Again, obtain a certified report from a qualified structural engineer describing the canal's condition and its working and nonworking components.

■ Buildings

Buildings that were developed during your corridor's previous uses are historically significant and offer diverse opportunities for trail development (figure 1.6). Since a building may have historic value, utilitarian value, or both, an evaluation is best made by a qualified historian or architect. A structural engineer, architect, or local building inspector must perform a structural evaluation of a building's foundation, framing, walls, stairways, windows, doors, roof, and other building components to determine whether

Figure 1.6: Historic buildings.

the building can be integrated safely into the completed trail.

In addition to evaluating the integrity of buildings, give some thought to possible trail-related adaptations you can make. For example, what will an industrial building look like as a snack shop, restaurant, or bike shop? Can a building within the corridor be converted into a trail visitor center? (See figures 1.7 and 1.8.) If your corridor is a former rail line, talk with a railroad history buff for insight into the building's historic significance and its possible functions. Contact local historical societies and also railroad and canal historical societies that may have special insight into the significance of corridor-related structures.

■ Other Related Structures and Facilities

These include mechanical devices associated with the corridor's prior use—millstones from a flour mill, fences built as a boundary, railroad switches, and other facilities adjacent to the corridor. Note the location, size, former purpose, and current status of these structures and facilities and determine whether they are opportunities for or constraints on your trail design.

Infrastructure

Infrastructure includes built elements that provide specific services, such as roads; gas, water, and sewer lines; and electrical, telephone, and cable television wires. Document infrastructure elements that are within the corridor, that run parallel to it, or that cross it (figure 1.9). Some of these services, like drinking water lines, sewer lines, and telephone wires, may be incorporated into the trail design to serve its users.

Figure 1.7: An abandoned, derelict building can be converted into a trail visitor center or ranger station.

Photo: Leona K. Jensen

Figure 1.8: A restored building along the Baltimore and Annapolis Trail in Maryland.

Photo: Sharon Alfinito

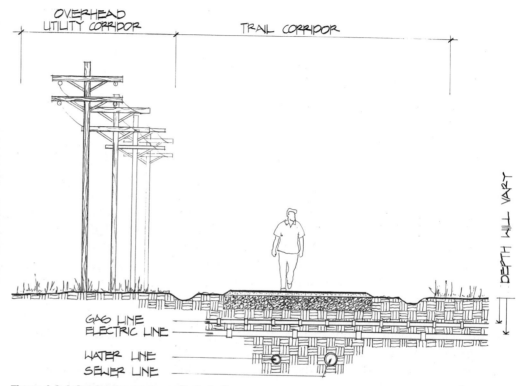

Figure 1.9: Infrastructure surrounding a trail.

When evaluating each infrastructure element, consider the following: What is the origin and destination of the service? What is its present capacity and likely future expansion? How does the location of the infrastructure element relate to the potential trail? This information will enable you to understand the compatibility of or conflict between existing or proposed utilities and your multi-use trail project. Evaluate the following infrastructure elements:

■ Utilities

Water, sanitary sewers, and electrical and telephone lines may be useful on your trail. Are these utilities already

17

present within the corridor? If so, are they capable of supporting additional use? Who operates the utilities? What is required to provide local connections for trail use?

Certain utility equipment, such as natural-gas pipelines and high-voltage electrical lines, can pose a formidable challenge to trail development. A utility-locating service can accurately determine the route and depth of these and other potentially hazardous utilities, so you can appropriately plan, design, and develop your trail around them. Do not underestimate the importance of this step! A utility investigation on a recent trail project in Colorado revealed a major fiber-optic line buried just 2 inches below an area to be regraded as a trail. Such lines cannot be simply spliced if broken—the consequences can be devastating.

Finally, when considering utilities, note not only the potential conflicts but the potential mutual benefits and economic opportunities of joint corridor use (see "Joint Ventures within Your Multi-Use Trail Corridor" in chapter 2).

Locate nearby utilities and services that are not available within the corridor itself. If potable water lines, sanitary sewers, storm water drains, and electrical and telephone services are nearby, perhaps they can be adapted for trail use.

Animal Life within the Corridor

Corridors cut through the habitat of a variety of domesticated and wild animals. In evaluating the corridor, try to quantify and describe the different types of animal life present in or adjacent to the corridor (100 feet on each side of the trail corridor). Also take note of all animal crossings and the frequency with which they are used. This information will help you determine your trail's route. For example, if your investigation shows that the nesting area for a wildlife species will be permanently disturbed by nearby trail development, you will want to reroute the trail to avoid this environmentally sensitive area (see "Wildlife and Multi-Use Trails" in chapter 3).

■ Domesticated Animals or Livestock

Catalog the domesticated animals and livestock you encounter and describe their habitat—meadow, cultivated field, natural forest, and so forth.

Also make note of any existing livestock crossings (figure 1.10), and talk with farmers and ranchers about their needs with respect to the corridor and trail development. Does the trail cut across two pastures? Will cattle crossings take place along the corridor? Are appropriate gates in place? How permanent or temporary are these animal populations? Will they pose any danger to future trail users?

■ Wildlife

Numerous species of birds, mammals, reptiles, and insects occupy the vegetated edges and adjacent lands of corridors in rural and urban landscapes. Seek professional assistance to identify wildlife within the corridor. In completing your wildlife evaluation, understand the potential impact of a

Figure 1.10: Livestock crossing.

Figure 1.11: A blue heron nesting area is located in a wetlands area adjacent to the West Bloomfield Trail Network in West Bloomfield, Michigan.

trail on wildlife nesting, breeding, and migratory habits (figure 1.11). Note particular wildlife that may be harmful to trail users, and vice versa. Look for ways in which trail development may improve a wildlife habitat.

■ Endangered or Rare Species
Because of the accelerating loss of ecologically sensitive species, it is important for you to use extreme care to identify species threatened by human activity. Note any endangered or rare species that exists in the area, identify potential threats to that species, and investigate trail routing or development options that would eliminate or minimize those threats.

Corridor Composition

In many transportation and utility corridors the corridor's original surface has been altered significantly. The alterations can make it difficult to determine slopes, soil composition, and texture of the corridor surface. If your corridor has been altered, you should analyze its surface and subsurface materials to determine their composition and structural integrity.

■ Composition
This refers to the materials that were used to form the subsurface and surface of the corridor. The composition of railroad beds, for example, includes ballast stone and, in certain cases, a surface-washed stone. A structural engineer and a geotechnical testing laboratory can properly identify these materials and their integrity.

■ Cross Section
This is the slope across the corridor perpendicular to the path of travel. You will most likely encounter four types of cross section as you evaluate your corridor: convex (or raised bed), flat, concave (or carved-out bed), and terraced (or along a side slope) (figures 1.12–1.15). Determine where each type of cross section is located within your corridor. How will this slope affect drainage along the corridor? Will the slopes prevent anyone from using the trail?

In evaluating the four cross-section types, you will want to look at surface drainage features and at the physical landscapes surrounding the corridor. Determine the degree of change, "rise," that occurs over a measured surface distance, "run." As a general rule, an acceptable cross slope for most trails is 2 percent (figure 1.16).

■ Longitudinal Slope
This is the slope that runs along the center line of the path of travel, often called the profile. For most transportation corridors, the longitudinal slope is generally flat to gently rolling (3 percent), depending on the type of prior use the corridor served. Railroad beds

Figure 1.12: Convex (raised) cross section.

Figure 1.13: Flat cross section.

Figure 1.14: Concave (carved out) cross section.

Figure 1.15: Terraced cross section.

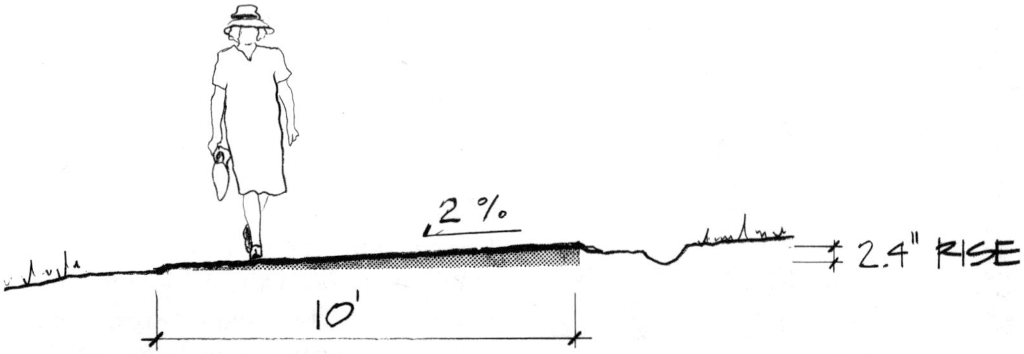

Figure 1.16: Preferred cross slope.

were almost always constructed with flat longitudinal grades. In evaluating the longitudinal slopes of your corridor, you will encounter three types: uphill slopes, flat slopes, and downhill slopes. To evaluate these slopes, you must determine the percentage of longitudinal slope. Generally, an acceptable, accessible longitudinal slope is less than 5 percent (figure 1.17).

Spatial Values of the Trail Corridor Landscape

The sequence of different landscapes that compose a trail corridor makes it an interesting place to walk, bike, and ride. As you evaluate your trail corridor, pay particular attention to the spatial components of its environment.

■ Viewsheds

Lines of sight within a corridor or out to a landscape or adjacent built feature are called viewsheds. Evaluate the view not only from the proposed trail, but also the view *from* adjacent lands *into* the corridor. Doing this is particularly important when you have a feature that should be highlighted, or when an adjacent landowner objects to the view of the trail.

There are two viewshed issues of concern to future trail users. The first is safety: the need for an unobstructed forward and rear view at all times. Following are the minimum acceptable sight distances: pedestrians, 50 linear feet each way; equestrians, 100 linear feet each way; bicyclists, 150 linear feet each way; snowmobilers, 400 linear feet each way (figure 1.18).

The second important viewshed issue is the need for trail users to see their surroundings, preferably wide views of the natural and built features of adjacent landscapes. Because view-sheds from the trail affect the quality of users' experience, you may consider creating view opportunities, even constructing an observation tower if your corridor is flat and potentially "boring."

■ Light and Dark Areas

These are determined by sun exposure, topography, surrounding vegetation, and adjacent structures. Light and dark areas alter the trail's environment, offering respite or energy for the user; they also affect the soil's moisture content, influence temperature, and vary the visual quality of the trail's features. Ideally, an assessment of light and dark areas should be made during different seasons and at various times of the day. Since your time is undoubtedly limited, try this: On your initial examination note areas of extreme light and dark, and assess them again at midday on your next visit, paying particular attention to soil moisture content, growth rate of

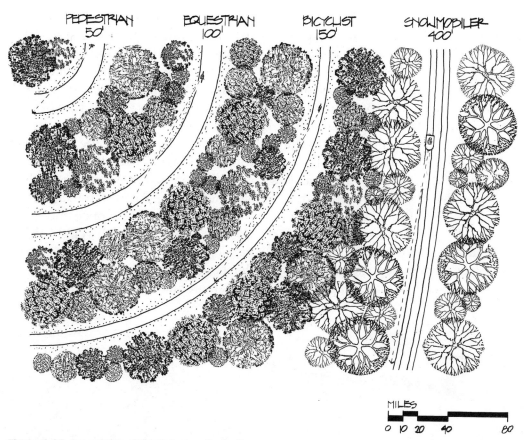

Figure 1.18: Acceptable sight distances for trail users.

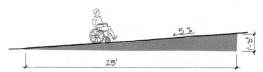

Figure 1.17: Maximum longitudinal slopes.

surrounding vegetation, amount of sunlight, and approximate sun angle. After compiling this data, characterize areas of the corridor on a scale from dark to light, depending on your observations. The ideal from a user's perspective is a mixture of light and dark areas.

■ Open or Closed Landscapes

These affect viewsheds and light, provide structure, and heavily influ-

21

ence the spatial sequence of a route's environment. Whether a landscape is open or closed is most often defined by vegetation, although topography and built structures can also be determinants. An example of an open landscape is an agricultural field or naturally occurring meadow (figure 1.19). A closed landscape may be a segment of the corridor surrounded by thick, overhanging vegetation, which creates a tunnel effect (figure 1.20).

To understand the importance of these landscapes, view the mass and voids of the corridor landscape, rather than the individual components making up the landscape. Does a series of steep slopes and overhanging trees create an unsettling "tunnel" effect over the trail? Does the trail corridor have extensive stretches that are void of vegetation?

Open or closed landscapes affect the trail user's experience and should be carefully considered when you are designing the trail. An ideal trail has a contrasting sequence of open and closed landscapes as well as light and dark areas (figure 1.21). Once you understand the spatial sequence of the trail environment, you can alter it or

Figure 1.20: Closed landscape.

leave it intact to provide trail users with a satisfying trail experience.

Intersections

Intersections can pose challenges during trail design and development, but they also can provide trail access. There are many types of intersections, and if you evaluate them properly you

Figure 1.19: Open landscape.

can incorporate them successfully into your trail design.

■ Roadways

Roads are the most hazardous and frequently encountered trail intersection. Consider how the trail will cross the road: at grade, below grade, or overhead. Is the traffic on the road too heavy to prevent a safe at-grade crossing? Is an alternative crossing located nearby? Determine how wide the trail should be and what is needed to make an adequate crossing. How much money is available to do the work? These answers will enable you to design appropriate and safe road crossings (see "Road Crossings" in chapter 3).

■ Active Rail or Canal Routes

Existing transportation routes crossing trails present a unique situation. These rights-of-way often are difficult to cross because their owners fear the liability associated with public access. Determine the activity associated with the rail or canal (for example, spur line, mainline industrial, or passenger service) and assess the quality of the surface, tracks, and structures within the rail bed or canal. Examine all available options for de-

Figure 1.21: Mix of open and closed landscapes.

veloping a safe intersection, including the possibility of going over or under the existing right-of-way.

■ Driveways

These may be residential, commercial, or industrial access points to prop-

erties adjacent to the trail corridor. Determine the type of driveway and the frequency of use on a daily or monthly basis. If the traffic on the driveway is less than anticipated trail traffic, then the trail should be designed to have the right-of-way at this intersection.

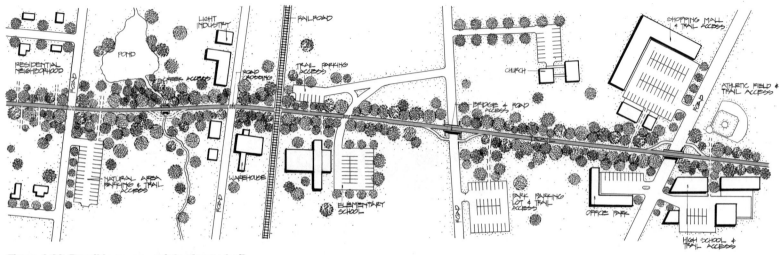

Figure 1.22: Possible access points along a trail.

■ Other Trail Corridors

Nearby trails allow you to link trails together. Assess any intersecting trails for compatibility and conflict, based on types of use, surface, signs, and regulations.

Access Points

It is important to take stock of all access points located within the corridor (figure 1.22). This assessment should include both vehicular and pedestrian access to and through the corridor. Vehicular access should take into account all forms of motorized and nonmotorized vehicles—cars, mass transit, and bicycles. Determine the impact of these access routes on your corridor. Do roads cause trail-crossing problems? Will it be possible for mass transit riders to access the trail easily? In addition to existing access points, where will new ones need to be located?

A proper assessment includes the type of access route—ranging from bicycle path to residential street to interstate highway—the route's capacity, its location in relation to the corridor, and its potential to serve as a trailhead. A potential trailhead should have space for parking and possibly offer services. Where are the major barriers to such access, and can they be overcome?

Pedestrian access includes all pathways, walks, or trails that intersect or lie adjacent to the corridor. To determine the type of pedestrian way, ask yourself if it is a footpath for local use or a regional hiking trail. What is its capacity and time of greatest use? Finally, how does it connect with your multi-use trail?

Using Your Assessment

After completing this assessment you should understand the constraints and opportunities, compatibilities, and conflicts present within and surrounding your corridor. The information you have collected, evaluated, and assembled during this analysis will be used throughout the design process, so store it in an easily accessible location. The conclusions of your evaluation—in conjunction with a cultural assessment—will serve as the starting point for designing your multi-use trail.

❖

CULTURAL ASSESSMENT OF SURROUNDING COMMUNITIES

Now that you have completed a physical inventory of the trail corridor, it is time to look at the community in which the trail will exist. The trail corridor will not function in a vacuum—a variety of individuals, businesses, and government agencies will have an interest in what happens along the way.

The corridor has a past: The people who came before left their imprint. The corridor also has a future. How will the trail be regarded by the users, by the people responsible for operating and maintaining it, and by the owners of adjacent properties?

It will be important to develop good relationships with all those who hold a stake in the trail corridor. You will be talking with a variety of people as you carry out your "cultural assessment." As you talk with them, try to be sensitive to the corridor's history, its politics, and its community character.

Community Character

Understanding the character of the people living and working along the trail corridor is essential for the success of the project. Most likely several communities and neighborhoods lie along the corridor, and they may vary significantly in character and type, combining rural areas, urban centers, suburban communities, and industrial zones. Consider the following critical elements when evaluating each distinct locale:

■ Socioeconomic Profile

What kinds of people live along the corridor? Is the area rural, suburban, or urban? Are the people high-income, low-income, professional, or blue collar? Are they highly mobile, or have they lived there for generations? Are the residents elderly, middle aged, or young families in starter homes?

For demographic information consult local planning agencies. Also consider reading recent U.S. Census reports and visiting areas to get a feel for the people and the neighborhoods. Meeting some local people and talking with shopkeepers will probably provide much of the information you need. Prepare a map showing the various neighborhoods, communities, and enclaves along the corridor. And keep written notes documenting the character, concerns, and perspectives of the people in each area.

■ Community Aspirations and Fears

Try to get a sense of how the people along the corridor view their neighborhood or community and how they see the trail fitting into their long-range objectives. How will the trail benefit them? Do they want access? If so, where? Be sure you are aware of and understand any community fears and concerns about the trail.

Some information can be gleaned during site visits along the trail and through informal talks with local residents and business people. Your presentations at community forums and workshops will also elicit local support and concerns. You will be gathering information throughout the assessment and public participation process (see "Public Involvement" in chapter 2).

Recreational Needs

"If you build it, they will come!" Or will they? Like any major capital undertaking, building a trail requires some thought about how the facility will be used and by whom. In other words, you need to market the trail. Marketing is the craft of determining the demand for a product, making the public aware of the product, and packaging the product for public consumption. In the case of trails, parks, and other public amenities where tax dollars are involved, marketing takes on an additional dimension—the political dimension. Many taxpayers may never use the trail but must sanction the project or, at least, not put roadblocks in its way.

■ Market Demand Investigation
There are several ways to assess the demand for your trail:

▶ Contact your state's department of natural resources (or equivalent agency), which is required to complete a "State Comprehensive Outdoor Recreation Plan" (SCORP)

approximately every five years. This publication often will document trail user demand.

▶ Determine the ratio of existing trail miles to the user population in the communities along the corridor. Compare this to the National Recreation and Park Association's "Open Space Standards," which suggest a ratio of 1 trail mile per 2,000 people for bicycling/jogging trails. (This number is intended only as a rough guideline and does not necessarily reflect local demographics, changing trends, uniqueness of the trail corridor, or myriad other factors. Such data may, however, help you make your case before community decision makers.)

▶ Contact the Rails-to-Trails Conservancy, American Hiking Society, National Park Service, Bicycle Federation of America, United Ski Industries Association, and other groups that may have literature about user trends related to trails. A recent national wire-service article showed that 66.5 million Americans walk for exercise, 59.6 million bicycle, 24.8 million run or

jog, 23.5 million hike, and almost 5 million ski cross-country.

▶ Check data from national opinion polls, which periodically survey participation in trail-related activities. In 1992, Rodale Press sponsored a Harris poll called "Pathways for People," showing that a significant number of Americans already walk, run, and bicycle for fitness, recreation, and commuting, and that even more would if safe and accessible transportation facilities were in place.

▶ Most important, talk with local bicycle, walking, jogging, equestrian, and other groups to determine interest.

■ Packaging the Product
Public acceptance of your trail will depend in large part on how you present it. Consider the full range of potential user groups—bicyclists, hikers, runners, nature enthusiasts, equestrians, in-line skaters, people in wheelchairs, parents with strollers, cross-country skiers, anglers, snowmobilers, students, conservationists, and elderly people. They all are potential trail users—don't leave anyone out.

Think also about your project's benefits to adjacent properties. Will the trail improve property values? Will the trail bring in tourists? Will trail users patronize the shops and restaurants along the corridor? Will the trail provide a much-needed, nonmotorized transportation option? Investigate these potential benefits as part of the planning process.

■ Selling the Product

During the planning process, think about likely supporters and opponents. Make a list of the people, agencies, and groups with a direct interest in the outcome of your effort (user groups, adjacent landowners, government agencies, railroad companies, construction contractors, developers). Another list could include all the potential opponents—people and agencies you must win over to succeed. Some groups, such as landowners and railroad companies, may be on both lists. Throughout the planning process, think about how you can make the plan appeal to both groups.

Historical Considerations

Trail builders and historians make great partners. More often than not trail corridors follow routes steeped in history. Rail lines, canals, and river valleys were the highways of settlement, the first passages for travel, commerce, and enterprise. They are often rich in artifacts and lore, and they offer unique paths to the past if their histories are preserved and interpreted (see "Historic Preservation" in chapter 3).

■ Local History of the Corridor

Most communities have local history books. You can probably ascertain what is available by visiting your local library or historical society. Try to find local rail or canal enthusiasts, and talk with teachers. You might convince a high school class or college student to research the corridor's history as a school project. Meet with adjacent property owners who may have interesting records or anecdotal material.

■ State and National Resources

Contact your state's historic preservation office, which is likely to have statewide historic surveys and knowledgeable contacts throughout your state. Federal programs such as the National Register of Historic Places maintain listings of sites, structures, and objects significant in American history. Consider also the Historic American Engineering Record/Historic American Buildings Survey (HAER/HABS) collection at the Library of Congress, which includes numerous drawings, photographs, and histories. All this information is available to the public.

■ Aesthetically Important Structures and Places

Inventory the artifacts and structures of aesthetic interest along the corridor. Does a retaining wall have especially attractive stonework? Are there old railroad artifacts? Are there historic residences, factories, or other interesting features adjacent to the corridor? Who owns these resources? Can they be safely restored, repainted, or otherwise preserved as a permanent part of the trail experience?

■ Archaeological Elements

Check with local historians and your state archæologist to determine whether any places of archaeological significance exist along the corridor. Consider interpreting archaeological elements and integrating them into your trail.

Political Climate

An inventory of politically oriented groups or agencies with a stake in the corridor is vital to your project's success. Listing these groups and later contacting representatives of each can avoid unpleasant surprises and help build the all-important alliances you will need during the implementation phase. Consider these key groups:

■ Political Jurisdictions

Identify and document all political jurisdictions along the corridor, preferably mapping their boundaries in relation to the trail corridor. Include special districts as well as cities, towns, counties, and states.

■ Local, State, Federal, and Utility
  Agencies

List (and contact) all governmental agencies with a potential interest in your project—they may have review authority. They also may be planning projects such as roads or sewers that will have an impact on your corridor, or they may be a source of potential funding. If applicable, include the U.S. Army Corps of Engineers, Environmental Protection Agency, Interstate Commerce Commission (if a rail-trail is involved), federal and state wildlife agencies, state and local park departments, state and local drainage and flood-control agencies, as well as state and local transportation and highway agencies. Others are possible, of course.

Also list any public or private utility companies that may have an affected interest, including electric companies, irrigation ditch companies, water and sewer utilities, fiber-optic companies, telephone companies, and gas pipeline companies.

■ Landowners and Tenants

Working effectively with adjacent landowners is critical to the success of a trail project. Nothing can hold up a project faster than opposition by adjacent landowners. Get to know them, and find out what they really want and what they care about (see "Meeting the Needs of Adjacent Landowners" in chapter 2).

To identify key landowners, take an inventory of public and private lands. Show rough property lines and, if possible, the names of the owners and information on how to contact them. Tax assessor maps at city hall or the county courthouse will be helpful. While these maps are not always reliable, they are usually sufficient for identifying most of the property owners. Also, be sure to keep in mind renters of land and buildings, even though you probably will not be able to identify all of them.

■ Community Organizations

Identify and list all community organizations with a potential interest in the project. Include recreation clubs (like bicycling, hiking, equestrian, skiing, and snowmobiling clubs), environmental organizations, groups for the elderly and the disabled, historical societies, homeowners' associations, business associations, civic clubs, farmer and farm organizations, educational groups, trade associations—anyone who may have a stake in what you are planning. Involve at least one person from each group in your trail's development. You need the help of these groups for your trail to succeed (see "Public Involvement" in chapter 2).

Adjacent Land Uses—Size, Facilities, Type of Ownership

Research and map the types of adjacent land uses; consider existing and proposed development. Pay special attention to properties directly abutting the corridor. Also, think about the trail's role in linking the following land uses and activity centers and whether they are opportunities for or constraints on trail development:

■ Residential

If possible, identify the type and density of housing near the corridor—single-family, townhouse, low-rise, high-rise, senior housing. Acknowledge any potential privacy or security concerns arising from the trail corridor's use.

■ Commercial

Include offices, theaters, restaurants, and stores, noting likely destination points, such as a shopping mall.

■ Industrial

Identify heavy, medium, and light industrial uses of adjacent land, and note any possible conflicts (figure 1.23). A trail next to a railroad switching yard, for example, could create a potentially hazardous situation if children using the trail were attracted into the rail yard. One midwestern trail passes a chemical plant where highly flammable rocket fuel was once stored. These problems

Photo: Leona K. Jensen

Figure 1.23: A trail corridor that passes four large grain bins is located in an industrial area of Yates County, New York

must be solved with fencing or other security measures, so be sure to document them in your analysis.

■ Recreational

Include important recreational destinations like ball fields, forest preserves, museums, and recreation centers. Certain recreational areas like golf courses can present a potential conflict, so note these as well.

■ Agricultural

The size and kind of agricultural activity are important (figure 1.24). Consider potential conflicts arising from users trespassing on private farms, the use of toxic chemicals, and livestock wandering onto the trail.

■ Institutional

Note schools by type—elementary, middle, high school, and college. Schools can be important destination points, and trail links to schools may go a long way toward helping you sell your project.

■ Vacant Properties and Others

Take special note of vacant properties adjoining the trail corridor. Are any in public ownership, and do they have the potential to be developed as trailside parks or future trailheads? Is any future development planned on large vacant tracts? Do opportunities exist for future trail-related development? Can proposed developments be linked to the trail?

Economic Development Factors

The popularity of multi-use trails has steadily increased, and many trails attract tens of thousands of commuters and recreational users. This growth has benefited adjoining neighborhoods beyond the obvious recreational

Photo: Charles E. Dressler

Figure 1.24: A trail corridor (shown at right) runs through vast tracts of farmland in south-central Ohio.

amenity that these corridors provide. A two-year study of three rail-trails across the country, called "The Impacts of Rail-Trails," concludes that rail-trail users create significant economic activity. Annual income resulting from the trails studied ranged from $1.2 million to $1.9 million. In addition to this "trip-related" revenue, trail users reported

spending considerable amounts on equipment, clothing, and accessories for use on the trail—ranging from $133 to $251 per user each year. Another study, on the 32-mile Elroy-Sparta rail-trail in rural southwestern Wisconsin, shows that each trail user traveling to the trail spends as much as $25 on trip-related expenses (lodging, bicycle rental, food, entertainment), generating more than $1 million per year for the local communities. Moreover, restaurants along urban trails and greenways find that many of their customers arrive by bicycle via the trail, and homebuilders and realtors often market trails as amenities. Talk with businesspeople and community residents to get a sense of how a trail might benefit the area economically.

Transportation

How will your trail system fit into overall local and regional transportation objectives? Trails are legitimate transportation systems even if they are used primarily for recreational purposes because they move people from one place to another.

To promote your trail, you need to understand how it fits into the larger transportation system (see "Comprehensive Trail Planning" in chapter 2). Begin your analysis by contacting city or county planning departments, highway departments, or state departments of transportation. Federal transportation legislation requires each state to employ a bicycle coordinator, who can offer expertise and useful information. Some large metropolitan areas also employ a bicycle transportation planner. Consider these elements of a transportation system:

■ Existing Systems

How does the current transportation system work? Where are the important "trip generators"—schools, places of employment, and large residential enclaves? Can you identify heavily traveled corridors, such as those between a large bedroom community and a downtown area? How might your trail fit into these corridors?

■ Motorized Counts vs.
    Nonmotorized Counts

Is there any data in your community comparing motorized travel with nonmotorized travel in general and within certain corridors? Nation-

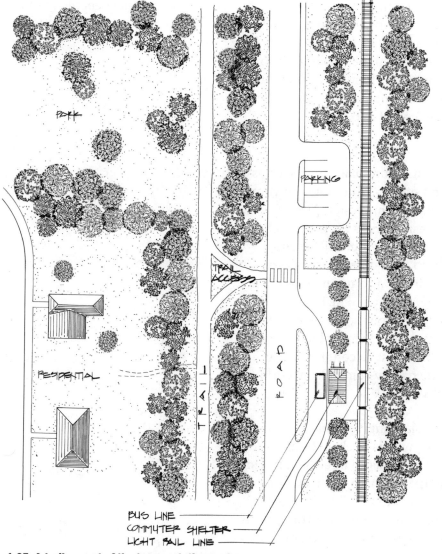

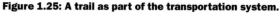

Figure 1.25: A trail as part of the transportation system.

wide, bicycle trips account for about 1 percent of all trips, according to the U.S. Department of Transportation. Is the percentage higher in your community? Could it be higher, reducing fuel consumption and pollution, if a trail system were put in place?

■ Future Plans

What are future plans for the transportation system? And how can your trail be part of this system? (See figure 1.25.) Consider mass transit as well as auto travel. Can your trail act as a feeder into a major mass transit station, serving as a component in a "bike and ride" system in which users ride their bicycles from home to the transit station and store them in bicycle lockers? Will it tie into a countywide or statewide trail system or transportation network?

When planning your trail, be sure you know who is likely to be affected by it and who has an interest in it. This knowledge will help you plan effectively and avoid possible disasters by exposing potential conflicts or opposition early in the process. You may also find opportunities for joint ventures and other mutual benefits with those holding a stake in the corridor.

CHAPTER

2

Planning Your
Multi-Use Trail

PUBLIC INVOLVEMENT

Public involvement is a major step in the process of creating a multi-use trail. If you institute and carry out a comprehensive public involvement campaign, you will create trust and support between your agency or organization and the public.

You may already have involved the public when you acquired the corridor, but you are now at a different stage in your project. The trail's future is more secure, and you need to develop a publicly supported trail design and management plan. If you successfully employed public involvement techniques thus far, build on them. If not, begin reaching out now.

Most trail projects have numerous "publics" or "stakeholders": trail users, friendly and hostile adjacent landowners, elected officials, and those unaware of the project. Know who the various stakeholders are, whom you need to inform, and from whom you need input. Your goal will be to get all the "publics" involved in the planning and design phase so that all develop a sense of "ownership" and "investment" in the trail. The following suggestions will help you advance your relations with all the various people who have a vested interest in your trail.

First, know more about the corridor than anyone else. This will give you the edge in a public setting: You will be prepared to answer any question that may come up; you (and your agency) will be viewed as credible; and you will be able to defuse potential opposition.

Compile a "resource book" for the proposed trail, including historic and economic information about the route. What were its previous uses? Did any interesting historic events take place along the route? Are there notable natural features along the route? If a cultural inventory was conducted, much of this information will already be assembled. Add news clippings and old photos to the book where possible (a three-ring binder works well). Include information about other trails in your region and articles on the national trails movement. Plan to display the book at public meetings and events to help generate excitement about the project.

In addition, develop an introductory manual to sell your project. It should supply interesting background information about the trail. Include maps of the route, highlighting the community resources it links (schools, libraries, parks, industrial centers). Also compile a list of potential user groups and some estimated development and maintenance costs. (A word of caution on cost estimates: Make sure your cost figures are solid before going public with them; your credibility will be undermined if they escalate.) This manual will introduce the trail to new groups. Also, visual elements, such as slides, are very helpful in a public setting.

Equipped with knowledge and materials, you are now ready to develop public interest and investment in the trail. Surveys, citizen advisory committees, public meetings, hearings, and meetings with individuals are all good ways to involve the public. A media outreach campaign may also be useful.

Before deciding which strategies will work best for you, consider the following questions: What kind of input are you asking the public to provide? What decision-making role will the public play? And when is public involvement appropriate or most effective? A successful public involvement program includes an appropriate mix of techniques that maximize inclusion of a large number of people and minimize confrontation.

Meetings

Meetings can be a good way to elicit community input on trail design and management (figure 2.1). But when planning a meeting, remember that too many meetings, or meetings without a clear purpose, waste time. Don't schedule one unless you know what you want to accomplish. Also, you may get better turnout if you bill the gathering as an "open house," with free flow of information for a few hours, rather than as a set meeting with a strict agenda. An open house provides more flexibility for people's schedules as they can come at their convenience during the allotted time period.

■ Issues Identification Workshop

This type of workshop enables the public to identify their true concerns. If successful, this meeting should assure the public that the trail's managing agency will work to address their concerns to the best of its ability. This meeting, which can develop real solutions to real problems, can be held for the general public or for a specific segment of the public. This meeting is

The Mayor of the Town of Hamden John L. Carusone Cordially Invites You to a Community Meeting on

Greenway Path

The Farmington Canal Line Park

Wednesday, February 6, 1991 7:00 p.m. at The Miller Senior Center 2901 Dixwell Ave. Hamden, CT

Dixwell Avenue Pedestrian Bridge

Figure 2.1: Announcement of a trail meeting.

quite effective when held specifically for adjacent landowners. If possible, schedule a workshop in a neighborhood setting—perhaps in a library— rather than at your agency's headquarters. Participants will be more at ease in a familiar setting.

At an issues identification workshop, each participant may list his or her concerns. But establish ground rules (for example, each person must speak in turn, there are no "bad" ideas, issues can be listed only once) at the outset.

After all issues have been identified and listed on a flip chart, workshop participants vote on which three to five issues are top priority. Allow time for a question-and-answer session with a panel of experts addressing the selected priority issues. The trail's managing agency should explain how it intends to handle those issues. At the close of the workshop, clearly inform participants how their input will be used.

At this workshop or another type of meeting, plan to use visual aids, particularly maps of the corridor and aerial views of it. These tools will help people pinpoint their residences (and community resources) along the route and see how the projects fits into the entire community.

■ Community Design Workshop

A community design workshop educates the public about the trail while eliciting input on design. An open public meeting is best, but be sure to include all relevant trail user groups and adjacent landowners. A member of the trail design team should also be present.

The workshop revolves around a large, user-friendly map of the trail corridor (figure 2.2) and a variety of miniature symbols representing trail-related objects such as signs, rest stops, trailheads, benches, drinking fountains, and trees for landscaping and buffers. With the map spread out on a large table, participants are encouraged to place the pieces where they envision them along the trail. This fun technique allows the public substantial input into the trail design and helps them visualize what the trail might look like when complete. A design specialist should take notes during the process and incorporate the ideas into the actual design.

Some community design workshops utilize computers to portray different scenarios of trail design. Others have televised a proposed design on a public station and asked the audience to phone in comments and recommen-

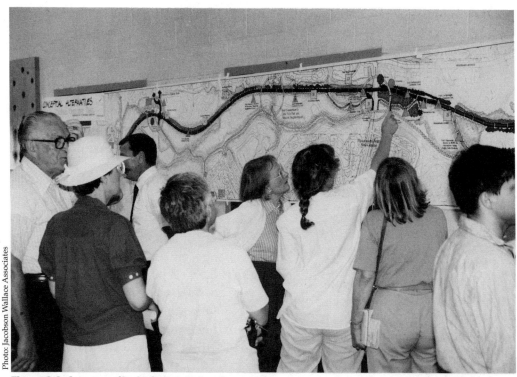

Photo: Jacobson Wallace Associates

Figure 2.2: A community design workshop in progress.

dations. In any case, participants should be aware that all the ideas will be considered but some may not be implemented in the final design.

■ Meetings with Individuals

To address difficult, emotional issues, one-on-one meetings with individuals can be the most effective technique.

Once out of a public setting (where pressure from friends and neighbors can be great), an individual will likely express his or her true feelings about the trail project. Often, people are neutral about a trail, but they are persuaded by others to oppose it. Or those who are truly opposed will not air their actual aversions in an open forum.

One-on-one meetings help you discern true opponents from potential supporters and genuine fears from false ones. This setting gives you and your opposition the opportunity to talk openly and discuss various options. What initially seemed an inflexible position may become quite fluid in this setting. Taking the time to talk with people one on one also demonstrates to the community your willingness to listen to different views and to work toward solutions.

■ Public Hearings

Many public agencies are mandated by law to incorporate public hearings — usually formal procedures with the air of a legal proceeding—into their planning process. They are one way of developing a permanent, "public" record. If you are required to use public hearings (or choose to), make your goals very clear.

Do not expect hearings to be consensus builders or forums for resolving differences. The hearing format can encourage those testifying to take strong positions from which it may be difficult to back down. Hearings may bring much of the hidden opposition out of the woodwork— be prepared for this.

Make sure that trail supporters are aware of any public hearings taking place.

Citizen Advisory Committees

Citizen advisory committees provide an outlet for each user group's views to be represented while also developing consensus among groups with differing perspectives. Depending on its structure, a citizen advisory committee can serve as a decision-making body or as a forum for information exchange, citizen advice, and input on the project. Typically committee members are selected by an agency and have a regularly scheduled meeting time (monthly, bimonthly, or quarterly).

In setting up a trail advisory committee, seek diverse representation as appropriate—a bicyclist, a hiker, an equestrian, a snowmobiler, a disabled person, an elderly person, a cross-country skier, an adjacent landowner, a historian, a law-enforcement official, and anyone else concerned about the design and management of the trail. Then, when working with this committee, clearly state each member's role and the decision-making abilities of the group. Effective citizen advisory committees can provide powerful insight into trail design and management.

Surveys

Although many people do not feel strongly enough about a trail project to attend a hearing or other meeting, they will anonymously express their views in a survey. If you do conduct a survey, make sure your purpose is clear. Is it to demonstrate community support for the trail? To show that people prefer the trail over another community improvement? To determine how many people will use the trail once it opens? Your purpose will determine the questions to ask.

In northwestern New Jersey, a newspaper conducted a reader's poll to determine whether or not the Paulinskill Valley Trail project was controversial— as had been reported by the local media. The survey results showed the true dimensions of public support: Of those who expressed an opinion, 97 percent (895 area residents) supported the conversion of an abandoned rail line into a trail, compared to 3 percent (27 people) who opposed it (figure 2.3).

Putting together a solid survey (with questions that cannot be misconstrued) is difficult. Keep your ques-

Susquehanna Railbed Update and Second Reader's Poll

by Laura O'Biso Socha

In April 1985, Robert Hughey, then the Commissioner of the NJ Department of Environmental Protection, authorized the DEP purchase of the New York, Susquehanna & Western railroad right of way for preservation as a multi-purpose trail. The abandoned rail bed is presently owned by the City of Newark—purchased by the city with the intentions of using it as part of a water pipeline from the Tocks Island Reservoir. The right of way is 26 miles long and roughly 66 feet wide, and runs from Sparta Junction to Hainesburg in Warren County. The railbed follows the Paulinskill River for most of its length. Supporters of the trail are calling it the Paulinskill Valley Trail.

There are about 169 parcels of land that abut the railbed. Of these, 68 do not meet required zoning ordinances for building; most of the land is zoned agricultural, and only 12 homes are located in close proximity to the trail. The landowners have formed the Railroad Right-of-way Repurchase Association in opposition to the trail. They would like to purchase the right of way and divide the property among them. The landowners fear that a trail would invade their privacy, result in litter and vandalism, noise from trail-bikes, interfere with agricultural crops and result in disturbance of the wildlife in the area.

The results of this year's poll again were overwhelmingly in favor of the trail. Response to the question, "Do you think that the 26-mile railbed in question should be purchased by the state to become a multi-use recreational trail?" was as follows:

Yes—895
No—27
Don't Know—46
Total Responses—968

Reader's Poll

ATTENTION READERS: The Sussex County Voice would like to introduce you to our first reader's poll. We appreciate your comments regarding current controversial situations affecting Sussex County, and we invite you to take this opportunity to VOICE your opinion regarding the proposed conversion of the NEW YORK, SUSQUEHANNA, AND WESTERN COMPANY RAILROAD BED into a public trail. The information we receive from our readers will be duplicated and forwarded to the involved officials, i.e., Senator Wayne Dumont, Assemblymen Robert Littell and Garabed "Chuck" Haytaian, Department of Environmental Protection Commissioner Richard Dewling, as well as the City of Newark. Please fill in your response, clip this section of the Sussex County Voice, and return it to us by August 31, 1986. Our mailing address is: Sussex County Voice Reader's Poll, Viking Village, Suite 5G, Vernon, NJ 07462.

1. Do you think that the state should negotiate to buy the railroad right of way with Green Acres funds to convert the former New York, Susquehanna, and Western Company's railroad bed to a public trail?

   Yes ☒   No ☐   Don't Know ☐

   Other _____

2. Do you agree with the landowners association that the conversion of this 26-mile strip of property would be an infringement on their rights and that the landowners' living adjacent to the proposed trail should be able to buy the land back?

   Yes ☐   No ☒   Don't Know ☐

   Other _____

3. Do you agree with the proponents of the trail conversion that this property is an ideal site for public recreation and leisure purposes?

   Yes ☒   No ☐   Don't Know ☐

   Other _____

4. Do you think that the Department of Environmental Protection will be able to adequately maintain and patrol the 26-mile site if it is converted to a public trail?

   Yes ☒   No ☐   Don't Know ☐

   Other _____

5. Do you think this public trail, if converted, would become an open invitation for trespassing and dumping on the privately-owned property adjacent to the proposed trail?

   Yes ☐   No ☒   Don't Know ☐

   Other _____

6. Do you think that the conversion of this railbed to a public site is an unnecessary duplication of the Appalachian Trail?

   Yes ☐   No ☒   Don't Know ☐

   Other _____

7. Do you think that neither solution proposed thus far is the correct solution for the use of this property?

   Yes ☐   No ☒   Don't Know ☐

   Other _____

Poll Supports Paulins Kill Trail

The plan to purchase the Susquehanna right-of-way and convert it to a trail has sparked controversy in Sussex and Warren counties since its proposal. The Commitee for the Proposed Paulins Kill Valley Trail feels, according to member Len Frank, "The flat cinder railbed is an ideal, multi-purpose trail that can be used for hiking, bicycling, cross-country skiing, horseback riding and dog sledding. It would provide access to long stretches of the Paulins Kill River, a favorite river with fishermen and canoeists. It can even be used by the elderly and the handicapped."

As Controversial as Apple Pie?

How popular does a trail proposal have to be before the media will stop calling it "controversial?" That's what advocates for New Jersey's proposed Paulinskill Valley Trail are wondering.

Although the Paulinskill has been bogged down in so-called "controversy" for years, with a handful of politicians preventing state acquisition of the corridor, a 1987 poll in the *Sussex County Voice* showed the true dimensions of public support. When asked if the 26-mile rail line should become a public trail, the response was 895 yes, 27 no.

One pundit quipped, "That has to make it more popular than either motherhood *or* apple pie!"

Figure 2.3: Trail opinion polls.

tions clear and unambiguous. Make sure the sample you survey represents the groups you are trying to reach. You will likely get a low response rate — 10–20 percent is average. Know how you will tabulate, analyze, and utilize every question in your survey. Make sure that your survey explains its purpose and the way the information will be used. Finally, share the results with your respondents. If possible, you may want to consult the sociology department at a local university or a professional with survey experience.

Mass Media Outreach

The media can help inform the public about your project and generate public input and support. But before reaching out to the media, remember that any newspaper or television coverage can stir up opponents as well as supporters. The media loves controversy, and a reporter is unlikely to take the story without looking at other opinions. As with a survey, be sure that you are communicating a clear message with little danger of being misinterpreted.

Once you feel sure that the time is right for some press coverage, you can use a wide array of techniques to at-tract the media. Press releases, press conferences, public service announcements (PSAs), newsletters, and public events can all stimulate the attention you are seeking (see "Promoting and Marketing Your Trail" in chapter 5).

❖

MEETING THE NEEDS OF ADJACENT LANDOWNERS

Of all the obstacles trail developers face, opposition by adjacent landowners can be the most troublesome. Resistance from even a few opponents can result in both bureaucratic inactivity and financial difficulties.

Regardless of your trail's support, you are likely to face opposition from some adjacent landowners who will voice concerns about trail design and management. Their proximity to the corridor often fosters anxiety about the trail's effect on their quality of life. With this in mind, you need to work closely with this key group of citizens.

Some trail proponents have waited until construction is about to begin before informing local residents—only to meet disastrous results. It is critical to communicate with adjacent land-owners from the outset and respect their opinions. You must provide them with opportunities to express themselves because only by listening to their fears and concerns can you begin developing solutions and moving toward a successful trail project.

Crime, Property Values, and Liability

The overriding concerns most often voiced by potential trail neighbors are fear of increased crime, decreased property values, and liability. Many adjacent owners, particularly those abutting the corridor, view the trail as a new public thoroughfare that provides quick access to their property by "undesirable" outsiders. Many of these concerns stem from a fear of the unknown and disappear once the trail is open. Be sensitive to landowners' concerns, yet also inform them of the benefits realized by residents near other trails. Often, residents who are ambivalent about the trail project become opponents when they hear the concerns of others. Continuing with the public involvement strategy discussed in the previous section should help neutralize many fears at the outset and begin building landowners' commitment to the trail.

Be prepared to address potential landowner concerns and think through your answers to possible questions. You will find extremely useful information in various studies that highlight the realities of rail-trails and refute claims about their negative impact. The most comprehensive study to date, "The Impacts of Rail-Trails," looks at the effects of rail-trails in three diverse areas across the country. Overall, landowners agreed that living next to a rail-trail was better than living next to abandoned tracks. Moreover, the vast majority of landowners use the trails frequently. For example, in the East Bay region near San Francisco, 99 percent of neighbors living along the suburban Lafayette/Moraga Trail use it; in fact, members of their households use it an average of 132 days each year.[1] A study of Seattle's Burke-Gilman Trail shows similar results, with adjacent owners making frequent use of the trail. The study points out that two of the trail's most vocal opponents now believe the trail is the best thing that ever happened to the neighborhood.[2]

The Burke-Gilman study and another of trails in Minnesota specifically address crime on rail-trails. Both studies show that landowner concerns about crime diminish once the trail is established. The studies also refute the idea that trails foster crime toward trail neighbors; the incidence of crime is actually lower in homes near the trail than those in surrounding neighborhoods.

The studies also addressed concerns about property values. No negative effect on property values has been found, and in some cases property values have increased. Along the Burke-Gilman, homes directly adjacent to the trail showed no increase or decrease, but those located a block from the trail realized a 6 percent increase in property values according to local real estate agents.[3] In "The Impacts of Rail-Trails," landowners said they believed the trails either increased or had no effect on property values. Some landowners thought their proximity to trails might make their homes easier to sell. In suburban areas of Chicago, Tampa, Washington, D.C., Seattle, and elsewhere, home-sale advertisements promote the properties' proximity to trails as a selling point.

Liability is another common concern among landowners. They fear that a trail user will wander onto their property, get injured, and then sue the landowner for liability. Fortunately, liability has not been much of a problem on multi-use trails, primarily because recreational-use statutes (RUS) are on the books in forty-nine states (all except Alaska and the District of Columbia). Under these statutes, no landowner is liable for recreational injuries resulting from mere carelessness. To recover damages, an injured person needs to prove "willful and wanton misconduct on the part of the landowner."[4] However, if the landowner is charging a fee for access to his or her property, the recreational-use statute does not apply.

Admittedly, the RUS does not necessarily prevent landowners from being sued, but it will grant them certain protections. Obtain a copy of your state's statute and find out to what extent it has been tested in court. Sharing this information with concerned trailside residents, many of whom are probably unfamiliar with the protection they receive under the statute, will do much to alleviate their concerns about liability.

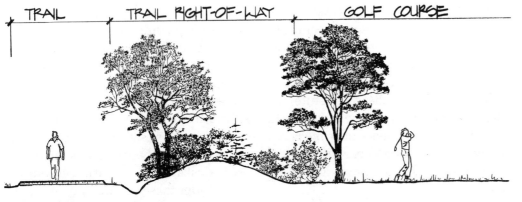

TRAIL   TRAIL RIGHT-OF-WAY   GOLF COURSE

Figure 2.4: Berm and planting screen.

Other Concerns

Additional concerns you will likely encounter are fear of careless maintenance, trespassing, and loss of privacy, all of which require specific management solutions.

Although most trails are more attractive than abandoned, rundown corridors, many adjacent landowners fear that a developed trail will not be well maintained after its opening. Trail neighbors are often concerned about weed control, tree pruning, drainage control, and trash pickup. Develop a regular maintenance schedule and share it with future trail neighbors to demonstrate that you are addressing their concerns. Only by living up to your promises and performing consistent maintenance functions will you truly gain trust on these issues.

Landowners also fear that trail users will leave the trail via their property in search of phones, bathrooms, and trail exits. You can reduce the potential for these problems by locating public parking lots, emergency telephones, access points, restrooms, and drinking fountains at regular intervals along the trail. To allay their fears, assure landowners that you will build proper amenities into the trail design.

If funds do not allow all desired amenities to be included at once, seek input from trail neighbors as to which are most crucial from their perspective. You could plan to install temporary facilities (including portable toilets and drinking fountains) until money permits construction of permanent structures.

The New River Trail State Park in southwestern Virginia produced a development plan outlining facilities to be constructed over twenty years. This plan complements the park's "guidelines for opening," which include required features (such as stop signs before road crossings and informational kiosks at major access points) that had to be in place prior to the trail's opening. Together these documents allowed the trail to open without all facilities in place while they reassured landowners that desired amenities would be installed over time.

Loss of privacy may be one of the most difficult issues you will face because it is so personal for each landowner. The heart of this issue is making people feel comfortable with their proximity to the trail, which is typically accomplished through some form of screening. Undoubtedly, all trailside tenants will have a different idea of how to shield their properties from the trail—and from the sight of trail users (figure 2.4).

In residential areas landowners often insist that fences be installed (at the agency's expense) to prevent trespassing and to maintain privacy. Keep in mind, however, that there are other less costly and more natural options than fencing, such as trees, shrubs, and other plantings (figure 2.5), that they may accept. Typically, fences should be considered as a last resort because of their high cost.

The manager of New Jersey's Delaware and Raritan Canal State Park faced a difficult dilemma when adjacent landowners strongly opposed a trail extension. The landowners would agree to it only on the conditions that fencing would be installed along the route to keep trespassers off their properties and that breaks would be located in the fence at regular intervals so the neighbors could access the trail. The manager developed a model solution: the trail would be installed with no fences in place, but at any time landowners could individually request fencing along their properties if they found it necessary. After five years, the trail manager has yet to install a single fence.

If this scenario doesn't satisfy your trail neighbors, urge them to try natural screening on a trial basis. Try an involvement technique to get them on board: Plan a tree-planting ceremony

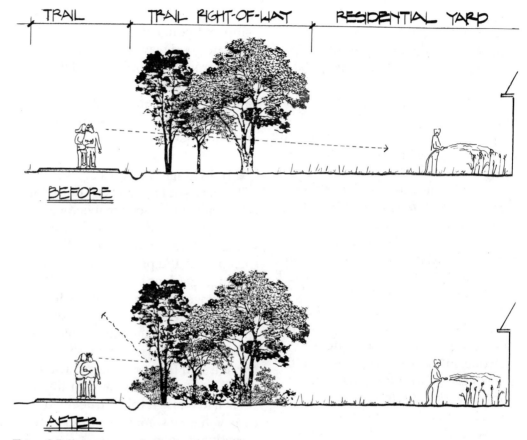

Figure 2.5: Natural screening for trail neighbors.

hosted jointly by the agency and trail neighbors. Once the trail is open and neighbors' concerns subside, they may be less anxious about fence installation.

In areas where a railroad company constructed or maintained fences (often in livestock-grazing areas), you will need to continue the upkeep. But again, talk individually with landowners to ascertain their needs.

Whatever screening works best in your situation, you need to consider the cost and who will cover it. Is there money in the trail development budget to cover plantings for the adjacent landowners? Will the adjacent landowners be required to split the cost with you? Who will pay the maintenance costs? No matter how much screening you require, these are critical questions to consider during the planning phase.

After thinking through all these issues, consider different strategies for working with future trail neighbors. As with any other "public," treat landowners with respect. Listen to their concerns, but also try to educate them about the many positive aspects of the trail.

You may want to open lines of communication with adjacent landowners by sending a personalized letter to each one, introducing yourself and the trail concept, and stating that you want to work with him or her in developing the trail. This gets these future trail neighbors involved at the outset, before they can feel shut out of the process.

Strategies for Landowner Involvement

Employ various strategies to gain the support of adjacent landowners and to address any concerns that develop. Individual meetings and trail tours are good ways to involve this critical group of people. In isolated cases, you may need to move into mitigation and negotiation with certain landowners who are unyielding on a particular issue.

■ Individual Meetings
The best strategy you can undertake is to conduct face-to-face meetings with adjacent landowners. This allows you to make a personal contact with each person and proves that you are making a genuine effort to take his or her feelings into consideration. It also gives the trail a human side—you become the "face of the trail." Unfortunately, in many cases, there is not enough staff time or there are just too many adjacent landowners for this approach to work. If this is true in your case, you may want to consider an alternative strategy.

■ Trail Tours
Organize a tour of a nearby multi-use trail to gain support from adjacent landowners (or to neutralize opponents). Such a visit allows future trail neighbors to experience an existing facility firsthand and should allay some of their fears. If possible, set up meetings with landowners along the trail, especially those supporters who were once opposed. Speaking directly with other landowners can do more to win people over than any statistics you can offer.

■ Mitigation
Negotiation and mitigation are tools that can help you and adjacent landowners develop creative solutions together. Often a landowner will compromise on an issue in exchange for an amenity connected to the trail. Examples: To address fears of increased crime along the route, you might agree to hire a full-time patrol person (to be augmented by volunteer patrols); if people are concerned about illegal nighttime use, you might designate the trail closed from dusk to dawn; to relieve privacy concerns, you might plant shrubs and trees to shield adjacent properties; and, in rural areas, you might allow access to private property via the trail.

As you forge relationships with adjacent landowners, you will learn to distinguish actual fears from those used to mask something else, perhaps a landowner's desire to acquire the property for private use. Listen carefully to the concerns of adjacent landowners and discern in what areas they may be willing to compromise in exchange for some personal benefit. You can develop creative solutions to landowners' problems without hindering the trail project.

In addition to these strategies, include the future trail neighbors in other public involvement efforts (trail advisory committees, community design workshops) to make them part of the entire trail-planning process (see "Public Involvement" in this chapter).

Although adjacent landowners have the power to slow down a trail project, there are many ways to involve them in the planning and design process. Providing them with a role, while allowing their concerns to be heard and addressed, will ultimately lead to a higher-quality design, reduce the potential for opposition, and enhance overall community support for the trail

❖

COMPREHENSIVE TRAIL PLANNING

During the 1970s and early 1980s, almost every state and metropolitan area developed comprehensive bicycle plans, the majority of which were never implemented. Bicycle proponents have come to realize that the success of bicycle programs and facilities depends on their integration into the policy and planning documents that are actually used by planners, engineers, and other decision makers; if they are not, they are ignored. Comprehensive multi-use trail plans produced as independent documents face the same fate if they are not also integrated into policy and planning documents.

Institutionalization

The key to having your trail integrated into official policy and planning is institutionalization. A project is institutionalized when an entire organization, not just one or two staff members, pursues it. Integrating a comprehensive trail plan into existing policy and planning documents is an effective institutionalization strategy because it generates familiarity, awareness, legitimacy, and funding opportunities.

■ Familiarity and Awareness
Planners, engineers, designers, and other decision makers, like everyone else, will support and promote things with which they are familiar and comfortable. While most people are not anti-trail, many are not aware of the opportunities associated with trails. The more visible and positive the presence of multi-use trails in documents they use, the more likely multi-use trails are to receive support.

■ Legitimacy
The old saying, "It's not what you say but who says it," also applies to trails. For multi-use trails to be "legitimate," they must appear in the documents considered legitimate by the professional involved. For an engineer, this may mean that trails are included in the local transportation plan. For a park planner, it may mean that trails are included in the local parks plan.

■ Funding
Perhaps the most important reason to integrate multi-use trails into all appropriate plans and policies is funding. For example, to use "transportation" dollars (the most likely funding source) to build trails requires trails to be included in transportation plans. The same is true for "recreation" and "open space" dollars. Failure to include trails in these various documents will se-

verely limit possible funding sources for these projects.

Policy and Planning Documents

Comprehensive trail plans should be integrated into transportation, recreation, open space, commercial, and industrial plans and policies. While the specifics of local and regional policy and planning documents will differ for each community, they will generally fall into one or more of the following categories:

■ Transportation Policies and Plans

Most state and local governments have transportation policies and plans because they are required for funding. In most cases, a department of transportation (DOT) or public works is responsible for developing and implementing its plan; in some cases, a separate planning department develops it.

Each state DOT is required to have a state planning process and a statewide transportation improvement program. Each metropolitan area (with a population base of at least fifty thousand) has a metropolitan planning organization (MPO) that develops a metropolitan transportation plan. All state and met-

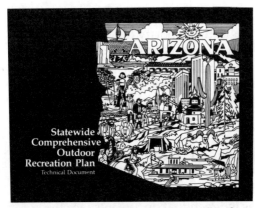

Figure 2.6: Arizona's *Statewide Comprehensive Outdoor Recreation Plan.*

ropolitan plans must address development of bicycle and pedestrian facilities.

Transportation plans are perhaps the most important place in which to include multi-use trails projects because there is more money available for transportation than there is for recreation. When including trails in transportation plans, be sure to identify them as "transportation" facilities and not "recreational" facilities because federal and state funding guidelines usually require that money spent on nonmotorized facilities be spent for "transportation" purposes. Labeling it as such should not have a negative impact on the trail's design.

■ Recreation Policies and Plans

All states have a recreation plan (figure 2.6), with the local or state parks department (or natural resources department) responsible for developing and implementing it. This is another important place in which to incorporate a multi-use trail plan. When you include a trail in a park plan, position the trail as a "linear park" or "greenway" that connects traditional parks.

■ Open Space Policies and Plans

Open space policies and plans are appearing in more areas, and multi-use trails should be part of them. Abandoned railroad rights-of-way and utility corridors are frequently the only undeveloped open spaces in urban areas.

■ Commercial and Industrial Plans and Policies

Urban areas often have commercial and industrial policies and plans. These should not be ignored because they frequently include railroad rights of-way that may be suitable for trail purposes. When incorporating trails in commercial and industrial plans, include language stating that government policy encourages railroads to stay in service and that the railroad rights-of-way are desirable for trail use only when they are no longer needed for rail use. A negative public backlash can result if trails are perceived as having "pushed" trains out of service.

Principles of Comprehensive Trail Planning

Comprehensive trail planning is the creation of a "system" of trails, not only an individual trail. The local, regional, or statewide system must be interconnected and must work as a whole. To take advantage of the full range of trail opportunities, keep the following principles in mind when developing transportation, recreation, commercial, and industrial plans:

■ Continuity
Facilities should be continuous and interconnected. While this may seem obvious, trails frequently end abruptly—especially in urban areas—with no provision for integrating them into a larger trail system. The relationship between continuity and trail use is direct: disjointed, short sections of trail, no matter how aesthetically pleasing, will not be as useful as trails interconnected with a larger trail network and multiple destinations.

■ Potential Use
Multi-use trails should be located along corridors that assure maximum use by the intended user group. For example, bicyclists and walkers generally have the same trip origins and destinations as motorists and need to get to and from the same facilities, services, and places of work and recreation. Of course, access, climate and perceived safety may also affect potential use.

■ Destinations
Multi-use trails should link neighborhoods, parks, and open space facilities. Trails should also connect neighborhoods to schools, universities, commercial areas, and employment centers. Strive to create a system that meets the both the utilitarian and recreational needs of a diverse population.

■ Safety
Safety considerations should be given top priority when selecting trail corridors. Routes with the fewest number of intersections should be selected, and steep grades should be avoided. Trails should not be routed directly through the middle of plazas, transit stops, and heavily used recreational sites such as

children's play areas (see "Trail Maintenance and Safety" in chapter 4).

❖

PLANNING FOR THE FUTURE

There is only one constant for trail planners—things change! Wise trail planning, therefore, always means looking ahead. Because trail development funds are usually limited, planners often try to go as far as they can before the money runs out. This can lead to a trail of minimal width and minimal capacity. Planners eager to get a trail built may be reluctant to think about the trail's surroundings a decade or two hence. But considering future needs and planning for them is important. In many instances, an informed decision early on will save dollars and aggravation later.

Try to anticipate trail-use levels accurately—they can expand explosively as word spreads. A new trail may fill to capacity within a few years after opening, leaving trail managers at a loss to accommodate the flood of users. Other factors change as well, including equipment used on the trail. The mountain bike introduced a whole

Figure 2.7: The former rural landscape adjacent to northern Virginia's Washington and Old Dominion Railroad Regional Park is now dotted with suburban residential developments.

new set of opportunities and needs. And now there are racing wheelchairs and in-line skates. Each has its own specialized equipment and user needs. Undoubtedly the future will present new variations not even considered today.

New trail construction technologies are also emerging. Crushed rock has proved an excellent surface, especially for mountain bikes and the "hybrid" mountain/street bike combination. Some trails are already testing surfaces made from recycled asphalt, discarded tires, and broken pottery. Prefabricated bridges and other premanufactured trail products will continue to emerge as the trails movement accelerates.

Demographic change is also constant. One large segment of the population—the baby boomers—are moving well into middle age. How will this affect trail demand? Will the fifty-year-olds of the late 1990s slow down, or will they increase trail-related activities? Will the desire to remain fit lead to even more trail use? Will these people bicycle long distances, or will they prefer a shorter stroll?

Anticipate Future Development

Future residential, commercial, and industrial development along trail corridors will likely impact trails in two ways. First, projects like new roads, utility crossings, and drainage projects can make trails impassable—at least temporarily. Second, land-use changes along the corridor will alter the experience or feeling of using the trail (figure 2.7). State and local comprehensive plans and land-use plans should give you information about projected growth and development.

■ Road Crossings
New streets, highways, and possibly even transit rail lines are likely to cross your proposed route at some

point before or after trail construction. Get the latest regional transportation plan from your local planning, public works, or transportation department. The plan should show existing routes and those planned for the next five to twenty years. Learn about phasing and schedules by talking with planners. What projects presently are budgeted and which will receive funding soon? Note where these projects will intersect your trail corridor. Also, plan now to develop a policy to protect your trail from development pressure, so that future projects do not disrupt the trail corridor (see "Trail Protection" in chapter 4).

■ Utility Projects
A power line, gas line, or water or sewer line may be slated for installation along or parallel to your corridor—now or in the future. Although utility construction may disrupt a trail, consider opportunities for joint use and the benefits for trail builders as well as utility companies (see "Joint Ventures within Your Multi-Use Trail Corridor" in this chapter).

■ Development along the Corridor
Prudent trail planning includes looking at existing land-use maps and

the comprehensive plans of the communities involved. How is the corridor currently zoned? What new projects are planned? How will these affect the trail project? Work with local planning and zoning departments. Find out who is requesting building permits for large projects. Where are projects likely to be located? Talk to area developers and realtors as well as planning officials.

Many city, county, and regional planning agencies maintain mailing lists for notifying interested agencies and groups when a development project is submitted for review. Be sure your organization or agency is on those lists.

While you may need to accommodate some development, be sure to adopt strategies and policies that protect the trail corridor and lessen the likelihood of future conflicts. Protective strategies could include the establishment of buffer zones between the trail and adjacent properties and the creation of access points from new developments where appropriate. The buffer zones could be landscaped to screen unpleasant views that result from nearby development.

■ Detours

Nothing is more annoying to a trail user than to set out on a trail only to discover that it has been closed because of work under way on a road crossing, a sewer line, or other public works project. Develop a "detour policy" for your trail in advance. Public agencies and utility companies must be made aware that the trail is a legitimate transportation corridor and, like any street or road, cannot be simply closed. Rather, a safe, clearly marked detour should be provided. An inter-agency policy and set of procedures including adequate notification regarding projects in the trail corridor should be adopted. Signs informing trail users of the start date and the reason for the detour (posted in advance) will help reduce complaints from trail users.

Know Your Trail User "Market" Now and in the Future

Remember that your trail is both a recreation and transportation "product." Its use will depend on the array of trail users in the community—the trail user "market." User groups can include road and mountain bicyclists,

walkers, snowmobilers, runners, equestrians, in-line skaters, and cross-country skiers, to name a few. And there are many types of users within each category. For example, just within the cycling category are racers, commuters, fitness trainers, family recreational bicyclists, and maybe even children riding to school. Each group has special needs, and the composition of these groups will change as people age and new recreational equipment is introduced. Look at the demographics of your community—consider age groups, lifestyles, and trends—and envision the situation ten years down the road.

Talk with sporting-goods and bicycle shop operators, since they may have a sense of future trends. Look to various trail organizations, national manufacturers associations, and magazines for additional insight. National opinion polls and trend watchers like National Demographics and Lifestyles, Inc., issue reports on recreational trends. Contact such a polling service or work through a local demographic and marketing consultant. And follow your instincts: Getting a sense of the market is art as much as it is science.

Design for Flexibility

Once your trail is built, it will become an integral part of the community through which it passes—areas that are ever-changing. With this is mind, make sure your trail can adapt to changing needs.

■ Anticipate Possible Expansion
When planners laid out the Washington and Old Dominion Railroad Regional Park near Washington, D.C., in the early 1970s, they were told by trail experts that a 6-foot-wide trail would suffice for the 45-mile linear park. As added insurance, they paved an 8-foot-wide trail. They never imagined that by 1990 some two million people would visit the trail annually. Because of the explosive growth, the Northern Virginia Regional Park Authority awarded a $248,000 contract in 1991 to widen and resurface a 5½-mile section of trail from 8 to 10 feet. Additional sections will follow until the entire width of the trail is at least 10 feet, 12 feet in the most heavily used areas.

A successful trail will fill up quickly, but overcrowding can cause serious conflicts among users. The best policy is to build a trail with adequate capacity initially. Gauge this by looking at trails in comparable communities. What trail width do they use and how well does it work? Would they have made it wider if they had known the volume of traffic it would receive?

Your trail should be a minimum of 10 feet wide with shoulders when it is first built—wider if you are in an urban area or anticipate heavy use (see "Meeting the Needs of Different Users" in chapter 3). If you cannot afford a wider trail now, get wider easements for future expansion. If possible, bridges and other infrastructure should be made extra-wide to accommodate any expansion.

Deciding which components to build to wider standards first will depend on the type of trail. A concrete trail is virtually impossible to upgrade safely once it is in place as joints created where the new surface is attached are extremely hazardous for bicyclists. Widening an asphalt or crushed stone trail is not as difficult because the materials are less costly and can be blended.

Bridges and tunnels should be built to the ultimate future width of the trail because replacing them later will be extremely costly. Drainage culverts and basic grading should also be designed for the maximum future width if site conditions allow this.

Note that different segments of the trail are likely to have different levels of use. It may be necessary to widen the trail only in certain areas where peak use occurs, such as through a downtown area or near a college campus.

Another option is to plan for two separate paths (or "treads") within the same corridor, with the possibility of separating types of users, such as bicyclists and in-line skaters from horses or runners.

Weigh the cost of extra width against extra length now. It is better to develop the first section at an ample width as opposed to the whole trail at an inadequate width. If a shorter section is open at the proper width, pressure will build (and money will become available) to develop additional segments. However, a longer trail may help spread out users and lessen crowding, or it may attract more people. It depends on the trail's location and demographics. Building more length now (even if it is not an ideal width) may make the trail appealing to a larger audience, which could help broaden public and political support for the project. This strategy may work best when a trail is the first of its kind in an area. As the trail gains in popularity, a stronger case can be made for widening it.

Clearly, decisions about widening a trail now or later are based on case-by-case judgments that reflect economics, political considerations, user safety, and the ultimate goals of the project.

■ Plan for Future Operations and Maintenance

An often-overlooked planning element is the long-term cost of operations and maintenance. Take this into account now. Your trail master plan should include a detailed maintenance schedule that lists various maintenance tasks such as sweeping, litter pickup, vegetation pruning, and graffiti removal (see "Trail Maintenance and Safety" in chapter 4).

Also consider the long-term replacement costs of such major trail components as trail surfaces, bridges, and retaining walls. While there are no definitive rules for calculating lifespans of trail components, here are some guidelines:

▶ **Asphalt** needs resurfacing every seven to fifteen years, depending on site conditions and construction quality. In 1992 dollars it cost a minimum of $10 per linear foot to remove and replace asphalt (without subgrade preparation). In some cases, it is possible to overlay the old asphalt with a 1½-inch top coating, costing approximately $5 per linear foot.

▶ **Concrete** lasts approximately twenty-five or more years; replacement costs approximately $25 per linear foot in 1992 dollars.

▶ **Crushed stone** should last seven to ten years, although it does require frequent patching and spot repairs; replacement costs approximately $5 per linear foot.

▶ **Bridges, tunnels,** and other structures can last more than fifty years when well constructed, although they will need painting and other repairs, including the replacement of wood decking.

Estimate annual costs by dividing each item's construction cost by its anticipated lifespan. Both routine maintenance and replacement costs should be factored into an annual maintenance budget.

Once you have approximated these costs, think about how they will be borne. Which agency will operate the trail—a local parks department, a state parks agency, or a private organization? What is the agency's financial condition? Is the tax base that funds the agency likely to expand or shrink? What will the long-term annual maintenance costs look like, and can the agency handle them? Planning for the future should take these matters into account.

How the managing agency actually budgets maintenance costs is another matter. Most agencies budget annually for routine maintenance costs, while long-term replacement costs are usually distributed over a number of years. Many communities fund items like trail replacement as a "capital fund" appropriation when the work is needed rather than setting aside a portion of the money each year. This may not be sensible, but sometimes it is more politically expedient. Nevertheless, there is value in annualizing these costs to gain a true picture of long-term needs (see "Developing a Comprehensive Budget and Management Plan" in this chapter).

The way in which you present these future costs depends on the approach of the local trail management agency and your project's unique situation. Consider a long-term endowment, user fees, or contributions by adjacent property owners who benefit from the trail as ways to cover ongoing maintenance costs.

❖

JOINT VENTURES WITHIN YOUR MULTI-USE TRAIL CORRIDOR

The linear nature of your multi-use trail corridor will be of interest to other agencies, corporations, or individuals who want access to the corridor. Although your first priority should be to develop a high-quality trail facility, you should also consider the benefits of joint use within the right-of-way.

Your multi-use trail corridor probably passes through an area several miles long and therefore links a number of points. Since it also borders other properties, your corridor is desirable for nontrail uses: neighboring homeowners wanting to expand their gardens onto trail property, utility companies proposing to place cables underground or overhead, or highway departments planning to construct a road across the trail.[5] These "nontrail" interests may present challenges as the trail is developed and managed. Nontrail uses may threaten the linear integrity of the multi-use trail and may disturb its natural, scenic, and historic qualities. However, such uses are the result of growth in an area, so you need to develop a strategy for dealing with them. Ideally, your trail will benefit from certain nontrail uses.

Potentially Compatible Nontrail Uses

The Northern Virginia Regional Park Authority (NVRPA) owns and manages the Washington and Old Dominion Railroad Regional Park (W&OD), a 45-mile multi-use trail developed from a former rail line. The authority has established a set of policies and procedures as well as a comprehensive licensing program to address all nontrail requests. Through coordinated planning, stringent standards, and close supervision, NVRPA has discovered that not only are many uses compatible with the trail, but also that joint ventures can provide the trail with a new source of revenue.

As you plan your trail corridor, consider the following examples of *potentially* compatible uses that might generate income:

▶ Telephone cables

▶ Fiber-optic communication cables

▶ Cable television wires

▶ Gas pipelines

▶ Sanitary sewers

▶ Electric transmission and distribution lines

▶ Water transmission lines

▶ Low-volume driveways

▶ Garden plots

▶ Private parking lots

▶ Storage areas

▶ Road crossings, with grade separation or with crossing signal

▶ Private trail connectors

A few of these uses may not be appropriate along your multi-use trail, but many others may prove compatible (figure 2.8).

Compensation

In exchange for access to the corridor, you should seek compensation. The fact that your corridor already exists makes it very valuable. In many cases, your right-of-way may be the only continuous passage along which an agency or company can lay its cables or pipelines. Without your corridor, the utility may be forced to purchase numerous easements over private property. Clearly, your trail can benefit financially from such joint uses.

Wisconsin's Glacial Drumlin Trail issued a perpetual 10-foot-wide easement to U.S. Telecom, which paved the 48-mile trail (a $375,000 value) in exchange. Near Seattle, the King County Parks Department set up a five-year renewable lease with U.S. Sprint on a 2¼-mile rail-trail. The phone company's fee increases by 10 percent each year for use of the right-of-way.[6]

Through its licensing program, the Northern Virginia Regional Park Authority has gained fair compensation for use of the W&OD trail corridor while it regulates and controls nontrail uses and protects the linear nature of the trail. The licensing program serves other uses as well: It discourages unnecessary encroachments, controls activities of licensees, minimizes inconvenience to trail users, reduces damage to the trail facility, defines standards for construction and restoration, and enables the authority to re-

Figure 2.8: Compatible joint use of a corridor.

cover its administrative and overhead costs and to receive appropriate compensation.[7] The authority administers and collects fees through license agreements, which often need to be renewed annually. It also attempts to recover 100 percent of its costs. NVRPA receives approximately $450,000 per year from fi-

ber-optics license fees, one-time and recurring rental fees (primarily for businesses using adjacent property), and administrative and review fees.

You should consider developing a similar licensing program or at least establish forms of compensation for particular outside uses:

■ Land-Use Fee

This can be either a one-time payment or, ideally, a renewable rental agreement. In Montgomery County, Maryland, a local power company agreed to pay $100,000 for development of a portion of the Capital Crescent Trail in exchange for placing power lines near the corridor.

■ Trail Improvements

A corporation may agree to upgrade your trail in exchange for access to the property. In the East Bay region near San Francisco, a development company agreed to pave a portion of the Iron Horse Regional Trail (at an estimated cost of $350,000) while constructing an office complex adjacent to the trail corridor.

■ Overpass or Underpass

If a transportation department plans to develop a road across your right-of-way, call for the creation of a trail bridge over the road (or a suitable underpass) to mitigate the adverse impact on trail users.

■ Adjacent-Use Fees

Local residents often like to make use of the land between the trail and their properties. Charge a small fee for them to use the land. Landowners adjacent to the Washington and Old Dominion Railroad Regional Park, for example, pay a $25 annual fee for garden plots within the right-of-way. A similar arrangement can be developed for private driveways.

Basically, do not underestimate the value of your trail corridor. A clear tract of linear space, particularly in a developing area, is extremely precious. Joint use of a corridor for trail and utility purposes can be mutually beneficial to all parties involved.

❖

COMPLIANCE WITH LEGISLATION

All trail projects must be reviewed for compliance with local, state, and federal laws. In most cases, permits will be required to construct a trail, particularly when it follows a waterway or is in an urban area. Most permits address environmental concerns, although permits frequently are required for construction activities such as installing an electrical conduit and plumbing.

Working through the maze of local, state, and federal requirements is complicated, but it need not be overwhelming. The key is to have a general understanding of the types of permits required and then to set up a process for identifying exactly what is required for a particular project.

For purposes of clarity and organization, think of regulatory legislation in four broad categories: environmental policy acts, which include requirements for environmental impact statements; shoreline and wetland regulations; permits and licenses; and construction regulations to which the contractor must adhere during construction.

Environmental Policy Acts

An Environmental Policy Act (EPA) delineates when, where, and how an environmental impact statement (EIS) must be conducted. Most states and many cities and counties have adopted an environmental policy act based on the National Environmental Policy Act (NEPA), passed by Congress in 1970. NEPA applies to all projects using federal funds even if the funds are funneled through a state agency.

The primary purpose of EPA legislation is to disclose the environmental consequences of a proposed action, thus alerting the public, government agencies, and other decision makers of the risks involved. The law is intended to ensure that environmental values are considered before a proposed action is taken. EPA legislation, when applied to a project, will likely have one of three outcomes:

■ Categorically Exempt

Certain types of projects are deemed "categorically exempt" through federal, state, and local EPA legislation. In other words, no further environmental documentation, including an EIS, is needed. In Washington State, for example, all bicycle lanes, paths, and facilities are categorically exempt, except when they are built over water or are on land classified as environmentally sensitive. Typically, an agency working on a trail project believed to be categorically exempt is required to fill out a standard form, which is submitted for approval to the local or state official responsible for administering the EPA law.

■ Environmental Checklist

If a project is not categorically exempt, an environmental checklist (ECL) must be completed. This stand-ard "fill-in-the-blank" form requires a detailed description of construction and project impacts. Once completed, the checklist is submitted to the correct local or state official, who makes a "threshold determination," declaring the proposed project as having "significant" or "nonsignificant" environmental impacts. At the time the checklist is submitted, the lead agency is usually required to provide notice of the proposed project to allow for public comment.

■ Determination of Significance or Nonsignificance

If it is determined that a proposal will probably have no significant adverse environmental impacts, the lead agency usually will be asked to prepare and issue a "determination of nonsignificance" (DNS), usually using a standard, preapproved form. The DNS is then filed with the appropriate state or local offices. Typically, there will be a public appeal period of fifteen to thirty days once the DNS is issued. If the project is "determined significant," an environmental impact statement must be drafted.

If you are required to prepare an environmental impact statement, you may want to consider contracting it out to a consultant. The EIS typically requires the following information:

▶ A detailed description of the proposed action, including information and technical data adequate to permit a careful assessment of environmental impact

▶ Discussion of the probable impact on the environment, including any impact on ecological systems and any direct or indirect consequences that may result from the action

▶ Any adverse environmental effects that cannot be avoided

▶ Alternatives to the proposed action that may prevent some or all of the adverse environmental effects, including analysis of the environmental impacts of the alternatives and their costs

▶ An assessment of the cumulative, long-term effects of the proposed action on the environment

▶ Any irreversible commitment of resources that might result from the action or that would curtail beneficial use of the environment

The EIS process begins with a scoping phase to identify potentially significant environmental impacts and issues that should be addressed in the study. Agency and public comment is taken during a subsequent time period (twenty-one days), which may include a public hearing. The next step is preparation of a draft environmental impact statement (DEIS) (figure 2.9). Once it is published, there is usually another comment period (thirty days) during which agency and public comment is encouraged. The last part of the process is to prepare a final environmental impact statement (FEIS), which responds to all comments received on the DEIS. This is issued within a specified time period (sixty days) from the end of the DEIS comment period. If substantial changes are made in the plan at any time prior to construction that may cause environmental impacts not addressed in the EIS, a supplemental environmental impact statement (SEIS) must be prepared.

Based upon the analysis in the FEIS or SEIS, the appropriate agency or department will issue its final decision approving, conditioning, or denying the project. Typically, a project may be denied only if the impacts are signifi-

INTERSTATE HIGHWAY 95 NEW HAVEN HARBOR CROSSING, NEW HAVEN/WEST HAVEN/EAST HAVEN, CONNECTICUT DRAFT - ENVIRONMENTAL IMPACT/SECTION 4(f) STATEMENT

Submitted Pursuant to 42 U.S.C. 4332 (2) (c)
and 49 U.S. C. 303 and Section 22a-1a-1 to 12 Inclusive
of the Regulation of Connecticut State Agencies by the
U.S. Department of Transportation
Federal Highway Administration
and
State of Connecticut, Department of Transportation

Coorperating Agencies

U.S. Army Corps of Engineers
and
U.S. Coast Guard
and
U.S. Fish and Wildlife Service
and
National Marine Fisheries Service

November 1991

Table 1-1 (Continued)

	1 Do Nothing	2 Transit/TSM	3 New Bridge 2-Parallel	4A New Bridge South-NB	4B New Bridge South-Thru.	5A New Bridge North-SB	5B New Bridge North-Thru.
Natural and Water Resources							
Intertidal Flats	No Impact	No Impact	L	L	L	L	L
Finfish	No Impact	No Impact	L	L	L	L	L
Benthos (acres)	No Impact	No Impact	0.19	0.13	0.13	0.42	0.38
Shellfish (hard clams)	No Impact	No Impact	75000	53000	53000	126000	86000
Leased Shellfish Beds (acres)	No Impact	No Impact	0.09	0.06	0.06	0.22	0.23
Inland Wetlands	No Impact	No Impact	L	L	L	L	L
Tidal Wetlands (acres)	No Impact	No Impact	1.0-1.4	1.0-1.4	1.0-1.4	1.0-1.4	1.0-1.4
Wildlife	No Impact	No Impact	L	L	L	L	L
Public Water Supply	No Impact	No Impact	L	L	L	L	L
Floodplains	No Impact	No Impact	L	L	L	L	L
Waterbody Modifications	No Impact	No Impact	L	L	L	L	L
Culture Resources							
Architectural (No. of Resources)	No Impact	No Impact	24	20	20	21	21
Archeological	No Impact	No Impact	H	H	M	H	M
Noise Impacts	No Impact	No Impact	24	20	20	21	21
Air Quality							
Emission Burden	Worst Case	I	I	I	I	I	I
CO Hot Spots (No. of Locations)	I	I	I	I	I	I	I
Hazardous and Toxic Sites (No. of Sites)	No Impact	No Impact	1	No Impact	No Impact	1	1
Visual Impacts	No Impact	L	H-Struct.	L-Struct.	L-Struct.	L-Struct.	H-Struct.
Energy Use (equiv-gasoline- million gallons)	2270.3	2257.5	2375.5	2365.2	2373.6	2379.7	2384.9
Construction Impacts Permits Required	No Impact	L	M	M	M	M	M

LEGEND:

L Low Impact Potential   H High Impact Potential
M Moderate Impact Potential   I Improvement

Figure 2.9: Environmental impact statement.

cantly adverse and cannot be mitigated. Once the final decision is issued, there is usually a time period (fifteen to thirty days) during which the decision can be appealed.

Projects on federal land (or those fully or partially funded with federal money) are subject to the requirements of the National Environmental Policy Act. The process, similar to that stated above, should be carried out by the lead federal agency.

Shoreline and Wetland Regulations

Many states, counties, and cities have adopted legislation to protect the vegetation, wildlife, water, and aquatic life of shorelines and wetlands. These laws vary greatly from one jurisdiction to another.

Shoreline and wetland protection laws typically include a purpose statement defining the intent of the legislation, as well as the procedures for obtaining the necessary permits. Also included may be shoreline and wetland overlay zoning and sensitive areas designation, each with its own specific development standards. Determining the need for shoreline and wetland permits typically occurs during the environmental review process. Most projects that do not require a full EIS usually are still required to secure shoreline permits. Permits are typically required for dredging, filling, and any other construction activity that may upset spawning and nesting patterns. Permits frequently require that certain construction activities be completed within a limited time period to minimize disruption to fish and wildlife. As with an EIS, most shoreline permits can be appealed within a specified time period (thirty days).

Permits and Licenses

In addition to the permits required by shoreline and wetland legislation, several local, state, and possibly federal permits and licenses may be required. The local agency or department that issues the master use permit (the umbrella permit covering all zoning and environmental permits) for a project will usually have a "punch" list of all permits and licenses that may be required for your project. Again, the specifics will vary from community to community. Possible required permits at the local and state levels can include the following:

▶ Land-use permit

▶ Shoring and excavation permit

▶ Drainage permit

▶ View protection certification of compliance

▶ Foundation permit

▶ Building permit

▶ Electrical permit

▶ Mechanical permit

▶ Street-use permit

▶ Demolition permit

▶ Structural permit

▶ Sign permit

▶ Energy-code approval

▶ Fire-code inspection

▶ Plumbing permit

▶ Water permit

▶ Water-quality certification

▶ Hydraulic permit

▶ Tidelands lease or easement

▶ Floodplain compliance permit

Additionally, the U.S. Army Corps of Engineers requires permits for work in navigable waters, for filling waters or adjacent wetlands owned by the federal government, and for disposal of dredged material.

While the list is long, it need not be overwhelming. Many of the permits are routinely issued once the master use permit is approved. Others are handled within the context of the environmental review process. The best approach is to find someone at the local level who knows the permit system and is willing to help guide you through the process.

Construction Regulations

During construction, the contractor will be required to have certain licenses, obtain certain permits, and abide by certain regulations. These should be spelled out in the contract that the contractor signs. While many tend to be "boilerplate" requirements that appear in all contracts, it is critical to have professional help in developing the contract so as to avoid legal and quality-control problems. Most local and state governments have standard forms of construction contracts that include the following:

▶ Requirements for maintaining traffic

▶ Barricade and sign requirements

▶ Procedures for shutting off gas and electric lines

▶ A dewatering plan

▶ A sewer license

▶ Site maintenance requirements

▶ Street-cleaning requirements

▶ Air and noise pollution control

▶ Erosion and siltation control

▶ Materials specifications

In addition, contractors must meet federal, state, and local fair hiring and labor practices.

❖

DEVELOPING A COMPREHENSIVE BUDGET AND MANAGEMENT PLAN

Prior to construction of the trail facility, you should develop a comprehensive budget and management plan that includes all the costs of maintaining the trail.

When considering maintenance costs, keep in mind the following direct relationship: If you build it, you must maintain it. If you install informational and directional signs, for example, a certain percentage of them must be replaced each year. If you include an automatic sprinkler system, you will need to maintain it on a routine basis. Your trail design, therefore, must reflect the amount of money (and volunteer time) available for maintenance.

Unfortunately, maintenance dollars are difficult to secure. Foundation and government grants, while available for trail acquisition and development, are generally not available for maintenance. And it is not easy to get the public involved in raising funds for routine maintenance. The lesson is that maintenance costs are best addressed through prevention—by spending money during the design phase to avoid management problems later.

Key Factors in Developing a Comprehensive Budget and Management Plan

Keep in mind that developing an accurate maintenance budget is a step-by-step "process," not an exact science. Differences in bookkeeping methods, wages, trail design, topography, availability of maintenance equipment, community expectations, and a host of other variables make it impossible to say categorically that a certain type of trail will have fixed maintenance costs per mile per year. Two identical trails in different communities may have radically different per-mile maintenance costs. Even so, it is feasible to develop an accurate estimate of maintenance costs for a particular trail system if the following components are included.

■ Existing Costs

An easy first step is to check the current per-mile cost for maintaining a similar existing trail in a similar community. (If your trail is the first in your area, check with a neighboring jurisdiction.) Get the maintenance costs for a trail that is nearby and analogous to your project; cost figures from distant trails may not be relevant.

When obtaining cost information, go over the budget with someone who can explain all the items included. For example, does the budget include labor and overhead costs? Does it include one-time costs on major equipment such as sweepers and trucks? Does it include charges for bringing debris to the local landfill? Is some maintenance done by volunteers? Every agency budgets differently, and the answers to these questions often explain the discrepancies in per-mile maintenance for similar trails.

■ Bookkeeping

A second important step is to find out how your trail managing agency assigns charges to various maintenance activities. In particular, you will want to look at major equipment, labor, and overhead costs. If you need to purchase a sweeper for trail maintenance, for example, there may be a separate capital fund to pay for it, in which case you pay only the labor costs of the operator. Or the trail maintenance budget may be charged a per-hour fee that covers the amortized lifetime costs associated with the sweeper's purchase and maintenance. Labor and overhead costs can also vary greatly. The cost of a maintenance employee making $10 an hour may actually be charged to the budget at $20 an hour if all overhead costs are included. Some agencies maintain separate budgets for benefits, office space, and management support while others account for these items as per-hour labor costs. The bottom line is that all agencies keep their books differently, so be sure you know how yours are set up. The bookkeeping methods used by the agency managing your trail will have a major impact on how you develop a maintenance budget.

■ Maintenance Checklist and Cost

The next step in developing a budget and plan is to create a checklist of all possible maintenance activities. Begin by listing every aspect of the trail's design. Once again, the general rule is that you will have to maintain whatever you build. Next to each maintenance activity list its frequency, its cost per application, and its annual cost. Calculating the annual cost may seem like a lot of work, but you can do it if you understand the bookkeeping system and how charges will be assigned.

Sample Maintenance Activity List

Consider this partial list of maintenance activities as you develop your maintenance budget and plan. Of course, you will need to modify it to reflect the needs and community expectations of your particular trail.

▶ Replace missing and damaged regulatory and directional signs.

▶ Repaint worn pavement markings.

▶ Trim trees, shrubs, and grass to maintain sight distances.

▶ Patch holes, fill cracks, and feather edges.

▶ Clean drainage systems; modify to eliminate ponding.

▶ Sweep to remove leaves, mud, gravel, and other debris.

▶ Mow trail shoulders (2½ to 5 feet back from trail).

▶ Mow other selected areas where groomed look is desired.

▶ Pick up trash; empty trashcans.

▶ Clean out ditches, culverts, and other drainage structures.

▶ Maintain furniture and other support facilities.

▶ Clean restrooms and drinking fountains; repair as needed.

▶ Remove graffiti from restrooms, retaining walls, rocks, and other surfaces.

▶ Prune dense understory growth to promote user safety.

▶ Inspect structures for deterioration.

▶ Remove fallen trees.

▶ Clean and replace lights (in tunnels and at road crossings).

▶ Spray for weed control.

▶ Remove snow and ice.

▶ Maintain emergency telephones.

▶ Maintain irrigation lines.

▶ Install and remove snow fences.

■ Routine and Major Maintenance

Once you have completed a draft list of maintenance activities, divide them into "routine" and "major maintenance" categories. In general, frequent maintenance activities such as mowing are considered routine. Activities done once every several years, such as repaving a trail surface, fall under major maintenance. Although major maintenance is needed only infrequently, it should be budgeted on an annual basis to avoid the periodic need for a major infusion of cash.

■ Maintenance Priorities

The next step is to set maintenance priorities by identifying which activities are critical to the trail's safe operation and which are key to other objectives, such as maintaining the infrastructure, protecting the environment, and protecting the overall appearance of the area.

While some priorities may vary according to local community expectations and the trail's needs, safe operation of the trail should never be compromised. Trail maintenance should conform to the design guidelines used to build the trail. And where proper guidelines were not used, maintenance should include improvements that will enhance the trail's safety and operation.[8]

■ Tracking

The final task in developing a budget and management plan is to create a tracking system that ensures the timely and systematic completion of all maintenance activities. You will probably want to develop a checklist for field crews and volunteers that includes instructions on each maintenance activity and its frequency. You should also develop a system for requesting specific maintenance improvements, such as sign replacement, and a standardized work instruction form.

■ Budget and Management Plan

Once the above steps have been completed, the budget and plan are ready to be put into final form. You should include a checklist of all maintenance items, the frequency of each activity as well as each activity's annual cost, and the individuals who will perform the activities. Priorities related to safe operation of the trail should be clearly identified and a tracking procedure clearly outlined.

As you enter the design phase, remember that the best solution to maintenance problems is prevention. If potential problems become apparent during the planning phase, address and solve them during the design phase. For example, the single biggest cause of maintenance-related safety problems is drainage, and fixing damage caused by drainage is often the biggest line item in a maintenance budget. The solution is to solve drainage problems before a trail is built by including drainage facilities in the trail

design. In the long run, it will be money well spent.

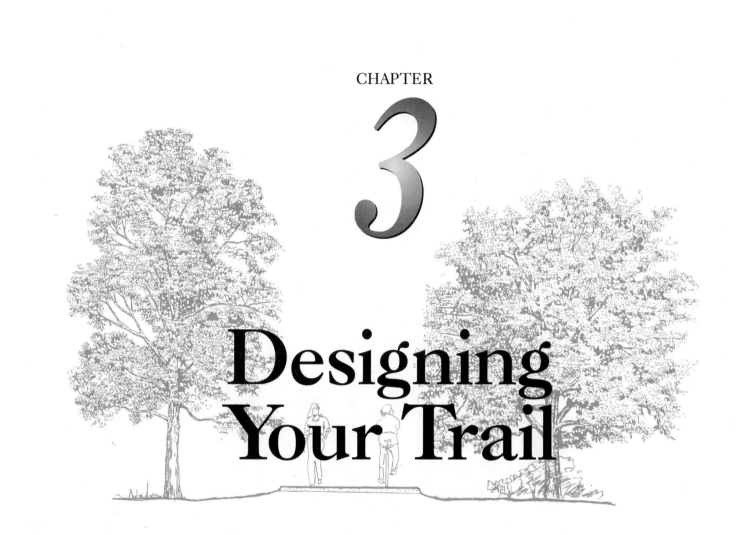

CHAPTER

3

Designing Your Trail

63

MAKING YOUR MULTI-USE TRAIL UNIQUE

Your multi-use trail will be an integral feature of your community, so its design should reflect the identity of its surroundings and should satisfy your community's needs. The following suggestions are designed to help you create a trail that is not like any other, one that highlights the uniqueness of your area.

Emphasize Local Conditions

When local topography, climate, flora, fauna, and local materials and traditions are incorporated into trail design, the result is a trail that is a memorable reflection of your area. Refer to the notes that you made during your initial assessment of the trail corridor (see "Physical Inventory and Assessment of the Site" in chapter 1); it should highlight special features along the route.

■ Topography

A trail should be skillfully incorporated into its surrounding topographical features. For instance, the path could extend onto a hill to take advantage of a special vista or pass near rocky crags and rock formations. A marshy terrain could be a potential bird and wildlife preserve, and a flat plain will offer good views of sunrises and sunsets. While not a multi-use trail, the Blue Ridge Parkway is a fine

Figure 3.1: Ramada – trail user rest structure.

example of how to emphasize unique local features. Skillful layout and design by a landscape architect more than fifty years ago opened up views from the parkway onto landscapes that are characteristic of the region, such as old Virginia tobacco farms. Payments made to the owners protected the farms from developers looking to subdivide them. The parkway passes by fields and features local styles of fences and barns.

■ Climate

Climate can also add to the distinctiveness of your trail. If your trail is in a hot, sunny desert area, shade will be one of its most important and desirable features. If appropriate to your region, you can plant trees for shade, or you can build rest stations. These can be "ramadas," simple wood-frame structures overlaid with branches (figure 3.1) or trellis structures covered with vines. A cold, snowy climate calls for the planting of evergreens. When placed strategically, they add color and act as windshields for windy sections of the trail (see "Landscaping" later in this chapter). Responding to the region's most difficult yet typical climatic condition in your design will increase the trail's usability.

■ Flora

Consider the most distinctive plant of your area. Maples? Hemlocks? Saguaro cactus? Readily available and easily identified by local people, native vegetation is a point of pride and should form the foundation of any trail design. In

65

Figure 3.2: Northeastern vegetation.

Photo: Virginia McGinnis

Elaborating on or accentuating the landform through which the trail passes enhances the land's inherent specialness and brings it to the user's attention. For example, a multi-use trail could offer fruit-bearing plants, such blackberries, blueberries, or even the forgotten paw-paws. Users should be encouraged to take advantage of these treasures by picking and eating fruit along the way (figure 3.4). Local garden clubs could be tapped to help maintain the trail and to develop interpretive signs.

■ Fauna

Certain areas attract wildlife because of their proximity to water or forest cover. A local bird-watching organization may wish to help create an environment along your trail that fosters the presence of birds. Talk with an ecologist at a local college or university about establishing or preserving wildlife along trail corridors. Also consider plantings that provide food, shelter, and nesting areas for wildlife.

■ Local Materials

When designing your trail, consider using local or regional materials to construct the trail's built elements, includ-

parts of the Northeast, for example, the autumnal show of fiery red, gold, and orange leaves is emblematic of the region's character (figure 3.2). In certain areas of Connecticut, hemlocks, which are particularly attractive after a snowfall, appear as silvery etchings on the landscape. Similarly, the dramatic image of the saguaro dotting the desert has come to represent the Southwest (figure 3.3).

There are endless other possibilities. Consider plants that attract local bird populations or those commercially grown in the fields around the trail. A cluster of lemon trees within a trail corridor linking urban and rural regions may be appropriate in California. The Baltimore and Annapolis Trail in suburban Maryland is dotted with patches of wildflowers to attract butterflies to the trail. People so much enjoy seeing the butterflies fluttering about that they donate money specifically for wildflower plantings.

ing the surface material, fences, bridges, and signs. If, for instance, the trail winds through cuts in rock, the use of that crushed local stone will echo the topography of the site (of course, it must have the proper composition for a trail surface).

In York County, Pennsylvania, broken plates, cups, and saucers from a local dinnerware factory will be crushed into fine stone and used as a subsurface material on a rail-trail. Tires and glass are also recycled for trail use. The Willard Munger State Trail in Minnesota is testing rubber asphalt on a section of the rail-trail; and a $100,000 project in Portland, Oregon, will use rubber-modified asphaltic concrete on nearly two miles of paved strips. Ground glass has also been used to supplement asphalt. Often added to asphalt in New York City streets, ground glass not only extends the surface's use but also gives the street a pleasing mica-like sparkle at night.

Familiarize yourself with local factories and companies dealing in materials such as stone, plastic, wood, and metal. You may be able to obtain materials for a reduced price in exchange for free publicity, or some companies may even donate materials as a contribution to the

Photo: Balmori Associates

Figure 3.3: The vegetation of the Southwest is striking in this trail in Tucson, Arizona.

Figure 3.4: Fruit-bearing plants along trail.

Photo: Sally Matthews

Figure 3.5: This memorable "shorthorn cow" along a rail-trail in England is an interesting way to recycle former railroad parts.

community. Even if these materials must be purchased, money stays in the local community, and the trail displays something produced in the area.

Also consider using local materials for signs and facilities along the corridor. In the South, for example, the use of cypress lends local character to signs and fences. Cypress is highly durable, even when exposed to extreme weather for long periods.

■ Local History
Incorporating local history into a trail project can provide a memorable experience for many trail users. The Farmington Canal rail-trail project in Connecticut has designed a pedestrian bridge over a busy street to highlight the tradition of New England's covered wooden bridges. The Farmington trail also features American chestnut trees along the section of the trail that passes the Connecticut Agricultural Experiment Station in New Haven. In 1980, Dr. Sandra Anagnostakis discovered a treatment for the fungus that threatened the chestnut's extinction in the Northeast. By passing a nursery of chestnuts at different phases of their growth (donated by the experiment station) trail users can observe a living laboratory. Thus, the uniqueness of the trail is directly related to New England's history, and it reflects the work of a local citizen, Dr. Anagnostakis, whose contribution to the land will be felt by all trail users.

Incorporating historic sites and structures—canal locks, railroad depots, and historic buildings—into the trail also will enrich trail users' experiences. Interpretation of these structures will further enhance the trail. In addition, you can highlight the history of the people who lived along the route as well as those who helped to develop the original rail or canal corridor.

You might also consider asking local artists and designers to create artworks based on local history. In England, old railroad equipment is converted into sculpture and placed along rail-trails, like the grazing cow fabricated from a collection of abandoned railroad paraphernalia shown in figure 3.5. Not only are the sculptures memorable, but they also remind trail users of the route's history. In Washington State a collection of folk windmills and whirligigs built by local artists is displayed next to an electric power substation in a local park (figure 3.6), juxtaposing the modern power station against a much older method of generating power. Consider seeking a grant from a local or national arts organization. City and state arts councils and the National Endowment for the Arts offer funds encouraging the use of local talent for innovative projects. You may also seek money for a national talent when local artists are not available.

Accommodate Users

A multi-use trail can also reflect its predominant users, adding to the trail's uniqueness. For example, if a demographic study of the trail's sur-

Figure 3.6: Local artists fabricated these "windmills" near a power sub-station in Washington State.

rounding area shows a high concentration of older residents, you will want to develop your trail to accommodate them, possibly by building additional benches and other support facilities. If, however, you anticipate mainly young, fitness-conscious users, per-

haps a self-guided fitness course adjacent to your trail is most appropriate. Offering extra features for a particular age group—such as a small play area for children—will give your trail special character.

These guidelines are only starting points. Allow regional characteristics and local history to guide you through the design process. In every aspect of design, consider different ways of using available local resources to give your trail some interesting local flavor.

❖

DEVELOPING A DESIGN PLAN: IN-HOUSE STAFF VS. OUTSIDE CONTRACTOR

As you enter the design phase of a multi-use trail project, you will need to determine whether you have the staff to design the project in-house or whether you need to hire a consultant to do the work. If the two options appear equal, you should probably go with in-house staff because it will likely be simpler than hiring a contractor and you will have more direct control over the project.

There are two basic questions to ask before deciding who will design the trail. First, is there a competent, preferably experienced, member (or members) of your staff who could carry out the work necessary to design a multi-use trail? Does the staff have the time to develop a design plan? If the answer to both questions is yes, go with a staff person. If not, you should probably hire a consultant. Another option is to develop a design team composed of in-house staff and outside contractors.

Politics may have a bearing on your decision to hire a consultant, such as a landscape architect, civil engineer, or land-use planner. Presumably your agency has a solid reputation for doing good work in the community or throughout the state. However, if problems have occurred in the past or there is a perceived lack of public trust in your agency, you may want to consider hiring a consultant. In some cases, a consultant is viewed as a neutral third party hired to develop the best possible project for the community.

Depending on their location and previous experience, consultants may be viewed as outsiders who do not understand the needs of a community.

For example, residents of a small town in central Iowa may be skeptical of a big Chicago-based consulting firm, particularly if most of its experience has been centered in the Chicago area. Since public involvement is an important aspect of the design phase, be sure to hire someone with whom the public feels comfortable.

Working with a hired consultant may have advantages. Many consultants are able to meet tight deadlines and move more quickly than an in-house person can, especially if the staff member is already working on several projects. If you are feeling pressure to move the project forward quickly, a consultant can often provide the relief you need. If your staff is small or has little experience with multi-use trail projects, a consultant can provide the necessary expertise.

The positive aspects of working with an in-house staff person should also be weighed. If you are fortunate enough to have an experienced staff, make use of their skills. Communication is likely to be better with a close-at-hand staff person than a (possibly) distant consultant, and your staff probably knows the community better than an outside contractor would. More-

over, the job can probably be done more cheaply by your staff.

The disadvantages of working with your own staff include other work priorities, which can take time away from the trail design effort, and possibly a lack of necessary expertise. As you would expect, there can be negative aspects to working with a consultant as well, including possible cost increases as the project progresses, poor follow-through on what has been promised, and gaps in communication.

When deciding between consultants and in-house personnel, be sure you know their strengths and weaknesses. You are probably familiar with the abilities of a staff member, whereas a consultant's abilities are relatively unknown. It is possible that your consultant may need a good deal of training to get up to speed on the project. Do not assume that because someone is a consultant, he or she is an "expert." In fact, there are many incompetent consultants in business. And many consultants do not have the proper expertise or experience to develop your design plan. With the growth of the trails movement in recent years, a number of consulting firms have developed specialties in trails and green-

One way to avoid hiring an incompetent consultant is to prequalify a list of consultants (annually or biennially) who can bid on projects for your agency. You can send out a request for qualifications; pare down the list of applicants if necessary, based on previous experience; and then observe and evaluate these prospective consultants when they are not in a competitive situation.

If you have not gone through a prequalification process and decide to employ the services of a consultant for a complex job, you should issue a "request for proposals" (an RFP), which allows a number of consultants to bid on your project by outlining their plans and associated costs. Your RFP should be very detailed so you can weed out most of the unqualified consultants early in the process. If a consultant is not qualified to do the job, he or she will not be able to complete a detailed RFP.

The next step is to choose two or three finalists from the best proposals submitted and interview them. You will want to get acquainted with them while learning about their relevant experience and assessing their abilities to do the job. You should examine the consultant's attitude, understanding of the project, and ability to communicate during the interview. A good consultant will use this time to ask questions and become more familiar with the project.[1]

The decision to use one consultant over another should be based on the quality of the interview and proposal, as well as on recommendations from previous clients. It is extremely important to obtain references, just as you would if you were hiring a new employee. The cost of the contract also will play a role in your decision, but remember that the lowest price is not always the best buy. In fact, some consultants put in a low bid to win contracts but then add expenses as a project progresses.

It is wise to document the factors that entered into the decision to hire so that if it is contested in court, a jury can see the logic of your choice. In hiring any consultant, avoid personal favoritism.

Once you hire a consultant, you will need to ensure that project deadlines will be met. One option is to provide incentive payment for completing portions of the project early. You can also stipulate penalties for each day the consultant is late.

If you do not have the money to hire a professional consultant and your staff has little expertise, consider having your project designed by the landscape architecture department at a local college or university. This can be a "win-win" situation for everyone involved. Your agency and the community can benefit because they get design assistance for minimal cost; students get real-world, hands-on experience; the professor has a ready-made class project for the semester; and the university is recognized for its expertise. When considering this option, however, you should realize that it may not result in a completed plan. The professor controls the process, and his or her first priority is providing a valuable learning experience for the students. A project must fit within the academic time frame and meet course objectives. Therefore, your request for assistance should be made well in advance, and with an acceptance of possible constraints. For example, the class project may result in a concept plan,

71

Figure 3.7: Pedestrians along the Ojai Trail in Ventura, California.

face material, and trail amenities. Consider hosting a "community design workshop" during this phase (see "Public Involvement" in chapter 2). A sampling of the trail users you may need to accommodate includes walkers, hikers, joggers, bicyclists, equestrians, cross-country skiers, and snowmobilers. In addition, you need to make the trail accessible to all people, regardless of age or ability.

Pedestrians

Pedestrians include a wide variety of people, such as walkers, hikers, joggers, runners, people pushing baby strollers, and birdwatchers (figure 3.7). These users travel at fairly low speeds (an average of 3 to 7 miles per hour) and tend to have fewer specific design requirements than other users. Many

and you will need to have construction drawings prepared by others.

A university may require a memorandum of agreement that covers costs involved with the project, such as travel expenses related to site visits and photography, printing, and administrative expenses. Many universities with planning and design programs offer assistance to communities. Investigate what resources are available in your region.

❖

MEETING THE NEEDS OF DIFFERENT USERS

Before you embark on your design, you need to know what type of users your trail will serve. Users vary in their needs and expectations, so you should take them into account during the design phase. This is especially important with regard to trail width, sur-

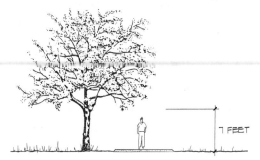

Figure 3.8: Vertical clearance for pedestrians.

pedestrians prefer a surface softer than asphalt (such as crushed rock) to prevent knee, shin, and foot injuries. If you are considering asphalt as your primary trail surface, consider providing at least a 2-foot-wide shoulder, preferably 5, on both sides of the trail for pedestrians. If a separate path is planned, it can consist of graded crushed stone, wood chips, or bare earth. In any case, trees, vines, and other vegetation should be trimmed to achieve a 7-foot vertical clearance (figure 3.8).

Trail facilities to consider for pedestrian users include benches, drinking fountains, restrooms, shelters, and picnic areas.

Bicyclists

When considering bicyclists' needs, keep in mind that there are several types of bicyclists; there are commuting, recreational, touring, and mountain cyclists. Each group uses different equipment and has somewhat different needs, and individuals vary in ability (figure 3.9).

The American Association of State Highway and Transportation Officials (AASHTO) updated its *Guide for the Development of Bicycle Facilities* in 1991.

Photo: Balmori Associates

Figure 3.9: Bicyclists along the Shinning Sea Bikeway in Falmouth, Massachusetts.

The AASHTO guidelines are viewed as the national standard for bikeway design, and many of its recommendations have been incorporated into this manual. Many of the AASHTO design guidelines, such as sight distances, trail width, and trail clearances, apply to all bicyclists; however, some aspects (such as trail surface material) may not apply to mountain bicyclists. Additional concerns specific to mountain bicyclists are addressed separately below.

AASHTO recommends a 10-foot width for bicycle paths, with at least a 2-foot-wide cleared shoulder on either side. Depending on the other anticipated uses on your multi-use trail, a 12-foot-wide trail with shoulders may be advisable.

An 8-foot-wide path is the absolute minimum for a multi-use trail that accommodates bicyclists, and it should be used only under the following conditions: bicycle traffic will be low even

Figure 3.10: Vertical clearance for bicyclists.

during peak times; the trail will have only occasional pedestrian use; good horizontal and vertical alignments will allow safe and frequent passing; and the path will not be used by heavy maintenance vehicles that may damage the trail edge. If your trail will not meet all of these criteria, develop your trail with a width of at least 10 feet. The vertical clearance for safe bicycle use is at least 8 feet (figure 3.10), although 10 feet should be the minimum for overpasses and tunnels.

To accommodate the speed of bicyclists, particularly on paved trails, you should develop your trail for a specific design speed, which is the maximum safe speed that a bicyclist can maintain over a specified section of trail. A trail's design speed should be set at a level that is at least as high as the pre-ferred speed of faster cyclists. In general, develop your trail for a minimum design speed of 20 miles per hour on level terrain, 30 miles per hour for up to 5 percent grade. On slower, unpaved paths, a 15 mile-per-hour design speed is adequate.[2]

Providing adequate stopping sight distance (the distance required to bring a bicycle to a full controlled stop) is critical for bicyclists' safety. Paved or unpaved multi-use trails should maintain a minimum sight distance of 150 feet for bicyclists. If you are building your trail on a former rail corridor or canal, sight distances will rarely be a problem and grades will be minimal. Ideal grades for bicyclists are less than 3 percent (typical for former transportation routes), although up to 5 is acceptable.

Bicyclists should yield the right-of-way to pedestrians and equestrians. Post signs along the trail to indicate this protocol. Signs should also be posted to encourage bicyclists to give a clear warning before passing and to reduce speed or dismount when entering tunnels or culverts.

Trail support facilities should include bicycle racks and, in some areas, bicycle lockers. Racks should be visible and easy to use, and they should be designed to prevent damage to bicycles (see "Trail Support Facilities" later in this chapter). Lockers, which are particularly helpful near mass transit stations and employment centers, should secure the entire bicycle and protect it from inclement weather.

In addition, maps should be displayed at kiosks along the trail to orient bicyclists and other users to their surroundings. Bicyclists will be particularly interested in connecting trails, designated on-street bike routes, and mass transit stations. Periodic rest areas, drinking fountains, and restrooms are also desirable.

Mountain Bicyclists

The mountain bicycle is a new phenomenon that has taken the recreation market by storm. Developed in the late 1970s, mountain bikes skyrocketed in popularity during the late 1980s. Mountain bikes now constitute half of all bicycles sold in the United States. The arrival of this new trail user group has sparked extensive debate as to whether trails, often already crowded, can accommodate an additional use. Of particular concern are mountain bikes' potential to compromise trail safety, degrade the environment, and increase user conflict.

Education is the key to solving these potential problems. Fortunately, the International Mountain Bicycling Association is working actively to educate mountain bicyclists about proper trail use, such as riding only on open trails, yielding the right-of-way to other users, and taking care not to scare animals. If mountain bicyclists will be using your trail, you should develop an educational campaign on proper trail use for all users.

Some mountain bicyclists seek a more rugged, challenging trail experience on steeper grades and softer surfaces than other cyclists do (figure 3.11), but the vast majority of mountain bicyclists ride on streets and trails. The biggest complaint against mountain bicycles is that they tear up certain trail surfaces and cause erosion, particularly after heavy rains or during a thaw. However, this is primarily a problem on steeper grades with natural surfaces or on trails that were not constructed properly (poor subgrade and subbase preparation). If your multi-use trail is on a former railroad, canal, or road, neither of these issues should be of great concern. Railroad corridors

Photo: Larry W. Earl

Figure 3.11: A mountain bicyclist in the Loop Creek Canyon near Avery, Idaho.

rarely exceed grades of 4 percent, and railroad engineers improved the subgrade and subbase problems when they built the line (see "Subgrade, Subbase, and Trail Surface" later in this chapter). Your facility is more likely to suffer damage from mountain bicyclists straying off the trail, a situation that can be best remedied through education and possibly by trail patrols (see "Trail Maintenance and Safety" in chapter 4).

Sight distances, vertical and horizontal clearances, and trail facilities for mountain bicyclists are the same as for other bicyclists. But be sure that any bicycle racks you use can accommodate the wide tires of mountain bicycles.

Equestrians

In many areas of the country, particularly urban centers, equestrians are finding it increasingly difficult to find places to ride. Multi-use trail corridors

Figure 3.12: Equestrians and bicyclists sharing the Little Miami Scenic Trail.

subbase and subgrade of your trail are solid and properly prepared. Horses are unlikely to damage a trail surface unless the subbase is poorly prepared, since the surface is merely a reflection of what lies underneath. Take time during the design phase to prepare your subgrade and thereby prevent future problems with the surface.

Vertical clearance for equestrians should be at least 10 feet (figure 3.13), with a horizontal clearance of at least 5 feet. Low-hanging tree limbs should be cut flush with the trunk (figure 3.14). Leaves, branches, and other protrusions that could injure or damage the horse, rider, or gear, should be removed; and within the tread, large rocks, stumps, and other debris should be cleared. Sight distances for equestri-

are often wide enough to accommodate equestrian use, but many trails prohibit the activity, fearing conflicts with other users and damage to the trail surface. If a trail is properly designed and developed to include equestrians, however, problems will be minimal.

Hard surfaces like asphalt and concrete are undesirable for equestrians because they can injure horses' hooves. Preferred surfaces include granular stone and dirt. If you are con-

sidering a hard surface, you should plan to include a softer 5-foot-wide tread for horses (figure 3.12). Although equestrians prefer a separate tread, a cleared shoulder will suffice if necessary. Equestrians may prefer to develop their own trail within the corridor where sufficient width exists; work with them to accomplish this.

If you plan to develop a single tread that will accommodate numerous users, including equestrians, make sure the

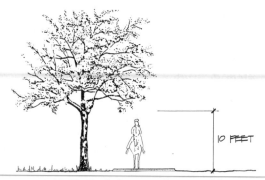

Figure 3.13: Vertical clearance for equestrians.

Photo: Charles E. Dressler

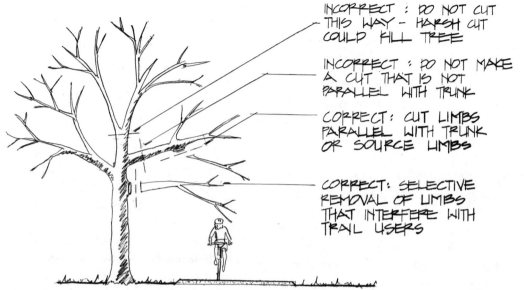

INCORRECT: DO NOT CUT THIS WAY - HARSH CUT COULD KILL TREE

INCORRECT: DO NOT MAKE A CUT THAT IS NOT PARALLEL WITH TRUNK

CORRECT: CUT LIMBS PARALLEL WITH TRUNK OR SOURCE LIMBS

CORRECT: SELECTIVE REMOVAL OF LIMBS THAT INTERFERE WITH TRAIL USERS

Figure 3.14: Proper tree pruning for clearance.

ans, who usually travel between 4 and 6 miles per hour, should be at least 100 feet.

Signs indicating that equestrians have the right-of-way on a multi-use trail should be included in your design plan. Signs can help educate other trail users about equestrians and encourage a "share the trail" ethic. The sign shown in figure 3.15 quickly and clearly indicates right-of-way protocol to trail users. Additional signs encouraging bicyclists to give a clear warning before passing also minimizes potential conflict between user groups.

You will need to provide support facilities for horses and their riders. Parking and staging areas are particularly critical and require a substantial amount of space (see "Trail Support Facilities" later in this chapter). In addition to restrooms and drinking fountains for equestrians, horses need water along the trail. Hitching posts should be installed at rest stops, picnic areas, and restrooms so that horses can be tied off the trail while their riders take a break.

For horseback riders, a water crossing is preferred to a high, narrow, and potentially scary bridge. Horses easily negotiate steep slopes and graveled stream beds. If a water crossing is not practical, provide mounting blocks or space at the ends of bridges and tunnels so riders can dismount and lead their horses. A large, firmly placed log located off the trail will suffice but a more elaborate design is possible. Work with equestrian groups to develop such facilities according to their needs.

Cross-Country Skiers

Many multi-use trails that are used for bicycling, walking, and horseback riding during warm months are ideal

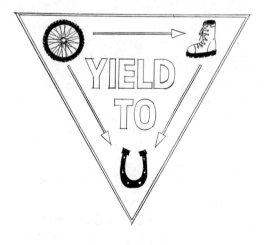

Figure 3.15: Trail etiquette sign.

77

Figure 3.16: Cross-country skiers along Idaho's Wood River Trails.

for cross-country skiing during winter months (figure 3.16). With a little preparation (and minimal maintenance) a multi-use trail can easily become a cross-country ski trail. Six inches of snow on the trail offers excellent cross-country skiing without damage to the trail or to ski equipment.

The width of a one-way trail used for cross-country skiing should be at least 4 feet; a two-way trail requires at least 7 feet. Clear the trail of shrubs, debris, and vines at least 2 feet on each side of the tread, and provide an overhead clearance of at least 7 feet above the average snow level.

Local retailers of cross-country ski equipment may be interested in promoting cross-country skiing on the trail by providing equipment rentals and skiing lessons. If cross-country skiing is popular in your area, you may actually consider grooming your trail during the snow season. Grooming creates a consistently packed snow surface so the skier can move more easily.

Snowmobilers

While some multi-use trails are designated snowmobiling trails during the winter months, snowmobilers have transformed many others into de facto snowmobiling trails (figure 3.17). In fact, many of these routes are used to access existing snowmobile trails. Multi-use trails can be converted into snowmobile trails with as little as 3 inches of snow, without causing much damage to the trail surface.

You should keep in mind several design requirements if snowmobiling is a potential use of your trail. For one-way snowmobile traffic, the trail tread should be at least 8 feet wide (10 is preferred); for two-way traffic, it should be at least 10 feet wide (14 is preferred). The trail should be free of branches and debris for at least 2 feet on either side of the trail and at least 10 feet above the expected snow base.

Horizontal sight distances should be 400 feet because of the high speeds that snowmobiles can attain. If this sight distance cannot be achieved, post caution signs at least 100 feet in advance of any problem area to encourage snowmobilers to slow down. Try to provide a 100-foot turning radius if possible.

Figure 3.17: Snowmobilers enjoy the Aroostook Valley Trail in Maine

Make sure any bridges or tunnels are wide enough to accommodate snowmobiles. They need at least an 8-foot-wide clearance and a minimum carrying capacity of 5 tons. Intersections can be dangerous areas for snowmobilers, so the approach grade should be 5 percent or less, and the intersection should be cleared to double the trail width if possible.

Conflicts can easily erupt between cross-country skiers and snowmobilers, particularly because of the noise and difference in speed. Many believe that the two uses are incompatible, although some multi-use trails have been developed to accommodate both user groups. If both groups want to use the trail, educating them about trail user etiquette is a must. Signs are critical, and speed limits for snowmobilers may be appropriate.

Some trail managers have developed creative solutions to the conflict between these two user groups. Minnesota's Luce Line Trail allows snowmobilers on half of the 60-mile-long trail and cross-country skiers on the other half. Other managers have set up a system whereby skiers and snowmobilers have access to the trail on alternate days. If you anticipate conflicts be-

Photo: Charles E. Dressler

Figure 3.18: In-line skater and bicyclists along Xenia to Yellow Springs Bikeway.

tween these two users, develop creative solutions during the design phase rather than after the trail is open.

Other Users

You may need to consider other users during your design phase, including in-line skaters (figure 3.18), people who want fishing access, skateboarders, people in wheelchairs, dog-sledders, and others. Try to involve them in your design plans and encourage them to identify their special needs. Consider how well your trail will be able to accommodate baby strollers, people with pets, and other occasional, often slow, users. In the end, you may not be able to accommodate every use, but you should consider all the possibilities before making crucial design decisions about trail surface material and facilities.

Making Your Trail Accessible

Your multi-use trail design should be accessible—free of barriers and obstructions and usable by people with disabilities. This is extremely important because most people have some temporary or permanent disability during their lives. And the 45 million Americans with permanent disabilities want to enjoy a trail experience with other people, rather than having a separate, "special" facility.

The primary sources of information for developing accessible standards for all buildings and facilities are the *Uniform Federal Accessibility Standards (UFAS)* and the "Americans with Disabilities Act Accessibility Guidelines," published in the *Federal Register* on 26 July 1991. You should also be familiar with the policies set forth in the Americans with Disabilities Act. (The guidelines and the law are available by calling 1-800-USA-ABLE.) Get a copy of all these documents, and consult any state and local codes before constructing your trail.

Another publication, still in draft form, is the *Design Guide for Accessible Outdoor Recreation,* developed by the National Park Service and the U.S. Forest Service in cooperation with the Ar-

Photos: Julia R. Maloney

Figures 19 and 20: People using wheelchairs along the Washington and Old Dominion Railroad Regional Park.

chitectural and Transportation Barrier Compliance Board. This publication takes an innovative approach, including a set of "challenge levels" for accessible outdoor facilities. People with disabilities have different capabilities and want different levels of difficulty (figures 3.19—3.20) just as other peo-

ple do. Thus, you may find it appropriate to designate a certain "challenge level" to your multi-use trail. According to *UFAS,* an accessible trail must meet a number of specifications including width, passing space, surface, slopes, clearance, rest areas, and signs. Most of these provisions relate to access for mobility-impaired people.[3]

Five feet is the minimum width to accommodate a wide range of users with disabilities, and your trail is likely to be double this width. Hard surfaces, such as asphalt and concrete, make a trail most accessible. Compacted crushed stone also works well, provided that the stones' diameter is less than 3/8 inch. Loose gravel is not recommended because it can pose problems for people using wheelchairs or walking aids.

An accessible trail gradient should not exceed 5 percent. If it does, build a ramp (not stairs) to accommodate all users. Although *UFAS* recommends a maximum ramp grade of 8 percent, a 6 percent maximum is strongly recommended. Ramps, which should have a level landing for every 30 inches of vertical rise, must have a hard, slip-resistant surface (figure 3.21). Install

32-inch-high handrailings on ramps and on bridges.[4]

An accessible trail calls for a rest area every 200 to 300 feet, preferably cleared, with a bench, outside of the trail tread. If installing numerous benches is not possible, plan to post (at trail access points) the distance between rest stops. Then users will know the distances before they set off on the trail.

At access areas, provide at least one accessible parking space. (For actual dimensions, see "Trail Support Facilities" later in this chapter) Also, if you plan to develop any barriers along the trail, such as bollards or gates to prevent motorized access, provide at least a 32-inch-wide clearance for wheelchairs. Be sure to install accessible trail support facilities, including restrooms, drinking fountains, and picnic tables. The more accessible your trail, the more users can enjoy it.

Recommended Tread Widths for Multi-Use Trails

Multi-use trails, by definition, should accommodate various users simultaneously, although this can be difficult given the diverse needs of each user group. Accommodating a range of users within

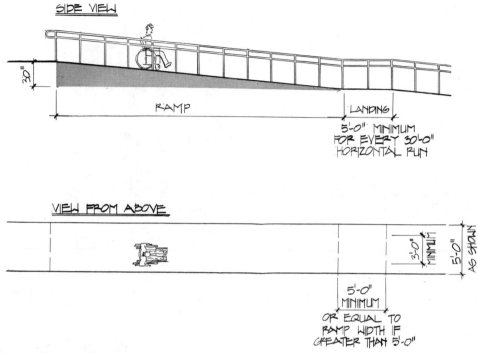

Figure 3.21: Accessible ramp.

a single trail depends upon trail width, trail surface, and speed of trail users.

The width of a trail depends on the land available within the boundaries of your project. For example, if an abandoned railroad bed is built up several feet above the surrounding grade, there is little opportunity for separated treads immediately adjacent to the railroad bed.

National standards for multi-use trail widths do not exist. For example,

the American Association of State Highway and Transportation Officials recommends a 10-foot width for bicycle trails, but some of these paths are too narrow to handle the ultimate volume of users. Consider the number of people who are likely to use your trail. Where "significant" trail traffic is anticipated (one hundred trail users per hour during peak periods), the width of a two-way, single-tread path should be at least 10 feet (figure 3.22). Significant traffic will occur in some rural areas and many suburban areas. In urban areas, where "heavy" trail traffic is anticipated (300 users per hour during peak periods), the width of a two-way path should be at least 12 feet.

The types of users who will use the trail adds another layer of complexity. To accommodate a wide variety of user groups in various settings, multi-use trails should have the following widths:

USER GROUPS	URBAN	SUB-URBAN	RURAL
All non-motorized users	14 feet	12 feet	10 feet
All non-motorized users, except equestrians	12 feet	10 feet	8 feet
Non-motorized and snowmobilers	14 feet	12 feet	10 feet

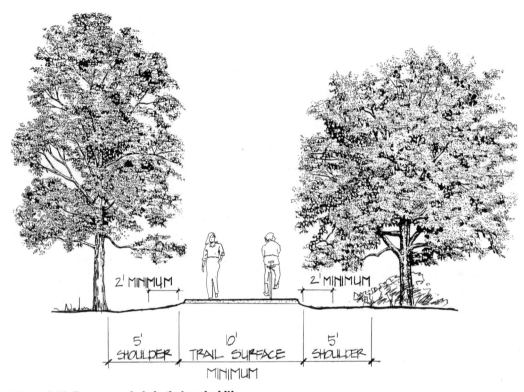

Figure 3.22: Recommended single tread width.

Under certain conditions it may be advisable to provide separate, parallel facilities for bicyclists and other users. When separating users, you need to decide what configuration will work best within your corridor: one primary, hard-surfaced tread primarily for bicyclists and other wheeled users, with a single shoulder for pedestrians and possibly equestrians; one main tread with a shoulder on each side; or two completely separate treads, segregated from each other by a few feet or by vegetation. Two treads can separate faster users requiring hard surfaces (such as bicyclists and in-line skaters) from walkers, runners, and equestrians, who prefer softer surfaces. During winter months, the two treads separate snowmobilers from cross-country skiers.

A primary tread should be developed at a minimum width of 10 feet in an urban or suburban area, 8 feet in a rural area. Develop a single shoulder for pedestrians and equestrians at least 5 feet wide (figure 3.23). (These widths are also appropriate when you are developing two separate treads). For dual shoulders, you need a minimum of 2 feet on each side of the primary tread.

❖

SUBGRADE, SUBBASE, AND TRAIL SURFACE

It is easy to assume that the difference between a smooth trail and a bumpy one is the material used to surface the trail. This is rarely the case. If you were to saw vertically through the surface and into the soil mass several feet down, you would reveal the three components of most multi-use trails: the subgrade, the subbase, and the trail surface (figure 3.24).

The subgrade is the native soil mass of the landscape; the subbase is a man-made layer of stone and rock constructed on top of the subgrade; and the trail surface is the material installed on top of the subbase. As a unit, the structural qualities of these three individual components determine the strength and quality of a trail. If you properly evaluate, design, and construct these layers, your trail surface will be smooth and should last for many years.

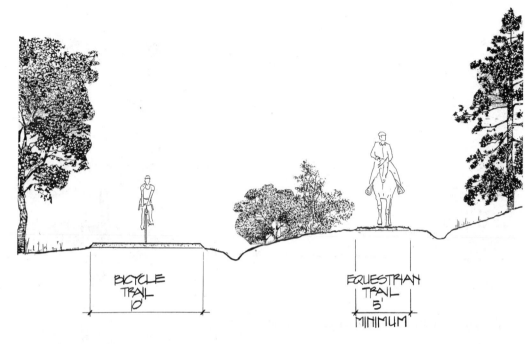

Figure 3.23: Recommended widths for double treads.

Ground Surface Concerns

As you plan the precise layout of your multi-use trail, examine the condition of the ground surface, especially the vegetation growing within or immediately adjacent to the corridor. Vegetation should be cleared and stumps and roots removed along each edge of the trail for at least 5 feet (figure 3.25). This is recommended for sev-

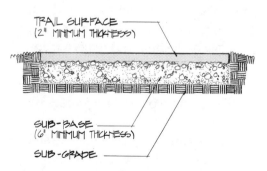

Figure 3.24: Three layers of trail composition.

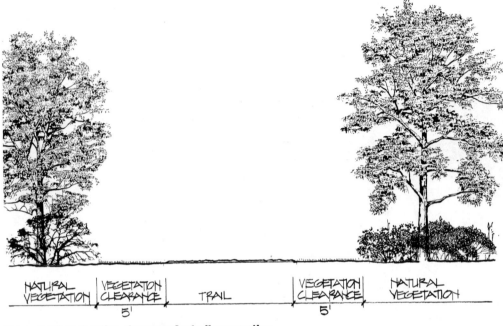

NATURAL VEGETATION | VEGETATION CLEARANCE 5' | TRAIL | VEGETATION CLEARANCE 5' | NATURAL VEGETATION

Figure 3.25: Vegetation clearance for trail preparation.

eral reasons: to prevent roots and later growth from eventually encroaching on the trail subgrade, subbase, or trail surface; to maintain clear sight lines along the edge of the trail; and to permit access by trail construction equipment and emergency vehicles. Eventually smaller shrubs, groundcovers, and grasses will grow back in the cleared area. They should be carefully maintained to stabilize exposed soils (see "Landscaping" later in this chapter).

Once the trail's user groups and width have been determined and any ground surface concerns noted, you (or the actual trail designer) are ready to proceed with the design of the trail cross section.

■ The Subgrade

The subgrade is the trail's foundation. To be suitable for trail development, the subgrade must be able to accommodate the trail's intended uses without overly expensive or severe al-

terations. The suitability and structural properties of the subgrade will determine how the subbase and trail surface must be designed and constructed.

Depending on its length, your trail may traverse a number of different landscapes, and, therefore, you may encounter several types of subgrade. A highly suitable subgrade has moderate slopes, good drainage, and firm, dry soils. In other words, topography, soils, and drainage are key factors in evaluating the subgrade.

■ Topography

Topography—the shape of the land—can be defined as flat, gently rolling, hilly, or mountainous. If you have conducted a physical assessment of your corridor (see "Physical Inventory and Assessment of the Site" in chapter 1), then you know the longitudinal slopes and cross slopes throughout your trail corridor. An accessible trail will have a maximum longitudinal slope of 5 percent (3 percent is preferred) and a maximum cross slope of 2 percent. The following table lists ranges of longitudinal and cross slopes acceptable for specific trail user groups. Fortunately, few rail corridors or canals ever reach longitudinal

TRAIL USER	AVERAGE SPEED	LONGITUDINAL SLOPE	CROSS SLOPE
Pedestrian	3 to 7 mph	no restriction	4 % max
Bicyclist	8 to 20 mph	3% prefer; 8% maximum	2% to 4%
Equestrian	4 to 8 mph	10% maximum	4% maximum
Skier	2 to 8 mph	3% preferred; 5% maximum	2% preferred

slopes of more than 3 percent, so most multi-use trails can accommodate virtually all users.

■ Soils

Soil composition is the most important factor in determining the subgrade's structural suitability (figure 3.26). In fact, the best foundation for a multi-use trail is firm and well-drained soil. Characteristics such as drainage, vegetation type, and composition are visually obvious, but others must be evaluated through scientific and engineering tests.

In addition to the structural suitability of your subgrade soil, you will want to evaluate the following four soil qualities:

Susceptibility to Freezing This is important because your trail can be damaged during cold winter months if the water in the soil freezes and pushes the fine-grained soil particles toward the surface. Known as frost heave, it will cause large lumps or mounds in the surface. You can prevent this problem by replacing fine-grained soil with coarser material, such as a graded aggregate stone.

Permeability This is the soil's ability to drain. Finer-grained or heavy clay soils will not drain as well as coarse-grained soils that contain more air pockets. Poorly drained soils will cause the trail surface to develop water ponds that can remain for more than a day. Replace poorly drained soils with a coarser material.

Bearing Strength This is the soil's ability to bear a specified load. Saturated soils cannot support as much weight as well-drained, moist soils. Low bearing strength can cause the surface of your trail to rut under normal or heavy usage. If your trail is on a former rail bed, then the railroad company probably solved this problem. If not, the solution is to modify soil com-

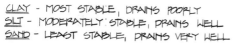

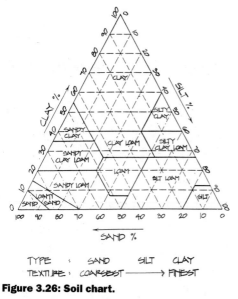

Figure 3.26: Soil chart.

position to obtain good compaction and permeability.

Shrink and Swell This is the soil contraction and expansion caused by water and temperature. A change in soil volume most often occurs with "expansive soils." Expansion and contraction of the soil mass can cause the surface of your trail to crack like an eggshell. Prevent this by replacing expansive soils with a coarser, better-draining material.

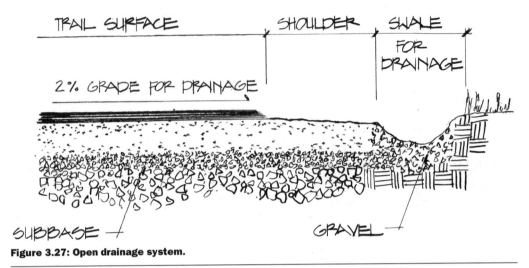

TRAIL SURFACE · SHOULDER · SWALE FOR DRAINAGE

2% GRADE FOR DRAINAGE

SUBBASE

GRAVEL

Figure 3.27: Open drainage system.

To evaluate the four soil qualities, ask the local Soil Conservation Service to test the soils and provide you with a complete description of the types located along the trail corridor. In most states this service is free.

■ Drainage

Proper drainage of surface and subsurface waters is the most important consideration in trail design, construction, and management. Improper drainage will have the greatest detrimental impact on the surface and subgrade of a trail. Proper drainage is the efficient removal of *excess* water from the trail cross section.

Proper drainage serves many functions: it prevents erosion of the subgrade and subbase by accommodating surface water flow; it mitigates the effects of flooding by providing areas where floodwaters can be absorbed naturally; it maintains or improves the water quality of adjacent or perpendicular streams; it maintains areas where surface waters can slowly percolate through the soil mass to recharge aquifers; and it helps ensure that wildlife is not permanently disturbed by trail development.

There are two types of drainage flow: surface water runoff and subsurface water runoff. Surface runoff is

water that moves on top of the ground, creating rills, troughs, and intermittent creeks and eventually draining into streams, rivers, and lakes. Subsurface runoff is water that moves through the soil horizontally or vertically, depending on the soil type and its permeability.

The trail designer must ensure that the trail does not interfere with proper on-site and off-site surface and subsurface runoff. On-site runoff typically results from rainfall. The design objective is to maintain the water-flow level that existed before the corridor was developed. Off-site runoff, usually in the form of adjacent or intersecting streams, should not be altered or obstructed. These are the two fundamental principles that will lead to successful management of drainage along your multi-use trail.

Three basic drainage methods are employed to mitigate surface water runoff. An open system uses swales (shallow drainage channels running adjacent to the trail), ditches, and sheet flow, combined with on-site detention ponds that absorb excess water flow (figure 3.27). Sheet flow allows the water to disperse evenly over the trail and surrounding landscape, preventing ruts and water channels on the

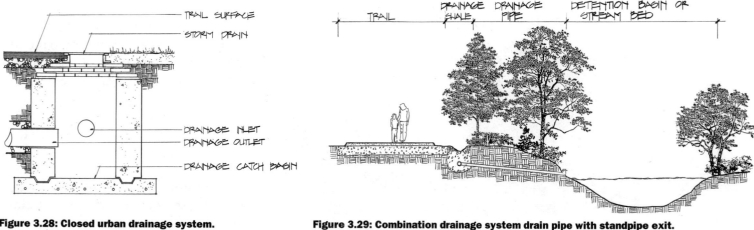

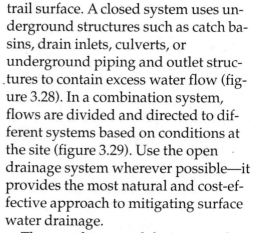

Figure 3.28: Closed urban drainage system.

Figure 3.29: Combination drainage system drain pipe with standpipe exit.

trail surface. A closed system uses underground structures such as catch basins, drain inlets, culverts, or underground piping and outlet structures to contain excess water flow (figure 3.28). In a combination system, flows are divided and directed to different systems based on conditions at the site (figure 3.29). Use the open drainage system wherever possible—it provides the most natural and cost-effective approach to mitigating surface water drainage.

Three underground drainage techniques mitigate subsurface water runoff: Installing piping to carry excess water away from the subsurface of the trail cross section (figure 3.30); con-

structing french drains, trenches filled with permeable material that collect water and route it toward a creek or stream (figure 3.31); and creating sloped and contoured underground drainage channels, where subsurface water is encouraged to flow through the trail cross section unimpeded (figure 3.32).

Work with professional landscape architects, engineers, or your local Soil Conservation Service for cost-effective and successful solutions to any drainage concerns throughout the trail design process. By no means should you underestimate the value of proper drainage systems in the design, development, and management of your trail.

■ Wetlands

Wetlands are a unique condition of the subgrade and surface areas of the soil mass—a result of topography, soils, and drainage. Because they are a valuable natural resource, people need to steer clear of them. The best way to direct traffic away from wetlands is by

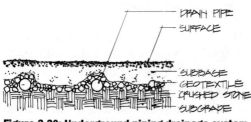

Figure 3.30: Underground piping drainage system.

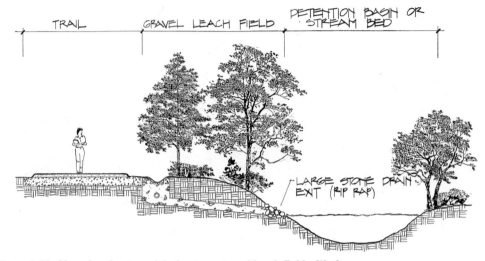

Figure 3.32: Sloped underground drainage — gravel leach field with rip rap.

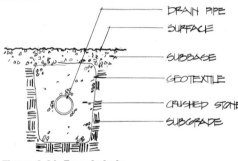

Figure 3.31: French drain.

constructing boardwalks, observation decks, bridges, or some other elevated structure. The use of impermeable surfaces and fill material is prohibited within wetlands, and any construction through them will require a permit from the U.S. Army Corps of Engineers. If you don't know whether there are wetlands in your corridor, or if you need assistance in selecting an appropriate trail surface through a wetland, contact a local environmental or design professional with wetlands expertise, your local Soil Conservation Service, the Army Corps of Engineers, the U.S. Fish and Wildlife Service, or your state's wildlife agency.

The Subbase

The subbase lies between the subgrade and the trail surface and serves as a secondary, built foundation for the trail surface. The purpose of the subbase is to transfer and distribute the weight from the trail surface to the subgrade. The subbase serves a vital drainage function, preventing water from migrating up from the subgrade into the trail's surface. It also allows natural cross drainage to flow through the trail cross section.

The subbase is usually a graded aggregate stone (gravel), which provides bearing strength and improves drainage. You can select from a variety of stones; your choice depends on local conditions and availability. The thickness of the subbase is dependent on the condition of your subgrade. Know the subgrade's characteristics before determining the subbase's thickness. As a general rule, the subbase should be 4, 6, or 8 inches thick. Four inches is sufficient if the subgrade is in excellent condition; up to 8 may be necessary if the subgrade is of poor quality.

The subbase can be placed either by hand or machine and should be compacted with a mechanical roller that weighs at least as much as the trail's anticipated design load (discussed later in this chapter). The subbase surface should be smooth and level because the trail surface will be only as firm, smooth, and resilient as the sub-base and subgrade.

It is *critical* that the subbase remain intact for the trail's lifespan if the surface and structural qualities of the trail are to fulfill their design function. Three factors—ballast, design load, and geotextiles—dictate the design and required depth of the subbase and determine how you should maintain the integrity of this layer during the projected life of your trail.

■ Ballast

A term used mostly by railroad workers, ballast refers to the layer of crushed rock used to elevate a railroad bed above the surrounding natural grade to provide proper drainage, a level surface for the ties and rails, structural stability for the track, and ease in maintaining the roadbed. Ballast retarded the growth of native vegetation and absorbed the shock from heavy loads. Railroad companies used different materials for ballast, ranging from cinders to gravel to fist-sized rocks (figure 3.33).

If your trail corridor is on an abandoned rail corridor, evaluate the condition and type of ballast still present; railroads sometimes remove ballast

Photo: Geoff Goodenow

Figure 3.33: Ballast surface.

when a line is abandoned. If the ballast is gone, evaluate the foundation soils and design your subgrade and subbase to support your multi-use trail.

A common question relating to ballast is, should it be kept in place, or should some of it be removed? The answer depends on the rail bed's condition and the surrounding natural landscape. Remember that the subbase

transfers weight from the surface to the subgrade and improves drainage. If you remove ballast, you are removing a valuable component of the roadbed cross section. Meanwhile, keep in mind that rail beds supported loads of 30,000 pounds per wheel, at speeds of 50 miles per hour—significantly heavier loads and greater speeds than your trail will need to support.

Occasionally, some reduction in ballast depth may be called for, but before embarking on an arbitrary reduction, employ the services of a structural or geotechnical engineer. This person can evaluate the existing ballast subbase and recommend the amount of ballast that can be removed without compromising your trail's structural integrity. Do not dispose of excess ballast as it does have some market value and could cover some of your development costs.

Another potential concern is "track-tie memory," the imprint left by the railroad cross ties on the ballast. Only some rail corridors are affected by it, particularly those with soft soils. To find out if you need to deal with track-tie memory, examine the rail bed where the cross ties have been removed. If you believe your corridor has track-tie memory, the top layer of ballast will need to be removed. The remaining ballast then needs to be regraded, recompacted, and then reconstructed to an elevation that can support the trail's design load. The use of geotextiles, discussed in this chapter, will prevent track-tie memory from appearing in the trail's surface.

Figure 3.34 illustrates the role that ballast can play in the development of a trail with a hard surface. If your budget is limited, however, graded ballast can serve as your trail surface; if you opt to upgrade the surface in the future, it can be layered on top of the ballast.

■ Developing the Trail's
   Design Load

The trail's design load is another factor influencing depth of the subbase. Design load is the *maximum weight* that the trail can carry at any point along its length. Your trail should be accessible by emergency vehicles, such as police cars and ambulances. Also, if you share your corridor with a utility company, the trail will be used by heavy trucks for maintenance and emergency repairs. Therefore, your minimum design load based on static wheel load (at

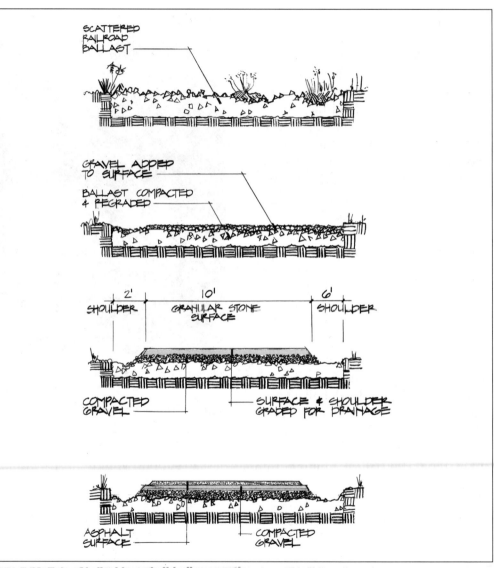

Figure 3.34: Role of ballast in asphalt trail preparation.

each axle) should be 5,000 pounds, and the minimum design load based on gross vehicle weight should be at least 10,000 pounds. The maximum speed for vehicles equaling the weight of your design load should be 15 miles per hour.

The design load is derived by evaluating and computing the combined structural properties of the subgrade, subbase, and surface as one unit. Determining the design load gives you the required depth of these component parts of the trail cross section. For example, if the subgrade is well drained, with a high bearing strength, it will not need modification and can sustain a thinner subbase and surface. If the subgrade is poorly drained with a low bearing strength, it will need modification, and the subbase and surface will need to be thicker to absorb and distribute the loads from trail use. Work with an engineer to make this determination and to define the proper design load.

■ Geotextiles

Geotextiles, which can help reduce subbase depth, are fabric mats that increase the strength of the trail cross section, especially in areas where soft or unstable soils are present. Geotextiles

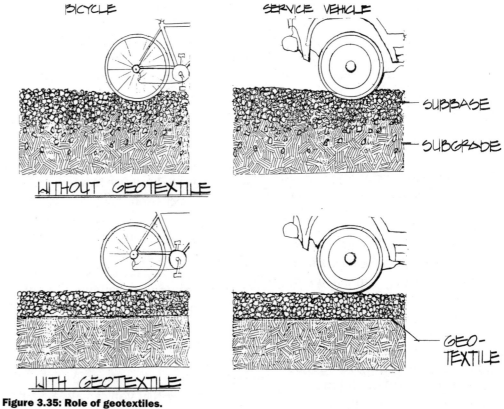

Figure 3.35: Role of geotextiles.

reinforce structural qualities of the subgrade and subbase, help prevent weed growth through the trail surface, and improve drainage.

Most often used between the subgrade and subbase, geotextiles maintain the integrity of the subbase by preventing it from migrating into the subgrade (figure 3.35). Migration, the downward movement of the subbase into the subgrade, damages the trail surface. Geotextiles keep the subbase intact, ensuring the strength and long life of the trail cross section. In some cases, this may allow a reduction in the thickness of your subbase material.

There are two types of geotextile fabrics, woven and nonwoven. Fabric selection depends upon your trail type and local soil and drainage conditions. A geotechnical engineer or landscape architect can help you select an appropriate fabric.

The Trail Surface

There are many surface types available to complete the cross section of your multi-use trail, including granular stone, asphalt, concrete, soil cement, wood chips, and natural surface.

Surface materials are either soft or hard, defined by the material's ability to absorb or repel moisture. Hard surfaces include soil cement, crushed stone, asphalt, and concrete. Soft surfaces include natural earth and wood chips.

Many single-use trails throughout the country, particularly hiking and equestrian trails, have soft surfaces.These surfaces often do not hold up well under heavy use or varying weather conditions, and therefore are not ideal for multi-use trails, particularly those with substantial use anticipated. Hard-surfaced materials are more practical for multi-use trails, particularly in urban and suburban areas. They are more expensive to purchase

and install but require less maintenance and can withstand frequent use. Hard surfaces also accommodate the widest range of trail users. Keep in mind that some "hard" surfaces are softer than others.

Trail surfacing can be used to encourage or discourage use. If you want to encourage as many users as possible, choose one of the hardest surfaces. If you want to limit use to a few groups, select a softer surface. You can also control the speed of trail travel by the surface type you select. The softer the surface, the slower the speeds.

Consider a variety of factors when selecting a surface: availability of the surface material, cost to purchase the material and install it, life expectancy, accessibility, costs of maintaining the surface, and user acceptance and satisfaction.

Remember that you can always upgrade the surface later. If you are dealing with a former railroad corridor and want an asphalt surface but cannot afford it at this point, open the trail with the existing ballast in place and upgrade it in the future. Dozens of high-quality trail facilities have been developed this way. After a trail is open (even with a modest surface), the

support for it quickly expands and public pressure builds to develop a higher-quality facility.

The Cannon Valley Trail in southeastern Minnesota began as a crushed stone trail but was later upgraded to asphalt to accommodate commuting cyclists and attract touring cyclists. The Northern Central Rail-Trail in Maryland, on the other hand, opened with crushed limestone, with plans to pave it later with asphalt. However, the adjacent landowners and local users liked the surface so much (in part because it deterred in-line skating and fast-paced bicyclists) that the agency decided not to change it.

■ Hard Surfaces

Following is a detailed description of hard trail surfaces, ranging from the softest to the hardest. These surfaces are the most appropriate if you will have only one trail tread. If you plan to have two parallel treads, the following surfaces should be used on the primary (that is, wider) tread. The cost estimates cited, which can vary significantly around the country, are in 1992 dollars. They are for a 10-foot-wide trail and cover some subbase preparation.

Photo: Stewart Watkins

Figure 3.36: Soil cement surface.

Soil Cement Used in some areas where stone is not readily available and the price of asphalt is prohibitive, soil cement is a mixture of pulverized native soil and measured amounts of portland cement (figure 3.36). This mixture is usually created at the project site. It should be spread approximately 4 inches thick on a prepared subgrade immediately after the mixture has been formed. It is then rolled and compacted to a very dense surface by machinery.

Soil cement will support most user groups; however, bicyclists and horseback riders will have the greatest impact on the surface. Results with this surface have been mixed: it can crack into large chunks with significant temperature changes or heavy use. Soil cement is inexpensive to install, costing approximately $45,000 per mile for a 10-foot-wide trail, but it may not be the best long-term option.

Drainage is very important to the upkeep of this surface. To prevent water erosion, you can permit sheet flow on longitudinal slopes of 4 percent and less. If the slope is steeper, however, you should crown the trail tread (make the middle slightly higher than the edges) and route the water into side ditches. Soil cement surfaces will last longer if installed on a well-prepared subgrade and subbase, although you will need to control vegetation and make spot repairs. The surface can be placed on longitudinal slopes of up to 8 percent and cross slopes not exceeding 2 percent.

Granular stone This is a very popular surface for multi-use trails because it accommodates a wide variety of trail users and can be compacted into a firm surface (figure 3.37). You can choose from a variety of stones including limestone, sandstone, and crushed rock. These stones can be crushed to a very fine material and densely compacted to hold up extremely well under heavy use. This surface is also compatible with the natural environment and complements the aesthetic appeal of surrounding landscapes.

If this surface is finely crushed and properly packed, it can accommodate virtually every multi-use trail user,

Photo: Geoff Goodenow

Figure 3.37: Granular stone surface.

from road and mountain bicyclists to equestrians. It also works well for people using wheelchairs as long as the stones' diameter are less than ⅜ inch. It is not suitable for in-line or roller skaters or skateboarders, however. For an ideal surface, spread the granular stone into a layer at least 4 inches thick over a prepared subgrade, and compact it with a motor grader.

The use of granular stone is increasing because of its moderate price. Depending upon availability and proximity to the trail, crushed limestone or sandstone costs approximately $65,000 per mile for a 10-foot-wide trail. Maintenance is minimal. Stones should be replenished (and the surface regraded) about every 7 to 10 years, although spot repairs and grading will be necessary in the interim.

Be aware that stones from different quarries can vary significantly. Stones from two limestone quarries within the same state may have noticeably different compositions, for example. This difference can affect how firmly the surface will compact and how well it will wear under heavy use. If possible, visit more than one quarry before selecting the stone for your surface.

Photo: Stewart Watkins

Figure 3.38: Asphalt surface.

It is critical to realize that fine-grained stones will retain moisture and vegetation may sprout within the surface. Use geotextiles to help prevent this problem. Heavy use of the trail also serves as preventive maintenance. Drainage can sheet flow across the surface, or the trail bed can be crowned so that surface water is routed into side ditches. Longitudinal slopes should not exceed 5 percent, and cross slopes should be limited to 2 percent.

Asphaltic Concrete Commonly known as "asphalt," this hard surface is very popular in a wide variety of trail settings and landscapes. It works particularly well on trails that are used for bicycle commuting or in-line skating. However, cross-country skiers may find that snow tends to melt more quickly on asphalt surfaces because the black pavement absorbs heat from the sun. In addition, equestrians generally cannot use an asphalt trail because it is hard on horses' hooves, and the hooves can leave imprints in hot weather. To avoid these limitations, you may want to construct a softer parallel tread along an asphalt trail or leave a wide-enough shoulder for those who prefer a softer surface.

Asphalt is actually a cement composed of tar and oils. In an asphaltic concrete surface a graded aggregate stone is mixed with asphalt (figure 3.38). Small aggregate stones result in a smooth surface with few voids. Coarse graded stones result in a rough, porous surface. When the proportion of asphaltic cement is increased, the surface is smoother and less porous.

Asphaltic concrete is a flexible pavement that conforms to the contours of the subbase and subgrade. If your subgrade and subbase have been prepared properly, the surface will be smooth and level. Asphalt should be installed 2 inches thick and smoothed out with an asphalt machine and rollers.

Asphalt is more expensive than crushed stone, approximately $110,000 per mile for a 10-foot-wide trail. It needs minor maintenance, such as crack patching, and has a life expectancy of 7 to 15 years. Actually, the surface will last longer with heavy use. Asphalt is a flexible surface that needs regular use to remain pliable and resilient.

Asphalt can be installed on virtually any slope, but cross slopes should not exceed 2 percent. Drainage should sheet flow across the trail. Contrary to what some may claim, asphaltic pavement will not "bubble up" or float away under normal surface drainage flow. Extreme flooding can ruin asphalt, however, just as it does almost all other trail surfaces.

Concrete The hardest of all trail surfaces, concrete is most often used in urban areas with severe climate changes, susceptibility to flooding, and anticipated heavy use. Like asphalt, it accommodates virtually all us-

ers, although a parallel path should be provided for equestrians and runners.

Although concrete is the most expensive surface, it lasts longer than any other—often twenty-five years or more. Approximate costs for concrete are $250,000 per mile for a 10-foot-wide trail. Concrete used for trail surfacing should be properly reinforced to prevent cracking. Typically a wire or fabric mesh is constructed over a well-

Photo: Stewart Watkins

Figure 3.39: Concrete surface.

prepared subbase, and then from 4 to 6 inches of concrete are placed on top with an on-site mixer.

Concrete can be shaped to fit most conditions, and it is the only surface that can be tailored at the time of installation—it can be colored with special pigments or scored with grooves in the surface. It should be rough finished with a stiff broom to avoid slipperiness when wet (figure 3.39). Joints should be saw cut (not troweled) to avoid bumpiness. When properly installed, concrete will need virtually no maintenance.

Soft Surfaces

The following surfaces may not be well suited for a multi-use trail that is expected to accommodate a high volume of many different uses. But these surfaces can work well in some rural areas and on parallel treads, particularly for equestrians, runners, and walkers.

■ Natural Surface
Natural surfaces include existing soil and vegetation (figure 3.40). The trail bed will require less preparation than harder surfaces, but you will need to remove rocks, tree roots, and other obstructions from the subgrade.

The only component of bridge construction that is generally not part of the bridge manufacturer's responsibility is the installation of bridge footings. However, most prefab bridge manufacturers will supply required drawings and specifications detailing how the bridge attaches to the footings, which you will need to have engineered and built.

■ Adaptive Reuse of Bridges

Old bridges, no longer sufficient to carry modern highway traffic, are available for adaptive reuse on trails. They often have a scale and character not found in new or prefabricated bridges. Designed for heavy loads, old bridges often need little upgrading for trail use. At the Fox River Trail in northeastern Illinois, for example, developers creatively adapted an existing bridge to meet their needs for a river crossing (figure 3.47).

Funding for bridge relocation and site-preparation engineering work (design of piers and abutments) is available from the Historic Bridge Program within the Federal Highway Administration of the U.S. Department of Transportation. Also, a California organization called BridgeMasters

Photo: Barbara Steinwart

Figure 3.47: Developers of Illinois' Fox River Trail added a trail bridge underneath an active train line, rather than re-construct a parallel bridge that had been removed.

serves as a clearinghouse for finding new sites and uses for historic bridges. BridgeMasters is establishing a national network with state transportation departments and could help trail developers locate a bridge.

■ Selecting an Alternative Crossing

In some instances reconstructing a bridge may be too expensive, particularly if the crossing is unusually long or if recent development prohibits it. If you cannot currently rebuild where a

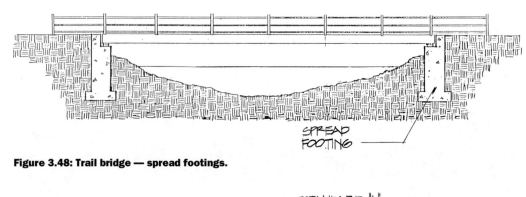

Figure 3.48: Trail bridge — spread footings.

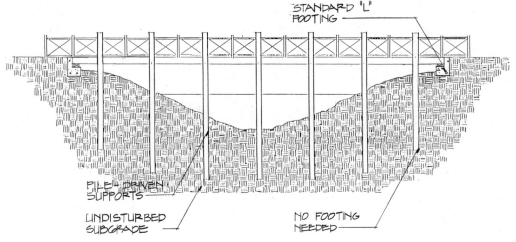

Figure 3.49: Trail bridge — pile driven supports.

acceptable crossing (see "Road Crossings" later in this chapter). If there are no roads, you may need to work out an access agreement with adjacent landowners. Or it may be necessary to purchase additional land to install a crossing that is shorter, safer, and more economical in the long run than a reconstructed bridge would be.

If Both the Superstructure and Footings Have Been Removed

If both the superstructure and footings are gone, you are starting at square one. If a bridge crossing is necessary, the first step will be to work with a geotechnical and structural engineer to evaluate the load-bearing abilities of the soils at the crossing. Once you have determined that, have a structural engineer design the appropriate footings for your bridge.

Evaluate several different designs, including spread footings, pile-driven supports, and piers (figures 3.48–3.50). Make your decision based on cost, design style, and environmental compatibility. Once you have completed the footings for your bridge, you are then ready to construct the superstructure, decking, and railings that are appropriate for your multi-use trail.

prior bridge existed, evaluate the corridor on both sides of the former bridge site to determine the feasibility of an alternate crossing. With luck, this will be only an interim solution until you are able to reconstruct the bridge.

You may find you need to develop a permanent alternative crossing. Find out if any existing roads can facilitate a crossing. In this case, you may need to work with a local or state department of transportation to come up with an

TUNNELS

Tunnels are among the most striking physical features of a trail and one of the most memorable aspects of a trail experience (figure 3.51). If your multi-use trail corridor is in a hilly or mountainous region, there is a good chance that you have one or more tunnels. A tunnel can present challenging structural, design, and management questions. Yet over the long term, many historic railroad tunnels have become, in effect, the signatures of their trails. One rail-trail manager calls his three tunnels "the main attraction of the trail."

Is Your Tunnel Structurally Sound?

If your corridor includes a tunnel, your first step is to have its structural soundness investigated. It is best to consult a geotechnical engineer, but a mining engineer or civil engineer is also suitable. The engineer should undertake a visual inspection of the tunnel and provide you with a written report. The report should address the tunnel's apparent condition; what work, if any, needs to be done to make the tunnel safe for trail use, and how much that work is likely to cost.

Each tunnel was individually created to meet a particular need and to serve a particular site, so some tunnels were lined and others were not. If the tunnel was bored out of strong and stable rock, it is probably unlined (figure 3.52). If it was drilled through weaker rock that tends to crumble, the tunnel was likely lined with wood, reinforced concrete, plain concrete, steel, or possibly bricks (figure 3.53). The liners generally do not hold up the tunnel's walls but prevent loose pieces of rock from falling off the ceiling (or crown) and sidewalls.

Unlined tunnels can be sound tested for structural stability by using a forklift truck and a hand-held steel bar. Stable rock will yield a characteristic ring. But if a piece of rock gives a distinctive dull response, it is judged loose and is mechanically removed. For example, inspection of the three-quarter-mile-long Tunnel Number Three on Wisconsin's Elroy-Sparta Trail, which takes a week, is carried out every other year. Schedule regular inspections for your tunnels, preferably during periods of low use because tunnels will be closed to the public during inspection.

Lined tunnels cannot be sound tested. The liner obstructs the sound; it also hides from view much or all of the geologic activity within the tunnel. Thus, the investigating engineer must look for liner cracking, bulges, flaking (in the case of concrete liners), seepage, movement, rotting wooden timbers, and other signs of trouble.

If these problems exist, the solutions include bolting, injecting "shotcrete" or another type of mortar mix to fill

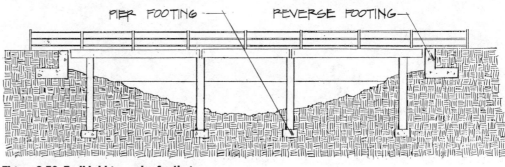

Figure 3.50: Trail bridge — pier footings.

Photo: Jane Whitaker

Figure 3.51: A historic tunnel along West Virginia's North Bend Trail.

voids in the liner, adding permanent liner material to hold the rock, and installing netting. For most trails, adding liner material is the best solution. Although this reduces the inside tunnel clearance, the clearance in most tunnels is sufficiently high for trail users, including equestrians. Reduced clearance poses a problem only if there is a chance that the corridor will return to its original use—for example, as a railroad. Before adding liner material to a tunnel, make sure that reduced clearance will not preclude any future use.

The portion of the tunnel most vulnerable to damage is the entranceway, or portal. Portals take the full brunt of the elements—erosion, freezing and thawing, falling tree limbs, rain and snow, and sometimes human vandalism. Because they are frequently built with one side against a hill and the other over the edge of a valley, they are particularly susceptible to uneven ground movement. Often portals are walls that extend out of the tunnel, so the footings of those walls should be checked for their structural strength.

In cold climates, some railroad companies installed huge wooden doors at a tunnel's opening. The doors were swung shut between trains to protect against winter winds, maintaining the natural 50-degree temperature of the ground. Such doors can be beneficial for a multi-use trail as well. On the Elroy-Sparta Trail, for example, the doors have been refabricated (figure 3.54) and are locked shut from mid-November through mid-April. They reduce the freeze-and-thaw cracking within the tunnel, especially at the portals. (The state of Wisconsin has built a steep alternative route for snowmobilers and skiers to get around the tunnels.)

Water is another potential problem in tunnels. As with any other segment of trail, proper drainage is critical and can be accomplished either by digging ditches at the sides of the trail or by adding a layer of well-drained ballast

Figure 3.52: Unlined tunnel (originally bored from stable bedrock).

in the center of the tunnel and raising the trail above any standing water.

If Your Tunnel Has Structural Problems

Most railroad tunnels were constructed as a "last resort," to provide a passage in inaccessible terrain. Thus, it is far better to utilize a tunnel than to reroute around it. If your tunnel has severe structural problems, however, you have four possible courses of action: raise the money to get the tunnel fixed; shut the tunnel with lockable gates but allow groups through periodically, preceding each tour with a certified safety inspection; issue permits to use the tunnel; or seal the tunnel shut.

If you seal the tunnel, you can do so with thick wood, steel, or concrete, or, preferably, you can install strong jaillike bars that allow users to peek into the tunnel and at least see what a major tunnel is like. (An interpretive sign would work well here, too.) Ideally, the long-term plan would be to unseal the tunnel, repair it, and incorporate it into your trail.

Most tunnels on multi-use trails were built long ago by railroads or canal companies. Occasionally, though,

Figure 3.53: Lined tunnel (used to reinforce loose bedrock).

the need arises for a new tunnel, particularly in places where a highway department has taken out a bridge or trestle over an abandoned railroad track and replaced it with soil and rock fill.

Ideally, your agency would cut a tunnel as beautiful as those constructed by the railroads, but with today's costs that is unlikely. Most new tunnels are constructed with large corrugated metal culverts or precast concrete culverts (figure 3.55). The hole is cut with standard soft-dirt tunneling equipment to accommodate the culverts, which are made in several sizes.

The tunnel's vertical clearance should be at least 10 feet, and the

Photo: Linda Hanlon

Figure 3.54: One of three tunnels along Wisconsin's Elroy-Sparta Trail.

in rural locations are often far from economical sources of electricity.

Many tunnels are short enough that even in the center a little bit of daylight is visible. Other tunnels, because of length and curvature, are literally blacker than the darkest night. If this is the case with yours, make every effort to publicize the fact that flashlights are necessary, and arrange to sell flashlights at convenient locations on or near the trail.

Trail managers usually post signs at the portals of dark tunnels requiring bicyclists and equestrians to dismount and walk through. This is prudent, considering the possibility of collisions or scrapes against tunnel walls.

❖

HISTORIC PRESERVATION

A wealth of resources is available to help you define and interpret the history of your multi-use trail, particularly if your trail is a former rail line. Museums, archives, your state historic preservation office, people living near the right-of-way, and retired railroad employees who ran trains over the former rail line can all help.

width of the tunnel must be at least as wide as your trail. The tunnel should be no less than 10 feet wide and preferably 14 feet wide.

If you opt to use the less-expensive corrugated metal culvert, attempt to improve the appearance of this utilitarian structure by angling each protruding surface down to the ground and facing each with rocks. (figure 3.56).

Special Considerations for Tunnels

Ideally, tunnels should have a source of light, not only for safety and convenience but also because the underground geology and construction techniques are interesting to users. In fact, tunnels are prime locations for interpretive signs and even for narrated tours. Unfortunately, however, tunnels

Figure 3.55: Along Idaho's Wood River Trails, a concrete culvert provides a passage under a highway.

throughout its history. Mergers and takeovers resulted in frequent name changes in the East and Midwest, and to a lesser degree in the West. Knowing the names under which your line operated gives you several advantages. First, you'll be better equipped to conduct research. Railroads generated a great deal of paperwork, and knowing all the names under which your line operated will help you make specific research requests. Otherwise, you might have to chip away at moun-

There are important questions to answer when researching your route's background. About former railroads ask: When and why was the line built? Was it a main line or a branch line? Who traveled over it, and what goods were shipped over it? What kinds of trains ran here? When and why was it abandoned? Similar questions should be asked about former canals and roadways.

Some of these questions have hard-and-fast answers, but others may yield varying data. A route that began life as a heavily used main line with ten express passenger trains a day may have been later bypassed by a shorter "cut-off" route and may have ended its days as a dead-end spur leading to a feed mill or lumberyard.

Researching an Old Railroad

Because most rail lines have existed for many decades (the oldest began about 1825), it is unlikely that your line had a single name or designation

Figure 3.56: A corrugated metal tunnel along the Cape Cod Rail-Trail.

tains of data that may not contain the information you want.

Second, knowing all the previous corporate names will be an important factor in choosing a name for your trail. Also learn what railroaders or local residents called the line as it may differ from the actual corporate name. Third, using the right terminology can give you credibility with the community at large and with the rail history community. Using accurate terms could be a critical element in winning a municipal body's approval or a foundation grant.

If an active railroad abandoned your line, the company may be able to provide access to track charts, bridge drawings, and other engineering data. If the line was abandoned by a company that no longer exists, you will need to get your information from bankruptcy trustees (who can function as real estate firms for years after the railroad is gone), a museum, a university library, or a railroad history society. Some local historical societies maintain railroad records, particularly in areas where a railroad was a large employer or had regional offices.

If the line existed as a common-carrier (public-use) railroad at the time

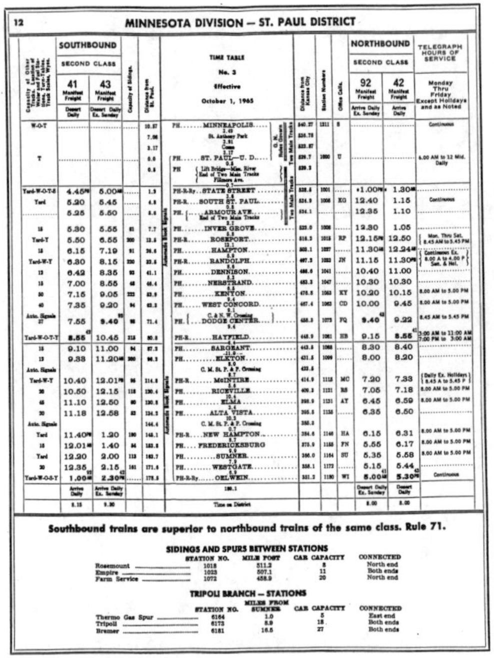

12 MINNESOTA DIVISION — ST. PAUL DISTRICT

Capacity of Other Tracks. Location of Water and Fuel Stations, Turn-Tables, Track Scales, Wyes.	SOUTHBOUND SECOND CLASS 41 Manifest Freight Depart Daily	43 Manifest Freight Depart Daily Ex. Sunday	Capacity of Sidings	Distance from St. Paul	TIME TABLE No. 3 Effective October 1, 1965	Distance from Kansas City	Station Numbers	Office Calls	NORTHBOUND SECOND CLASS 92 Manifest Freight Arrive Daily Ex. Sunday	42 Manifest Freight Arrive Daily	TELEGRAPH HOURS OF SERVICE Monday Thru Friday Except Holidays and as Noted
W-O-T				10.57	PH.......MINNEAPOLIS (G. N. Rules Govern; Two Main Tracks)	540.27	1211	S			Continuous
					2.49						
				7.08	St. Anthony Park	536.78					
					2.91						
				3.17	Como	533.87					
					3.17						
T				0.0	PH.....ST. PAUL—U. D.	529.7	1000	U			6.00 AM to 12 Mid. Daily
					0.5						
				0.5	PH Lift Bridge—Miss. River / End of Two Main Tracks / Fillmore Ave.	529.2					
					0.7						
Yard-W-O-T-S	4.45PM	5.00AM		1.3	PH-R-Ry..STATE STREET	528.5	1001		•1.00PM•	1.30AM	
					3.6						
Yard	5.20	5.45		4.8	PH-R....SOUTH ST. PAUL	524.9	1006	KG	12.40	1.15	Continuous
					0.8						
	5.25	5.50		5.6	PH. ARMOUR AVE. / End of Two Main Tracks	524.1			12.35	1.10	
					2.1						
15	5.30	5.55	81	7.7	PH.......INVER GROVE	522.0	1008		12.30	1.05	
					5.8						
Yard-Y	5.50	6.55	200	12.5	PH-R.......ROSEPORT	516.3	1015	RP	12.15PM	12.50	Mon. Thru Sat. 8.45 AM to 5.45 PM
					13.1						
15	6.15	7.19	91	26.6	PH.........HAMPTON	503.1	1027		11.30AM	12.24AM	Continuous Ex. 8.00 A to 4.00 P Sun. & Hol.
					5.9						
Yard-W-Y	6.30	8.15	220	32.5	PH-R.......RANDOLPH	497.3	1032	JN	11.15	11.30PM	
					8.6						
13	6.42	8.35	93	41.1	PH.........DENNISON	488.6	1041		10.40	11.00	
					5.3						
15	7.00	8.55	68	46.4	PH.........NERSTRAND	483.3	1047		10.30	10.30	
					6.5						
50	7.15	9.05	222	52.9	PH.........KENYON	476.8	1053	KY	10.20	10.15	8.00 AM to 5.00 PM
					9.4						
40	7.35	9.20	94	62.3	PH.....WEST CONCORD	467.4	1063	CD	10.00	9.45	8.00 AM to 5.00 PM
					9.1						
Auto. Signals 27	7.55	9.40[92]	98	71.4	PH. C. & N. W. Crossing ...DODGE CENTER	458.3	1073	FQ	9.40[42]	9.22	8.45 AM to 5.45 PM
					9.4						
Yard-W-O-T-Y	8.55[42]	10.45	315	80.8	PH-R.......HAYFIELD	448.9	1081	HB	9.15	8.55[41]	3:00 AM to 11:00 AM 7:00 PM to 3:00 AM
					6.4						
15	9.10	11.00	94	87.2	PH.........SARGEANT	442.5	1088		8.30	8.40	
					11.0						
13	9.38	11.20AM	200	98.2	PH.........ELKTON	431.5	1099		8.00	8.20	
					9.0						
Auto. Signals					C. M. St. P. & P. Crossing	422.5					
					8.7						
Yard-W-Y	10.40	12.01PM	96	114.8	PH-R....... McINTIRE	414.9	1115	MC	7.20	7.33	Daily Ex. Holidays 8.45 A to 5.45 P
					5.6						
30	10.50	12.15	118	120.4	PH.........RICEVILLE	409.3	1121	RS	7.05	7.18	8.00 AM to 5.00 PM
					10.4						
45	11.10	12.50	80	130.8	PH.........ELMA	398.9	1131	AY	6.45	6.59	8.00 AM to 5.00 PM
					3.4						
30	11.18	12.58	83	134.2	PH.......ALTA VISTA	395.5	1135		6.35	6.50	
					10.3						
Auto. Signals				144.4	C. M. St. P. & P. Crossing	385.3					
					0.7						
Yard	11.40PM	1.20	180	145.1	PH-R....NEW HAMPTON	384.6	1146	HA	6.15	6.31	8.00 AM to 5.00 PM
					8.7						
15	12.01AM	1.40	84	153.8	PH.... FREDERICKSBURG	375.9	1155	FN	5.55	6.17	8.00 AM to 5.00 PM
					9.9						
Yard	12.20	2.00	113	163.7	PH.........SUMNER	366.0	1164	SU	5.35	5.58	8.00 AM to 5.00 PM
					7.9						
30	12.35	2.15	161	171.6	PH.........WESTGATE	358.1	1172		5.15	5.44	
					6.9						
Yard-W-O-S-Y	1.00AM[92]	2.30PM[42]		178.5	PH-R-Ry......OELWEIN	351.2	1180	WI	5.00AM[41]	5.30PM[42]	Continuous
	Arrive Daily	Arrive Daily Ex. Sunday			189.1				Depart Daily Ex. Sunday	Depart Daily	
	8.15	9.30			Time on District				8.00	8.00	

Southbound trains are superior to northbound trains of the same class. Rule 71.

SIDINGS AND SPURS BETWEEN STATIONS

	STATION NO.	MILE POST	CAR CAPACITY	CONNECTED
Rosemount	1018	511.2	8	North end
Empire	1023	507.1	11	Both ends
Farm Service	1072	458.9	20	North end

TRIPOLI BRANCH — STATIONS

	STATION NO.	MILES FROM SUMNER	CAR CAPACITY	CONNECTED
Thermo Gas Spur	6164	1.0	5	East end
Tripoli	6173	8.9	18	Both ends
Bremer	6181	16.5	27	Both ends

Figure 3.57: Employee timetable.

the federal government ordered a national railroad-property-valuation survey (1915-1927), chances are very good that the National Archives' Suitland (Maryland) Reference Branch in suburban Washington, D.C., will yield some valuable information. These files contain mile-by-mile maps, photos, and many other kinds of data. Archivists there cannot conduct your research for you, so you must actually visit the center. If you live too far from the Washington, D.C., area, you might consider hiring a researcher to find the information for you.

Among the variety of forms issued by railroads, one especially helpful document is the track chart. It shows the tracks' alignment, number, locations, and degrees of curvature; steepness of grades; types of bridges; location and character of all structures (like wooden shelters and brick freight stations); sidings and yards; signals, tunnels, water tanks, and milepost designations; town populations; political subdivisions; and grade crossings.

Another good resource is the employees' timetable, often easier to find than the track chart because many more were published. Ranging from ¼- to ¾-inch thick, the employees' timetable differs considerably from a public timetable, which is usually a 4-by-9-inch brochure listing passenger trains and scheduled times at stations. (Public timetables, incidentally, can be a source of handsome graphics that you can reproduce in newsletters, fliers, and sign logos.) The employees' timetable (figure 3.57) includes station department times as well as operating information such as speed limits, types of engines allowed on (or prohibited from) certain tracks, types of signal systems and the rules for their use, town-by-town route mileage charts, and rules governing specific local conditions.

Another resource, railroad-published maps, vary widely in their usefulness. Older ones show the names of every town that ever had a flag stop, but newer ones may be computer generated and show only the locations at which customers existed at the time the map was compiled.

Books have been published on almost every facet of railroad history. These may help you find such facts as, for example, whether a U.S. president ever traveled over your line, or whether your route was part of the federal government's land-grant program to stimulate development and settlement.

Structures and Markers

If your property includes a railway station or shed, chances are good that it can be restored to its original appearance. Photographs and company records of standards for painting structures and trim are probably available to help you reconstruct the building's original appearance. Large railroads had many stations to main-

tain, and so most found it simpler to build them to the same specifications and to use the same colors of paint on many buildings. As a result, it is fairly easy to find references to original colors and, in some cases, even paint chips. Railroad history groups often have or know where to find this information. These groups may also be able to supply diagrams for re-creating station signs, which are among the most evocative and easily constructed details you can fabricate.

Railroad history groups also may have access to graphic materials such as lettering stencils and railroad logos. Resources like these are invaluable because designing your trail signs with the same style of type and colors as those used by the railroad honors the heritage of what was there before and promotes continuity. It's a giant leap over using punch-out manila stencils from the hardware store. Taking a serious approach to authenticity, even in these small details, will win you credibility and cooperation from rail history groups.

Seek a professional preservationist's help if converting a building into a trail amenity is a possibility. He or she can determine how much of the origi-

nal structure is left and whether it should be remodeled or restored. Well-meaning groups have needlessly gutted the interiors of some beautiful structures; in other cases, too much of the structure has already been modified or damaged to warrant restoration. Figure 3.58 shows two buildings that have been preserved at the Delaware and Raritan Canal State Park.

Railroad structures opened for public use often serve as small museums. Avoid accepting every railroad artifact people may offer for display—photos, books, timetables, lanterns, passes, switch keys, coal shovels, conductors' uniforms. Some items may be inappropriate. Carefully screen all items to determine their connection with your line. Too many exhibits are nothing more than a collection of trinkets with no theme, purpose, or interpretation. Visitors will gain much more from the display if they can easily understand the relationship between what they're seeing and why it's there.

Include a photo of a train on your line, preferably at an identifiable point, as well as of a station, bridge, or other local landmark. Do not include a paper placemat decorated with a train quiz from Irma's Diner. A crew member's

Rolling Stock

You may have the opportunity to obtain a piece of retired rolling stock such as a boxcar or caboose. You could use it for storage, for display, or even as an office. Make every effort to get a car that was used on your route or, at the very least, one formerly owned by the same railroad company of which your line was a part (or by a former shipper on the line). Nothing will chill the cooperation of railroad history groups faster than a preservation project built around a piece of rolling stock having no relationship to its surroundings. Such a car might be viewed as a caricature.

Do your best to avoid removing a car's wheels and mounting the car on concrete blocks. Take the trouble to buy or seek the donation of a few ties and rail lengths to put the car on a short stretch of track so that it looks genuine (figure 3.60). Imagine how a retired airliner would look sitting flat on its belly in the grass rather than with landing gear down on pavement.

Contact rail history groups to provide guidance in restoring a car to its original appearance. Some information is irretrievable if you're not careful about how you approach the restora-

Figure 3.58: Preserved Prallsville Mill buildings longt New Jersey's Delaware and Raritan Canal State Park.

Photo: Wilma Frey

time book showing a record of trips worked over your line would be appropriate. Often these books include dates, time on and off duty, engines, train or job numbers, notations of unusual events, and sometimes rates of pay. A plush, upholstered parlor-car seat would be inappropriate if it displays a logo from a railroad whose closest tracks are 200 miles away.

Also, try to incorporate any small structures remaining within the corridor, such as distance markers and mileposts. They will remind trail users of the corridor's heritage and may add an interesting interpretive element to the trail. On Minnesota's Cannon Valley Trail, a concrete slab lies below mile marker 80, serving as a small memorial for a 1912 train wreck (figure 3.59).

Human Resources

Railroad history groups can be a valuable resource for learning about your line's history. Some groups are composed of several local constituencies (the Western New York Railway Historical Society, for example), while others are devoted to a single railroad company (such as Friends of the East Broad Top). Still others are based on a common subject interest, such as depot photos or collectible artifacts such as lanterns or timetables. The two national rail history organizations find most of their strength in active local chapters. The National Railway Historical Society, founded in 1935, is the largest, with 20,000 members and 150 chapters; and the Railway & Locomotive Historical Society, founded in 1921, is the oldest. The American Canal Society works nationally to preserve and restore canals.

■ Historical Societies and Railroad History Groups

Local historical societies and railroad history groups can help you find people who worked for or used the railroad. To raise public interest and gain a higher profile, you might con-

Figure 3.60: Preserved caboose along the Washington and Old Dominion Railroad Regional Park.

sider organizing events such as an oral history day, in which you encourage people to come and be videotaped as they recall stories of working on or traveling over your line. Or you could coordinate a show-and-tell day, encouraging people to come and display photos or other artifacts in their collections.

■ Railroad Unions

Unions can be a resource for finding employees who worked on a line. Current union members may have worked on your route before it was abandoned, and union retirees may also have worked on the line. Unions often send their newsletters to retirees, so a notice in the newsletter from

Figure 3.59: Mile marker 80 along Minnesota's Cannon Valley Trail.

tion. Treat the car as if it were an archaeological site: don't rush into sandblasting it only to discover that you forgot to document its color, markings, and number, or failed to note whether different colors, markings, and numbers were hidden under a coat of paint. It is usually best to get professional preservation and restoration assistance.

113

you, requesting contact with anyone who ever worked the line, may bring surprising results. Keep in mind that labor organizations are specialized. If you want to follow this path, you'll have to work through one union for the locomotive engineers, another for train crews (conductors and brakemen), another for switch-tower operators, another for maintenance-of-way personnel, another for clerks, and yet another for shop workers.

■ Railroad Museums

Railroad museums can also serve as important resources. Two of the nation's largest are the California State Railroad Museum at Sacramento and the Railroad Museum of Pennsylvania at Strasburg. These state-owned facilities serve as hosts for a semiannual preservation symposium, held in California in the spring and in Pennsylvania in the fall. Other railroad museums are operated privately or by trusts and foundations.

Examples of institutions that are not exclusively devoted to railroad history but maintain railroad-related archival material include the Mercantile Library in St. Louis, the Smithsonian Institution in Washington, D.C., and the Hagley Museum in Wilmington, Delaware.

❖

WILDLIFE AND MULTI-USE TRAILS

Regardless of whether your trail's setting is urban, rural, or wilderness, it will run through some kind of environment that plants and animals require for survival. The nature and condition of this corridor as wildlife and plant habitat will depend on a number of factors—geographic location, climate, corridor width, species living in the corridor, previous use of the corridor, and the kinds of adjacent land uses.

A corridor running through the Rocky Mountains will be quite different from one crossing the prairie, and both will differ from one traversing coastal lowlands. In the case of prairie, rail lines and other corridors can serve as ecological threads of remnant prairie holding together a delicate network that was once a grassland "sea." In some midwestern areas, the only remaining "black soil" prairies lie along derelict rail lines.

Similarly, abandoned corridors through forests, wetlands, and even cities can be home to important plant and animal communities. A rail-trail corridor in the wilds of Montana may traverse big-game habitat. One skirting the edges of the Carolina coast may pass through important tidal wetlands. In urban areas, the edges of rail, canal, and utility corridors may offer viable habitat because the immediate edges of such corridors tend to remain undeveloped. A trail planner needs to understand the trail's effect on wildlife and plants and how to develop a trail that will enhance, not hinder, habitat.

Understanding Habitat

Understanding what constitutes habitat will assure a sensitive design process that matches the trail to its setting. This calls for visualizing your trail corridor as habitat—some creature's home—composed of water, food, territory, shelter, and a place to breed and bear young. Each must be present for a healthy habitat.

■ Water

A key component in almost all habitats, water is vital for drinking, bathing, and sustaining plants that provide food and cover. Consider how your trail will affect not only surface water (rivers, lakes, and wetlands), but also the vital unseen water system in aquifers and water tables beneath the ground. Will trail construction alter or block water flow, introduce contaminants, or inhibit subterranean water systems?

■ Food

A healthy habitat includes species ranging from microorganisms to plants to vertebrates. Most species depend on the survival of others in the food chain. Healthy habitats also have proper predator/prey relationships that keep populations in check. Will trail development affect any food sources or population balances?

■ Territory/Shelter

Most animals need a defined territory and migration routes in which to move, get to water, forage for food, and find mates. Many animals are sensitive to intrusion by people or pets. Most creatures need shelter or a place of cover. Some plants may need special growing conditions, including appropriate soil makeup and moisture and sun exposure. Will your trail and its users disrupt territory, disturb sensitive species, or disrupt vital wildlife movement patterns?

■ Breeding and Bearing Young

Animals need undisturbed places to mate, build nests, and raise their young. Again, some species are sensitive to intrusion. Will your trail affect important breeding areas?

The Impact of Trails on Sensitive Environments

A corridor's previous use, be it a railway, canal, or utility line, has had an impact on wildlife. Grading and construction activities altered drainage patterns, excavation and filling changed soil conditions, vegetation removal and herbicide application affected growing conditions, and human presence may have driven some species away. However, some corridors may have protected a special habitat, such as prairie in the Midwest.

Trails are a relatively benign component in the environment, but a trail and its users may alter it nevertheless. The trail surface, coupled with groomed edges, can result in a 10- to 20-foot-wide swath of land altered with surfacing and vegetation removal. While this may seem insignificant, the total habitat loss over several trail miles is noteworthy. Even a swath as narrow as 10 feet occupies more than an acre of land per trail mile—a significant land mass, especially if it traverses a sensitive area such as wetlands. Other components, such as parking areas and bridges, may impact habitat either by their use or during the construction process.

After the trail opens, people will use it and some may wander off the path, disturbing wildlife. Some sensitive species are disturbed by the mere presence of people and pets on the trail. The trail's impact on nearby wildlife, therefore, can be significantly wider than the 10- to 20-foot swath. It can range up to several hundred feet or more on either side of the trail depending on the sensitivity of the species in the area and the amount of buffering between the trail and surrounding habitat.

The width and significance of this impact zone also may vary by season. For example, a certain habitat may be occupied by wintering bald eagle between November and March but not be occupied by sensitive species during the balance of the year. Also, many big-game species, like bighorn sheep, may be more sensitive to stress during the winter and early spring months

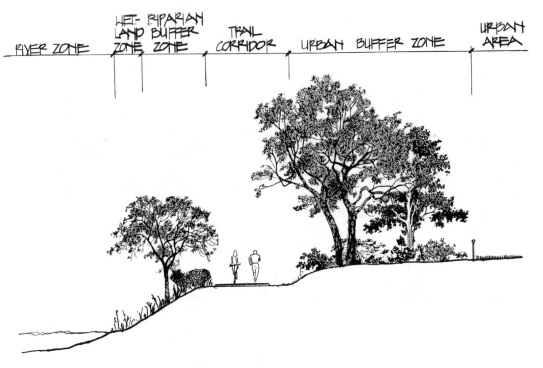

Figure 3.61: Buffer zones for wildlife.

than at other times. Early in the planning process, you should have conducted an assessment of your corridor (see "Physical Inventory and Assessment of the Site" in chapter 1). As you conduct the design phase, you need to review your findings, evaluate potential impacts on wildlife, and select design options that minimize or mitigate those impacts.

Planning and Design Techniques to Minimize Impact

Strive to make your trail "wildlife-friendly." Use the following tips to ensure that your multi-use trail is a good neighbor to nearby animals and plants:

▶ Think in terms of corridor rather than trail. Always consider the swath of impact—approximately 100 feet on each side of the trail's alignment.

▶ Design trails to discourage unwanted diversions off the trail surface, particularly shortcuts through sensitive areas. This can be accomplished with grading, plantings, and, if necessary, signs discouraging "cutoffs" from the trail.

▶ Using grading or vegetation, provide buffer zones between the trail edge and potentially sensitive areas such as stream edges or wetlands (figure 3.61).

▶ Direct the trail away from areas of critical or sensitive habitat. Leave a buffer zone between any critical area and the trail edge. In some cases, you may need to close your trail during critical times.

▶ Develop interpretive vistas and observation points for viewing wildlife where appropriate. You can point out or describe nesting areas, mating activities, wildlife food sources, medicinal values of certain local plants, and other interesting wildlife information. Be aware, however, that some sensitive species may be more jeopardized by overzealous viewers if their presence is made public.

▶ Provide informational and interpretive signs as well as leaflets that make the public aware of wildlife values along the trail corridor. Let people know that there may be sensitive wildlife and vegetation species. Ask them to stay on the trail and to avoid disturbing plants and animals. Phrase requests in positive terms such as "Please tread lightly and help protect this precious natural resource" rather than "Do not disturb wildlife."

▶ Include wildlife and habitat protection as a key component of the trail corridor's maintenance and management program once the trail is open—and be sure to budget accordingly in advance.

▶ If the corridor traverses sensitive areas, choose a trail surface that has minimal environmental impact. Generally, water-permeable surfaces such as granular stone are preferable to impermeable surfaces like asphalt and concrete.

▶ Minimize vegetation removal and soil erosion in your trail design. Special designs may be needed in certain areas. For example, laying boardwalk is preferable to filled causeway through a wetland.

▶ Locate high-activity areas such as trailheads, parking lots, visitor centers, and restrooms away from sensitive areas.

▶ Promote the preservation (or restoration) of natural and native landscape along the trail edges. Avoid turf grass, exotic species, and undesirable plantings. In some cases, significant healthy habitat may remain in your trail corridor. In other cases, the habitat may have been disturbed by the previous uses. Recognize that not all species are good for the habitat, such as noxious weeds. Emphasize plant material that provides the habitat's basics—food and shelter—for the wildlife species you want to encourage.

❖

ROAD CROSSINGS

Streets and roads typically are classified in a hierarchical system that deter-

mines which street has priority at intersections. The street with the higher traffic volume usually has priority. For example, users of residential streets stop at intersections with arterials. Public roads usually have priority over private roads and driveways. This consistency is critical to road safety since it provides predictability to road users.

The same principles should be applied to trail intersections with public and private streets. Where a trail crosses a high-volume public street, the street will have the right-of-way. Trail users will stop and yield to traffic on the public street. In some cases, however, a trail may have substantially more volume than a residential street, in which case the trail users should have the right-of-way. A trail should have the right-of-way when it crosses a private street or driveway, requiring road and driveway users to stop or yield to trail traffic. Avoid making exceptions, as they will create confusion and compromise safety.

Trail Crossings at Grade

When a trail crosses a road, you need to decide whether an at-grade crossing will suffice or whether a grade-separated crossing (bridge or tunnel) is necessary. Road crossings are extremely site-specific, so determining how to cross should be made on a case by case basis.

Ideally, a safe at-grade crossing has either light traffic or a traffic signal that trail users can activate. If neither of these exists, you need to work with a traffic or transportation engineer to evaluate the intersection's characteristics, including current traffic volumes and times of peak vehicle travel, speed of travel, sight lines to and at the intersection, unique features of the intersection that pose problems or offer opportunities for a safe crossing, and the anticipated number of trail users likely to pass through the intersection.

Once this information has been evaluated, your engineer should perform what is known as a "gap analysis." This is a determination of the times during each day when the roadway is most heavily traveled, and the times when vehicle traffic is lowest. (This can also vary by season, such as "beach traffic" in the summer months.) Understanding the gaps in traffic will help you determine the safest type of crossing. Perhaps the intersection can be made safe by adding a crosswalk

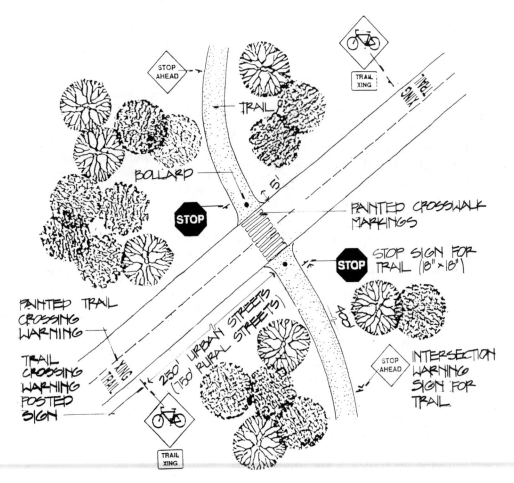

Figure 3.62: Typical road/trail intersection.

and some "Trail Crossing" signs on the road. Or you may decide that a traffic signal is vital. In that case, you will need to investigate with your local, state, or federal transportation agency the possibility of installing a special pedestrian signal light at the intersection to facilitate a safe crossing.

Trails should cross public streets as close as possible to an intersection (if one exists), in the same place a crosswalk would normally be placed. This creates a predictable movement for trail users and motorists who are used to pedestrians crossing at crosswalks. It also allows the stop bar for the motorist to be placed behind the crosswalk, thus reducing the likelihood of cars blocking the trail as they sit waiting to proceed. Opinions on the advisability and effectiveness of painted crosswalks for trail crossings differ, but in any case be consistent: Mark all crossings or don't mark any of them. Figure 3.62 illustrates a typical road/trail intersection.

If your trail crosses a street with curbs, the curb cuts should be the same width as the trail (for example, a 10-foot-wide trail should have a 10-foot curb cut). For crossings of high-volume, multilane arterials where signals are not warranted, consider providing a median refuge area for bicyclists and pedestrians.

■ Controlling Access onto the Trail
Barrier posts (bollards) are the most frequently used method of controlling motor vehicle access to multi-use

Photo: Jonathan Stoke

Figure 3.63: A typical bollard on a multi-use trail.

trails. However, they are largely symbolic and should not be routinely installed at all motor vehicle crossings. A barrier post is used only if operational problems demand it; for instance, if there is a need to indicate that a particular facility is open only to nonmotorized users. When locating such installations, ensure that barriers are well marked and visible to bicyclists,

day or night (usually by installing reflectors or reflector tape). Barrier posts must be at least 3 feet tall and should be placed at least 10 feet from the intersection. This will allow trail users to cross the intersection before negotiating the barrier posts (figure 3.63).

One post is generally sufficient to indicate that a path is not open to motorized vehicles. The post should be placed in the center of the trail tread. Where more than one post is necessary, a 5-foot spacing is used to permit passage of bicycle trailers, adult tricycles, and wheelchairs. Always use one or three barrier posts, never two. Two posts, both placed in the paved portion of a trail, will channel trail users into the center of the trail, causing possible head-on collisions. Barrier posts should be designed to be removable (figure 3.64) to permit entrance by emergency and service vehicles. In addition, it may also be desirable to remove the posts in the winter if snowmobilers will be using the trails. Figure 3.65 shows a typical bollard's design.

Once your trail is established, the need to prevent access may decrease. Many trail managers discover that after a few years unauthorized vehicle access is no longer a problem, so they

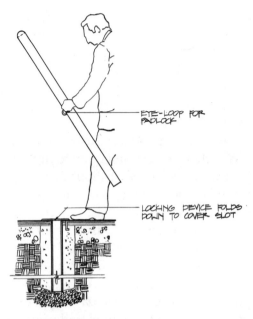

Figure 3.64: Removable bollard.

get rid of the bollards at all but their most problematic intersections.

An alternative method of restricting entry of motor vehicles is to split the entryway into two 5-foot sections separated by low landscaping. Emergency vehicles can still enter if necessary by straddling the landscaping. Other, more restrictive, methods of preventing motor vehicle access are generally not acceptable since they create a hazard for nighttime trail users and deny access to trail users in wheelchairs and

bike carts as well as those who cannot lift a bike over a barrier (figure 3.66).

■ Stopping Trail Users at
Intersections
Obstructions such as numerous barrier posts, fences, and speed bumps should not be used at intersections to force trail users to slow down or stop. The hazard they create is greater than the problem they are trying to solve. On an asphalt path, an 18-inch concrete strip (a pad, not a speed bump) can be placed across the trail, 30 feet from the intersection, to create a change in pavement texture that alerts the trail user to an upcoming intersection. A center line should be painted on the final 150 feet of the approach to alert users (especially bicyclists) to look up and concentrate on safely navigating the intersection.

■ Stopping Sight Distances
Multi-use trail intersections and approaches should be on relatively flat grades. Stopping sight distances at intersections should be checked, and adequate warning should be given to permit trail users to stop before reaching the intersection, especially on downgrades. For bicycles, the distance

required to reach a full controlled stop is a function of the bicyclist's perception and brake reaction time, the initial speed of the bicycle, the coefficient of friction between the tires and the pavement, and the bicycle's braking ability.[8]

Trail Crossings Above and Below Grade

Crossings above and below grade have their advantages and disadvantages. In terms of personal security, above-grade crossings are less threatening and are perceived by the user as safer than below-grade crossings. However, above-grade crossings can

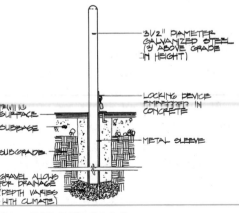

Figure 3.65: Bollard detail.

be unsightly and require long access ramps. Spiral ramps can invite improper use by roller skaters and skateboarders, and they are difficult to build to the recommended AASHTO design speed of 20 miles per hour. Moreover, trail users frequently ignore above-grade crossings, finding it quicker simply to cross the street and avoid the long climb up the access ramp.

Going under a roadway usually involves the installation of a pedestrian tunnel. If your trail borders a stream, you may be able to convert an existing drainage structure to a crossing. You should evaluate the feasibility of using existing structures for pedestrian passage with the help of a hydrologist and a structural engineer. The big disadvantage of below-grade crossings is that they can feel threatening and may attract trash and graffiti. They also have to be designed so they do not flood during heavy rainfalls. On the plus side, they work well for bicyclists, who pick up speed on the downhill ramp and get enough momentum to climb up the opposite side easily. Because of this, below-grade crossings generally will be used if built.

Photo: Jean C. Mooring

Figure 3.66: Steel gates on the Illinois Prairie Path prevent unwanted vehicular traffic but also pose a problem for people in wheelchairs.

For crossings at freeways and other high-speed, high-volume arterials, a grade separation structure—either an overpass or an underpass—may be the only possible or practical treatment. On a new structure, the minimum clear width should be 10 to 20 percent wider than the paved multi-use path, and the desirable clear width on both sides of the surfaced path should be 2 feet. This provides the minimum, safe horizontal clearance from the railing on a bridge or the wall of a tunnel. It also provides needed maneuvering space to avoid conflicts with pedestrians and bicyclists who may be stopped on a bridge or inside a tunnel.[9] This horizontal clearance also allows emergency vehicles to gain access to the trail on either side of the overpass or underpass.

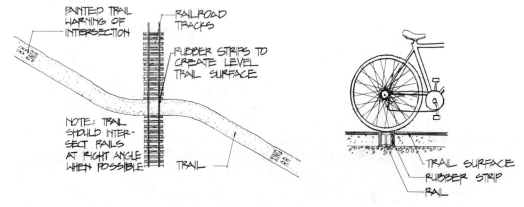

Figure 3.67: Trail/railroad intersection.

The preferred vertical clearance for a new multi-use trail bridge or tunnel is 10 feet. The absolute minimum is 8 feet, although this will not suffice if equestrians will be among your trail's users, and some emergency vehicles may have difficulty passing through an 8-foot clearance.

In the event that neither a tunnel nor a bridge is possible, investigate the possibility of routing trail users for a short distance to an alternative crossing off the trail: to a traffic signal, a bridge that crosses the road, or a tunnel beneath the road. If you choose an alternative crossing, be sure that the route is safe and accessible, and posted with signs providing clear directions to trail users.

Railroad Crossings

Ideally, trails should cross railroad tracks at a right angle to the rails for safety reasons. The more the crossing deviates from this angle, the greater the potential for a bicyclist's front wheel to be trapped in the rail flangeway, thereby causing loss of steering control. It is also important that the trail approach be at the same elevation as the rails—the maximum threshold.

Consideration should be given to the materials of the crossing surface and to the flangeway depth and width. If the crossing angle is less than 45 degrees, consider widening the trail to give bicyclists adequate room to cross the tracks at a right angle. Where this

is not possible, compressible flangeway fillers, which are commercially available, can enhance bicyclists' safety while allowing trains to continue operating (figure 3.67). Place railroad-crossing warning signs and pavement markings on the trail.

❖

SIGNS FOR MULTI-USE TRAILS

Signs play an important role in trail design. They give directions and offer needed information along trails. When developing signs for your trail, take time to think about how they influence perceptions of the landscape and how they can shape a trail user's expectation of what is around the next bend.

Role of Signs

A primary role of trail signs is to aid and instruct users along the linear route. Signs are of three types: regulatory, warning, and guidance. Generally, regulatory signs give operational requirements of the trail and are used for traffic control. Regulatory signs include stop and yield signs, right-of-way signs, speed-limit signs, and exclusion signs.

These are normally erected where the specific regulation applies.

Warning signs point out existing or potentially hazardous conditions on or near the trail and caution users to reduce speed or dismount a bicycle or horse for safety reasons. Warning signs are typically used near intersections, bridges, crossings, and tunnels; they indicate significant grade changes, upcoming traffic-control devices, and changes in surface conditions.

Guidance signs provide trailside information to orient trail users geographically. These signs can be both directional and informational. Directional signs often point out nearby support facilities and local points of interest. Informational signs include distance markers as well as "you are here" signs that orient a user within a larger area such as a park, a trail system, or the surrounding community. Informational signs can also serve an interpretive role, pointing out elements like historic sites, locations of historic events, and areas of ecological significance.

Some guidance signs are temporary signs offering public information. Such signs—announcing concert dates, festivals, lectures, and meetings—are most effective when clustered together in a central location. They are an important part of a community's involvement in the trail's use. Temporary signs also include information about trail closures, construction, or other short-term conditions. Although temporary signs are secondary to the design of permanent trail signs, bulletin boards or informational kiosks for their display should be erected in visible locations. Without adequate space for temporary signs, unwanted posters and fliers may spring up in inappropriate places along the trail.

Use of Standard Signs

Trails are transportation corridors, and therefore recognizable transportation signs should be adapted for trail use. The U.S. Department of Transportation's Federal Highway Administration (FHWA) has outlined size, shape, and color criteria for signs in the *Manual on Uniform Traffic Control Devices (MUTCD)*. Standard shapes and colors should be used for trail signs where feasible. Minimum sizes of signs for bicycle facilities are provided in the *MUTCD*.

Applicable Standard Sign Shapes

Figure 3.68 illustrates the standard sign shapes and sizes as indicated below.

▶ The octagon is reserved exclusively for the stop sign.

▶ The equilateral triangle, with one point downward, is reserved exclusively for the yield sign.

▶ The circle gives advanced warning of a railroad crossing.

▶ The diamond shape is used only to warn of existing or possible hazards either on or adjacent to the trail.

▶ The rectangle, with the longer dimension vertical, is for regulatory signs (except stop and yield signs).

Applicable Standard Sign Colors

▶ **Red** Background for stop signs, do-not-enter messages, and parking prohibition signs. Red is also used for the prohibitory symbol (circular outline and diagonal bar).

▶ **Black** Background color on one-way signs and the message on white, yellow, or orange signs.

123

White Background color for regulatory signs, except stop signs, where white is used for the message. White is the message color on blue, brown, and green signs, as well as stop signs.

Orange Background color for construction and maintenance signs.

Yellow Background for warning signs (except where orange is specified) and school signs.

Standards for guidance signs include the Sign Symbol system, a standardized set of pictographs developed by the American Institute for Graphic Arts for the U.S. Department of Transportation. These symbols—legible at a greater distance than text would be and understandable to people who do not read English—can be used to supplement text signs.

Design Guidelines for Trail Signs

Although trails should borrow the conventions of highway signs, it is not necessary to erect large highway signs on your trail. Large highway signs are made so that drivers of high-speed vehicles can recognize them in seconds.

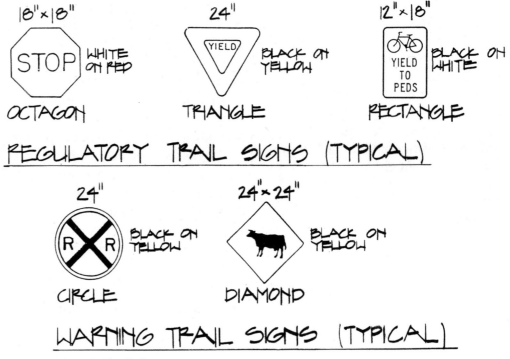

Figure 3.68: Standard trail signs.

The scale of trails is much smaller, so smaller signs are appropriate for your trail.

Intended to help users negotiate their way along a trail, signs should be clearly readable and easy to understand. Legibility is determined by visibility, user comprehension, sign shape, color contrast, text character height, and proportion. Information on a sign should be concise and direct; lettering styles should be simple and bold.

The effective viewing distance for multi-use trail signs is between 20 and 150 feet. Effective text height for most trail signs is between 3 and 6 inches. Guidelines for letter size suggest 1 inch of capital-letter height per 30 feet of required viewing distance, or 1 inch of lowercase letter height per 50 feet of viewing distance. Large lettering, which mandates large signs, would be out of scale and character for pedestrian-scaled systems.

Color, contrast, and shape can be useful for transmitting messages quickly but only if the meaning is easily understood. Symbols or logos should not be too abstract and should not be the exclusive means of communication. As a rule, use text and symbols together for the clearest message. Also, minimize negative messages on signs because they are more prone to vandalism and theft.

Use contrasting colors with light images on dark backgrounds to make signs easy to read, especially from long distances. But don't use color as the sole means of communication—nearly 12 percent of the population is color blind. Instead, use regularity in sign design. Similar shapes and sizes as well as consistent symbols, lettering styles, and color schemes help users quickly understand and utilize a trail's sign system.

Sign Sizes and Placement

Trail stop signs should measure 18 by 18 inches, trail yield signs should be 24 by 24 inches, and regulatory signs should be 12 by 18 inches, as required by the *MUTCD*. Various dimensions may be used for recreational and cultural-interest signs.

Where you place signs along your trail is extremely important (figure 3.69); improperly placed signs may present an obstacle or hazard to trail users. Place signs in a clear area, where they will not be obscured by parked cars, vegetation, or buildings. Place post-mounted signs at least 1½ feet, preferably 2 feet, off the edge of trail circulation routes. Signs should be raised between 4 and 5 feet off the ground.

Place non-traffic-oriented signs, such as information boards or interpretive signs, at least 4 feet off the sides of pathways. The greater distance allows groups of pedestrians, people using wheelchairs, and bicyclists to get completely out of the path of travel to read the signs, minimizing disruptions on the trail.

Placing signs within sight-distance limits and required stopping distances is critical, particularly for regulatory and warning signs. Adequate time to read and respond to traffic signs must be calculated into your sign layouts.

For a bicyclist traveling 20 miles per hour, the viewing distance for stop signs should be between 100 and 125 feet. To prepare riders or pedestrians, warning signs should be placed 125 to 150 feet in both directions from the conditions they address. And stop signs where the trail intersects with roads should be visible from at least 200 feet. Warning signs for intersections should be placed no fewer than 400 feet from crossing points.

Pavement Markings

Pavement markings are commonly used to reinforce signs along multi-use trails, but they should not replace signs altogether. Striping is the most common form of pavement markings, although warning and regulatory messages are sometimes used. However, use pavement markings sparingly and only where necessary to attract additional attention to a possible problem area since signs painted on pavement can be slippery when wet and can reduce the friction of bicycle wheels on the trail. Pavement signs often increase the danger of sideslipping and can make stopping difficult. Therefore, do not use pavement signs at critical turning and stopping points. Never use them as an exclusive signing method in areas where snow, sand, or leaf buildup is a problem, or where exces-

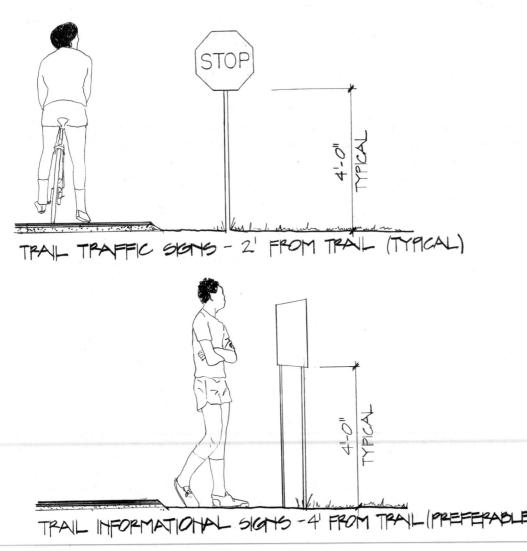

TRAIL TRAFFIC SIGNS – 2' FROM TRAIL (TYPICAL)

TRAIL INFORMATIONAL SIGNS – 4' FROM TRAIL (PREFERABLE)

Figure 3.69: Typical placement of trail signs.

sive wear is likely, because the signs may be obscured. Figure 3.70 demonstrates an effective use of pavement markings.

If you do opt for stenciled pavement markings, they should be white for best visibility. (The exception to this is a yellow center line, which you may opt to use to separate heavy trail traffic). The height of letters (or arrows) on the pavement should be between 3 and 4 feet. Pavement signs you may consider include "Stop," "Yield," "Slow," "Bike Lane," and "Pedestrian Lane." Messages should be placed at the beginning of your trail, before roadway intersections, or near intersections with trail facilities.

Design Principles for Signs

▶ Do not group regulatory or warning signs together. Make them clear, concise, and easy to read.

▶ Keep at least 75 feet between signs to allow users time to read and react to the messages.

▶ Group informational signs together, especially at trailheads, rest areas, and trail facility locations. Bulletin boards or kiosks work well for this (figure 3.71).

Figure 3.70: Typical pavement markings.

▶ Avoid placing signs where they may detract from natural surroundings and diminish the trail experience. Do not place a sign so that it diminishes a scenic vista or minimizes the dangers of a hazardous area.

▶ Balance the need for signs and their functions with the impact they have on the overall aesthetic appeal of the trail.

Materials for Signs

You should take into account several factors when choosing materials for a sign system: budget, aesthetics, durability, and maintenance costs.

▶ Plastics (especially acrylics, polycarbonates, butyrates, polypropylenes, and laminates) are widely available and adaptable to many fabrication processes. Select plastics based on color, appearance, impact resistance, durability, and suitability for certain fabrication techniques. Many plastics expand and contract with temperature changes.

▶ Fiberglass (fiber-reinforced polyester) is durable, impact resistant, and easily formed into customized shapes. Graphics and colors are often applied to the surface and sealed under coatings that improve finish and colorfastness. Fiberglass is available in opaque or translucent forms and is sometimes used for internally lit signs.

▶ Wood usually requires special treatment to protect against decay. Solid woods (especially cypress and redwood) are typically used for carved signs. High-density plywoods are widely used for sign faces and are relatively inexpensive. They are made with various exterior-rated adhesives and finishes, and all edges must be sealed. Wood signs can be easily damaged by vandals.

▶ Aluminum is widely available, is lightweight, and does not rust. But it does require specialized welding skills and equipment. Lami-

Figure 3.71: An attractive kiosk displaying trail information along the McHenry County Prairie Trail in northeastern Illinois.

127

nated products with aluminum faces and plastic or wood cores are also available. Some aluminums require a painted or anodized finish to protect against pitting.

▶ Steel is relatively economical, is available in many forms, and is easy to cut, form, weld, or rivet. However, steel requires galvanizing or special finishes to inhibit rust. Specialized alloys of steel (including stainless steel) offer increased strength and corrosion resistance but at a higher cost.

▶ Brass and bronze are often used for cast signs or cut letters. They can be allowed to develop an oxidized patina, or they can be sealed with lacquers. Both metals are quite durable but are comparatively expensive.

▶ Stone is extremely durable, but is hard to work with and expensive. If graphics are to be used on the sign, they generally will be sandblasted or carved into the stone. Some types of stones are susceptible to damage or discoloring from airborne pollutants.

▶ Fabrics (including nylon, cotton, and other synthetics) are used for awnings, banners, and flags. Translucent fabrics can be backlit to highlight text or graphics, and awning fabrics can be treated to improve durability and resistance to fading and dirt. Exterior banners suffer wind damage and fading and must be replaced periodically. Interior banners are durable but may require periodic removal for cleaning.

Using Signs to Make Trails Unique

In addition to serving important functions, signs can help define your trail's image. Ask yourself how signs can foster a feeling of specialness about the trail. The answer can be found in the way signs are presented along your trail.

Signs, especially guidance signs, offer you a chance to establish a dominant image or visual tone along a trail. By repeating logos or other forms along the trail's length you can create a sense of continuity and consistency.

Both the U.S. Forest Service and the National Park Service have developed well-recognized sign systems. Their white or yellow letters on a maroonish brown background generally connote conservation and the outdoors. Both include sign types for roadways and trails that are instantly recognizable.

If possible, reflect in your signs the unique character of your trail's location or highlight something associated with local communities. Interpretive signs can point out areas of interest that make the trail unique. Consider highlighting historically significant points by calling attention to sites of important political events or the location of historic architecture and bridges along the path. If appropriate, provide interpretive information on industrial relics such as bridges, canal locks, signaling devices, and switching stations. These remnants should be preserved to educate future generations.

You could also highlight the people who built the historic structures, especially since canal and railroad construction represent one of the most dramatic periods of U.S. immigration and labor history. A multi-use trail lends itself to educational displays documenting the struggles and history of the railroad's creators. You may also want interpretive signs relating to Native Americans who inhabited the area even earlier.

Planners in several areas are enriching the trail experience by incorporating local history. For example, signs along the Little Miami Scenic State Park Trail in southwestern Ohio point out a group of Native American burial mounds, a highlight of the pathway. And the citizens working to create the Farmington Canal Greenway are researching the history of Italian immigrant laborers who built the stone bridges dominating one section of trail.

Ecologically significant areas along the trail can also be interpreted. Native plant groupings, local animal habitats, or unusual geological features are all of interest. Signs should also point out particularly sensitive terrain and suggest appropriate trail etiquette. Educating the public about flora, fauna, and special terrain can be more effective than setting up barriers and "Do Not Enter" signs. Making your trail a place for environmental education and providing informative signs generates a new purpose for the trail, one beyond transportation or recreation.

Developing a trail-specific logo is another way to highlight the uniqueness of a trail and its landscape. You

Figure 3.72: Examples of trail logos.

can generate a logo by abstracting or simplifying an image, picture, or symbol into a graphic element. But keep your logo simple so it can be easily re-

produced in different sizes. Dominant landscape elements—mountain peaks, rivers, valleys—are all potential logo sources, as are footprints, bicycle tires, and other trail-evoking images. The first letter of your trail's name, the seal of your town or city, or an anagram of a local trail organization can also serve as logo models. Many trails have developed interesting logos (figure 3.72).

Repetition of logos and certain signs reinforce the image and uniqueness of a trail. Placing signs at regular intervals keeps the trail's identity in the trail user's mind. Distance markers at half-mile intervals, for example, are not only popular among trail users gauging their progress, but also make excellent opportunities to reinforce a trail theme. They can also facilitate quick response to medical emergencies. Interesting distance markers can be placed along the sides of trails or on the trail surface.

Similarly, informational signs can have logos included on them as part of their borders or color schemes. The Washington and Old Dominion Railroad Regional Park has developed a "Share the Trail" campaign, which includes numerous signs (printed with the campaign's logo) along the trail.

Trail logos can be affixed to benches, drinking fountains, gates, restroom doors, trashcans, and fences, serving the dual purpose of identifying the facility as trail property and advertising the trail system to users.

Temporary signs also provide opportunities for displaying logos. Fabric banners or flags for annual events such as road races, benefit events, and seasonal openings can be placed at entrances, at exits, and along special sections of the trail. Place a logo on any temporary signs posted on trail kiosks to reinforce trail identity.

❖

TRAIL SUPPORT FACILITIES

The types of facilities your trail will need—and their placement along the trail—depend on several factors: the setting and proposed uses of the trail, the trail's intensity of use, the level of servicing or maintenance that the facilities need, and the utility or infrastructure requirements of the facilities. Whatever the location, user groups, and desired activities along the trail, you must plan for trail facilities from the start. Even if you cannot afford to develop all facilities at the outset, know the types of facilities that you and your community ultimately want. Also keep in mind that some facilities will need upgrading as the trail's use increases.

Group your trail amenities together when possible (figure 3.73). Grouping makes them recognizable from a distance and saves space along the trail's edge. Clustering complex features such as restrooms, drinking fountains, and telephones also minimizes construction costs. By clustering facilities you also minimize the visual disturbance of the landscape along the trail corridor.

Consider establishing minor and major "rest stops." Minor ones include sitting areas, shade shelters, picnic areas, and informational or interpretive signs. These facilities are the least complicated to locate and accommodate. Your sitting and picnic areas could consist of commercially manufactured benches and tables, or they could be as simple as big logs or boulders arranged for sitting. Secure signs, furniture, and trash receptacles by bolting them to buried footings. A minor rest stop should require little maintenance over its lifetime.

Major rest-stop facilities will likely include restrooms, a drinking fountain, a phone, a recycling drop-off point, and possibly even vending machines for snacks and drinks. Locate ma-

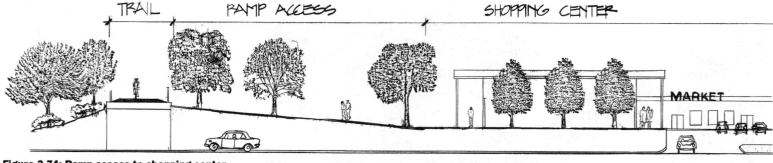

Figure 3.74: Ramp access to shopping center.

jor rest stops near more heavily used access points. Remember that restrooms and drinking fountains can be difficult to accommodate because they need running water, buried pipes, and access to sewage lines. When designing either major or minor facility

Figure 3.73: Clustered trail amenities along Iowa's Sauk Rail-Trail.

clusters, allow flexibility for change over time.

The text and illustrations that follow demonstrate a range of options for the design, materials, and placement of facilities along your multi-use trail. The components, configurations, and dimensions are not absolutes—they should serve only as guidelines.

Facilities at Access Points

When planning support facilities for a multi-use trail system, start with the trail's access points. What facilities will be located at these points? The answer is important because a trail user's first and last impressions are formed when entering and exiting the trail.

Think of access points as opportunities to link the trail with the surrounding community, including destinations

and points of departure known to the entire community, not just trail users. Where possible, locate access points in developed areas—next to public parks, shopping centers, or residential developments (figure 3.74). Many public amenities, including restrooms, telephone booths, parking areas, and refreshment facilities, will already be in place. When located in developed areas, access points tend to be safer because of their frequent public use. These locations are also more accessible to emergency help and maintenance.

Access points should link the trail to as many systems of transportation as possible. The proximity of trails to ample parking lots, bus stops, light-rail stops, and train stations allows users to make convenient connections to the

131

parks and residential developments (figure 3.76). Also consider access points from the trail to nearby rivers and streams (figure 3.77).

Parking Areas

The primary design consideration for a parking area is simplicity; parking areas should never be complex or designed to test a driver's patience. A parking area should meet other conditions as well. It should be designed in harmony with its surroundings and should be a functional space with an easy-to-understand circulation system. The lot should also have clearly marked spaces and a safe entrance and exit coordinated with traffic flows from adjacent roadways.

For efficient land use, parking lots should have 300 to 350 square feet for each car space required. Use this number to calculate the size and capacity of an efficient parking facility. The minimum area required to park a standard-sized car is about 144 square feet, or a rectangle 18 feet long and 8 feet wide. Compact cars require about 113 square feet, or a rectangle 15 feet long and 7½ feet wide. The larger-sized space should be used as a minimum for unsupervised or unregulated lots.

Figure 3.75: Major trail access point.

trail, thereby assuring its success as a true public amenity.

Access points, which need to be accessible to everyone, should follow a hierarchy. Rather than designing all access points similarly, decide which locations will serve as major access points and which will be minor ones. The difference will be the number of facilities and amount of parking at each point. Major access points should be established near commercial developments and transportation nodes, making them highly accessible to the surrounding communities (figure 3.75). Minor access points should be simple pedestrian and bicycle entrances at locally known spots, such as

Accessible parking spaces occupy between 234 and 270 square feet with 13-by-18- or even 15-by-18-foot spaces. Accessible spaces usually require a 9-foot width with a 5-foot access aisle on one side of the space (or between two accessible spaces). Provide at least one accessible space in every lot. Generally, the *Uniform Federal Accessibility Standards (UFAS)* recommends one accessible space for every twenty-five spaces. Consult the "Americans with Disabilities Act Accessibility Guidelines," published in the 26 July 1991 *Federal Register,* as well as local codes for all required parking dimensions prior to beginning any lot design.

You need to provide several significantly larger spaces if equestrian use of your trail is planned. Ideally, the spaces should be about 45 feet long, 35 feet to accommodate the vehicle and trailer and an additional 10 feet for unloading the horses. Spaces should be 15 feet wide, which will allow horses to be tied to the trailer, where tack and feed are stored. Another option is to install picket posts about 10 feet behind the trailer parking. Equestrians can tie ropes between the posts and tie the horses to the ropes, thus eliminating

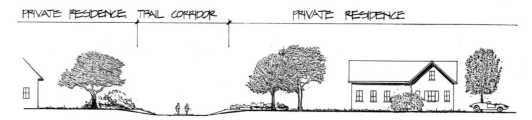

Figure 3.76: Minor trail access point.

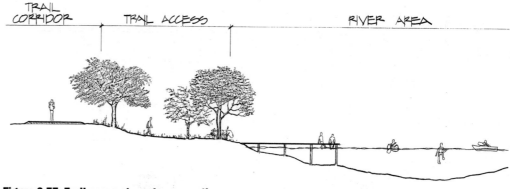

Figure 3.77: Trail access to water recreation.

the need to secure the horses at nearby trees.

Figure 3.78 depicts recommended parking stall dimensions.

To minimize conflict with adjacent street traffic, you should clearly define the parking lot's entrance and exit. Separate entrance and exit points work best along heavily traveled roads. Entrances and exits should be offset from street intersections by at least 50 feet.

Wherever possible, entrance and exit design should favor right-hand turns to avoid the hazards of left turns across through traffic. Single-lane parking lot entrances and exits should be 12 feet wide, and double-lane entrances should be 24 feet wide. Turning radii at entrance and exit points should be at least 15 feet, with a 5-foot minimum turning radius for getting into individual spaces.

133

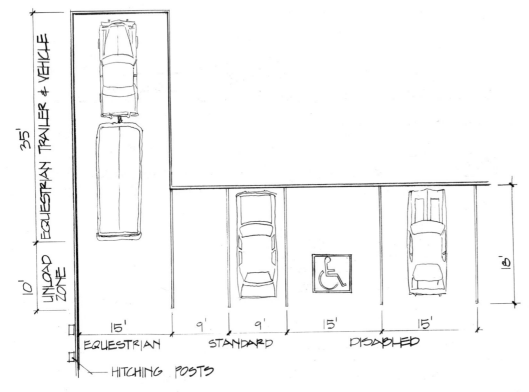

Figure 3.78: Dimensions of parking stalls.

A parking lot's layout and orientation are important if the lot is to function smoothly and safely. Lots can be laid out with either one-way or two-way circulation aisles, depending on the circumstances of the site. In general, orient parking-lot aisles so they are perpendicular to the major destination of the site (figure 3.79). This orientation minimizes the number of times pedestrians must cross the vehicular traveling aisles.

The design of aisle widths depends on the orientation of the parking spaces along the aisle. The standard 90-degree orientation between spaces and aisles, which only works with two-way traffic flows, requires a minimum of 22 feet, preferably 24 feet. Angled orientations, which work only with one-way circulation, require 18 feet at 60 degrees and 12 feet at 45 degrees (figure 3.80).

Your parking lot should be paved if you are planning on year-round use. Grading should provide adequate drainage, and the surface should abate dust. Parking lots should never exceed a 5 percent slope in any direction because too steep a pitch will make opening and closing car doors hazardous, and, on icy surfaces, cars can potentially slide under their own weight even after parked. Crushed-stone surfacing is adequate if proper drainage is provided. More rigid surfaces, such as concrete and asphalt, generally last longer, are easy to maintain, and withstand plowing in the winter. These surfaces (just like a trail surface) require adequate subsurface drainage if they are to last. Base your decision about surface material on climate and cost. Also, if you plan equestrian use, it is best to provide a softer surface in the area where horses will be standing prior to entering the trail.

Restrooms

Aside from parking lots, restrooms are probably the most expensive and complex facilities for a multi-use trail. They need utility connections for running water and sewage (unless you install a portable variety), and they require considerable maintenance and service. Restrooms must also meet local ordinance standards and accessibility codes. The number of stalls will vary depending on the predicted level of trail use. These and other requirements should be considered during the early stages of design.

Full-service restrooms that include running water and flushing toilets must be located near existing utilities and should be easily accessible to cleaning and servicing personnel. If existing utilities, such as sewage lines, are inconveniently located, consider portable toilets with holding tanks, a septic system, or composting toilets instead. The feasibility of these alternatives, however, depends on local codes, the characteristics of the site, the level of anticipated use, and the level of maintenance and security (particularly in urban areas) that can be provided.

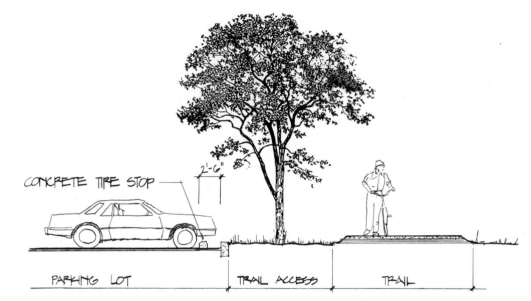

Figure 3.79: Trail section at a parking lot.

The space required for restroom facilities depends on the number of toilets to be provided at each station. Toilet stalls for the disabled should allow sufficient room for maneuvering a wheelchair. As a rule, at least one toilet must be accessible to wheelchairs. Therefore, if only one stall is provided, it should be a wheelchair-accessible unisex toilet. If single men's and women's toilets are provided, both should meet accessibility codes. Approximately 50 to 60 square feet should be allotted for each accessible toilet stall, including the toilet area, aisle space, and sink area.

Standard toilet facilities for a single stall require a minimum of 3 by 9½ feet with a sink and 3 by 8 feet without a sink. Wheelchair-accessible single-stall toilets require a minimum of 5 by 10 feet with a sink and 5 by 8 feet without a sink. In wheelchair-accessible stalls, grab bars should be located 30 inches from the floor. The height of toilet seats should be between 17 and 19

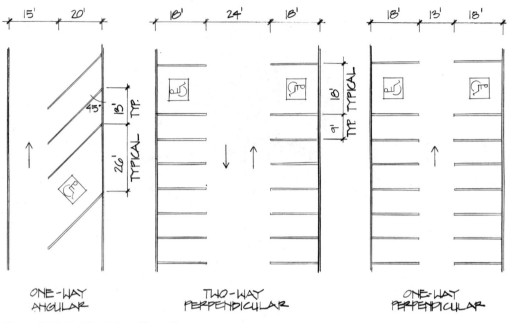

Figure 3.80: Parking lot configurations.

ONE-WAY
ANGULAR

TWO-WAY
PERPENDICULAR

ONE-WAY
PERPENDICULAR

inches above the floor. The minimum doorway width (for restroom and stall entrances) is 32 inches, preferably 36, and the doors should open outward.

As shown in figure 3.81, any restroom needs at least one mirror, sink, and towel dispenser, and all should be usable by people in wheelchairs: tops of sinks should be no higher than 34 inches from the floor; pipes and valves below the sink should be covered to prevent legs from

being burned or scratched. Towel bars, soap dispensers, and shelves should be no higher than 42 inches from the floor. The bottoms of mirrors should be located at the same height. Even better is a full-length mirror that accommodates everyone, including children. Floors should be even and level, extending to the outside without steps, lips, or barriers.

For cleaning ease, restroom interiors should be finished with concrete, tiles,

fiberglass, or metal. Adequate light and ventilation should be provided either naturally or mechanically. Provide a floor drain in case of toilet overflow. And, if possible, include a secure area that protects mechanical systems and provides storage for paper and cleaning supplies. Finally, make provisions for locking and securing the facility at night or during the off-season.

Drinking Fountains

Drinking fountains also require access to water utilities and disposal lines. Consider installing drinking fountains near restrooms to get the most out of utility access and improvements. But in locations where there is no access to water, consider providing bottled-water dispensers or vending machines.

The design of drinking fountains should incorporate the needs of all potential users. Spigot heights for adults should be 42 inches above the ground. Heights for disabled users should be no higher than 36 inches, with at least 27 inches below the basin to allow wheelchairs to pull up to the fountain. To accommodate all needs, provide both standard- and accessible-height spigots and install steps to the side of the standard spout for children to use. If you are providing a separate spigot for children, it should be about 30 inches from the ground (figure 3.82).

An additional spigot at the base allows people to fill water bottles and basins for uses other than drinking. If possible, provide for both hand and foot operation. You should locate fountains at least 4 feet off circulation pathways. The surface around the fountain should be accessible and well drained and should slope away from the direction of the trail. If a nonporous pavement is used, such as asphalt or concrete, provide a nearby drain. As with any outdoor public amenity, sturdiness is important. The best materials for drinking fountains are cast iron and precast concrete.

Benches

When designing or purchasing a bench, consider user comfort, simplicity of form and detail, ease of maintenance, durability of finish, and resistance to vandalism. Some benches are simply "slab type," meaning they have neither arms nor backs; others are double backed, and some are seating walls.

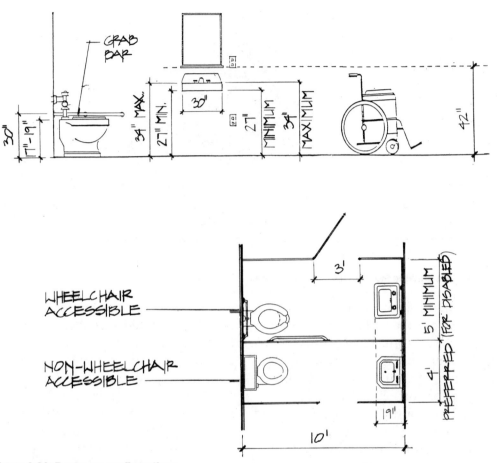

Figure 3.81: Restroom configurations.

Typically, a bench's seat is located between 16 and 20 inches above the ground, with handrails on the end between 6 and 12 inches above the seat. The depth of a bench seat ranges from 18 to 20 inches. Usually a width of 24 to 30 inches is allotted per person. A comfortable three-seater bench would measure between 72 and 90 inches wide. Bench backs are usually 15 to 18

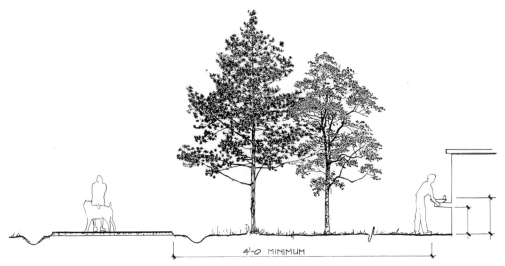

Figure 3.82: Drinking fountain and restroom area.

inches high and are set from 3 to 9 inches above the seat (figure 3.83).

Bench seats are not set parallel to the ground but are generally tilted back between 8 and 15 degrees for greater comfort. This tilted position also allows for the drainage of rain and snow. To keep a seat free of standing water requires a minimum tilt of $\frac{1}{8}$ to $\frac{1}{4}$ inch for every 12 inches of seat width (a slope between 1 and 2 percent). A slight angling of the bench back, between 5 and 15 degrees, allows for a relaxing resting position.

Benches can be made from a variety of materials. Simple, rustic benches can be made from flat-topped boulders or split-faced logs. Weather-resistant materials include treated wood, painted metal, and concrete. Whatever you choose, make sure that the seat and back are well drained, preferably by a cross pitch or slats, not just holes or perforations on a flat surface. Be sure the bench is securely anchored to the ground, so that it will not overturn. (People often use benches in curious ways—they sit on the backs, stretch against them, and employ them as workbenches for bicycle repair.)

Locate benches where they offer a good view or shelter from seasonal winds. Benches should highlight the trail's variety, taking advantage of sunlight or shade (figure 3.84). Place some in quiet areas and others in busier spots.

Benches and other furniture should be placed away from pedestrian and bicycle circulation paths, at least 3 feet from the trail edge, to allow adequate room for people's outstretched legs, walking sticks, and canes.

Hard pavement or a gravel bed may be laid 1 foot beyond the outside dimensions of a bench to ensure that puddling will not occur where people put their feet. As with any pavement or gravel area, grade the site to allow water to drain away from the bench and the trail. A slope of at least 2 percent should be maintained in these areas.

Provide wheelchair access alongside benches, at least a 30-by-48-inch area for adequate maneuvering. If benches are next to each other (either side by side or face to face), allow 4 feet between them. A distance of 1 foot between benches and amenities such as trash receptacles, light poles, and signposts is adequate. A distance of at least 4 feet between such facilities as restrooms, phone booths, and drinking fountains allows easy circulation.

Shelters

Shelters with roofs and protected seating areas will be well received by users, particularly on long multi-use trails. Shelters protect users from sun, wind, rain, and snow while providing a pleasant place to rest (figure 3.85).

Shelters should be located at least 3 feet, preferably 5 feet, from the trail's edge. The measurement of this setback should be taken from the point of the shelter nearest the trail. Shelters should never interfere with safe movement of trail traffic. When determining where to place a shelter, think about the location of existing and proposed utility systems, including fire hydrants, power and telephone lines, below-grade utilities such as water and sewer lines, other underground conduits, and existing and proposed plantings.

Existing objects such as trees, shrubs, utility poles, signs, and other natural and built obstructions should not substantially interfere with visibility into or out of the shelter. To ensure that shelters are perceived as safe, locate them as close as possible to the trail, clustering them with other facilities such as pay phones, parking areas, drinking fountains, and restrooms. Shelters should also be positioned to

Figure 3.83: Bench dimensions.

provide maximum protection from prevailing winds.

The exterior walls of shelters range from 10 to 16 feet in length and are from 5 to 8 feet wide. The interior height should be between 7 and 8½ feet. The roof should be sloped to permit adequate drainage and, where necessary, to prevent the buildup of snow. If wind is a problem, windscreens

should be provided along the front of the shelter. When a windscreen is used, entrances should be located at either end of the shelter. The windscreen's entry and exit openings should be unobstructed and at least 36 inches wide. In addition, shelters should meet structural wind and snow-loading requirements for their location. Check local building codes for requirements.

Figure 3.84: A well-placed bench along the Cannon Valley Trail in southeastern Minnesota.

Bicycle Racks

You need to consider three criteria when choosing bicycle racks for your multi-use trail: their locations, the way they secure bicycles, and the dimensions of the bicycles likely to be used on the trail. Bike racks should be located as close as possible to destinations without interfering with traffic flow. Bike storage areas or racks set more than 50 feet away from a destination encourage bicyclists to seek out the nearest light post, bench, or tree instead. Locate bike racks in areas where visual supervision is likely and where lighting and shelter are available.

There are several ways to secure a bicycle: putting it in enclosed storage;

locking it to a rack, post, or other stationary object; and making it inoperable by weaving a chain and lock through the frame and wheels.

The first two methods are the most effective. Among the various options available, coin-operated or leased lockers provide the greatest security and eliminate the need for bicyclists to carry locks and chains. But lockers are bulky and costly to install and maintain. The stationary rack or post is more affordable. Racks and stanchions that allow cyclists to lock both the wheels and the frame reduce casual theft, while devices that provide lateral support only at one wheel leave the bicycle vulnerable to wheel damage because it is easily tipped over. Racks or stanchions should be high enough that excessive cable or chain lengths are not needed to secure both frame and wheels.

A bicycle rack should allow 2 feet of space between bicycles, so that cyclists can move their bicycles into and out of the racks with minimal effort and damage. A rack should accommodate a bicycle length of 5 feet 6 inches and a height of 42 inches. The examples in figure 3.86 illustrate some possible options.

Picnic Areas

Locate picnic areas where they provide for the maximum comfort and enjoyment of users. Picnic areas should not be located near potentially hazardous areas—for example, areas with low-hanging branches or poisonous or thorny plants. Because of their relatively large size and high level of activity, picnic areas should be set back sufficiently from circulation pathways so they will not interfere with activities on the trail.

Typically, picnic areas consist of picnic tables and benches, but you can also include cooking facilities, restrooms, and drinking fountains. The simplest picnic facility includes just enough room for a picnic table with attached benches. As a general

Figure 3.85: An appealing shade shelter along the Ojai Valley Trail in Ventura, California.

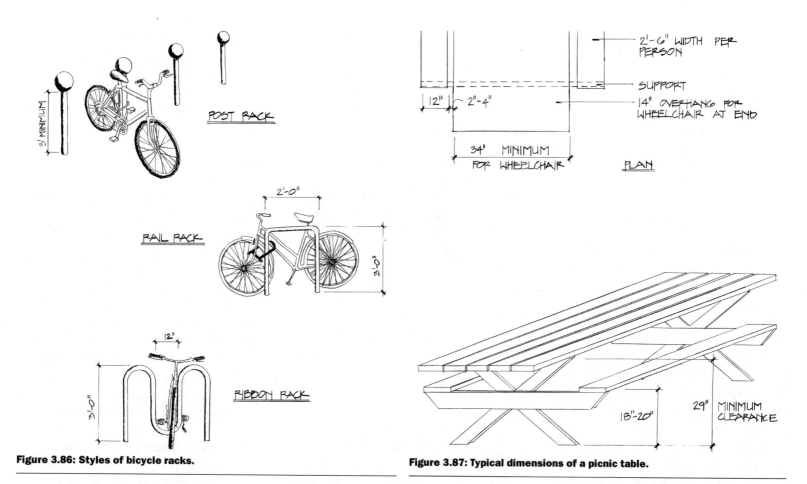

POST RACK

RAIL RACK

RIBBON RACK

2'-0"

12"

3' MINIMUM

3'-0"

3'-0"

2'-6" WIDTH PER PERSON

SUPPORT

14" OVERHANG FOR WHEELCHAIR AT END

12"

2"-4"

34' MINIMUM FOR WHEELCHAIR

PLAN

18"-20"

29" MINIMUM CLEARANCE

Figure 3.86: Styles of bicycle racks.

Figure 3.87: Typical dimensions of a picnic table.

rule, this requires about 168 square feet, a rectangle measuring 12 by 14 feet. A picnic table and bench unit usually measures 6 by 8 feet, and a circulation space of 48 inches for wheelchair access should be maintained on all sides of the unit. All tables should be accessible to wheelchairs and so should be situated on level, free-draining ground with a fairly hard, compacted surface. Tabletops should be between 30 and 34 inches high, with a 29-inch clearance at either end to allow for wheelchair access (figure 3.87).

Most picnic table units are made of wood, but metal and concrete are viable alternatives. If you are building or selecting a wooden unit, remember that wood decays easily and should be treated. Painting or staining will prevent rotting, but naturally weather-resistant and decay-resistant woods such as redwood, cedar, or cypress are preferable. The use of treated woods should be considered cautiously, as the additives used are often irritating to the skin and can be carcinogenic.

Fitness Courses

Fitness courses, also known as exercise courses, obstacle courses, and parcourses, are popular additions to a multi-use trail. A fitness course consists of a circuit or loop divided at intervals by stations, each equipped with apparatus and directions for specific exercises. A fitness system leads users through a progressive routine that includes warmup, strengthening, aerobic, and cool-down exercises. Since the stations generate activity, they should be located away from trail traffic. The areas where stations are located should be level, free draining, and clear of obstacles such as landscaping, boulders, or steep drop-offs. Wood chips, gravel, or coarse sand should be used to prevent excessive wear on the ground underneath the course and to avoid puddling;

more rigid surfaces such as asphalt and concrete can lead to injuries.

The fitness course usually includes equipment of two or three different sizes to provide varying levels of difficulty and to accommodate different-sized users. The first stop on the fitness course should outline the entire circuit and explain the different types of exercises. Signs at the remaining stations should be numbered and labeled with their specific routines, and each should include text and an illustration describing the exercise to be performed. To obtain equipment and plans for a fitness course that is appropriate for your particular trail, contact commercial manufacturers. Figure 3.88 shows typical fitness equipment and signs near a trail.

❖

LANDSCAPING

What does it take to create a great trail experience? It helps to start with a beautiful trail corridor. Fortunately, many corridors offer exceptional landscapes and rich experiences for the trail user. But in other situations, significant work is needed to give the trail a personality of its own.

To create a successful trail experience you must consider the perspective of the user. "Since landscape is usually experienced by a moving observer," author Kevin Lynch writes, "it is not the single view that is important as much as the cumulative effect of a sequence of views.[10]" Trails are multi-dimensional, with things to see, hear, smell, feel, and even taste along the way. Users will also have emotional, intellectual, and spiritual reactions to a trail experience. You need to keep all of this in mind as you plan your trail's landscape.

Early in the trail-planning process you should have conducted a physical inventory of the route (see "Physical Inventory and Assessment of the Site" in chapter 1). Much of the information you collected then will be used to develop a landscaping plan.

In developing your landscaping plan, you must factor in the costs of both installation and maintenance. Landscaping is not a one-time cost but an ongoing commitment. You also need to think of possible constraints in landscaping your trail. If your trail is in a dry area, will irrigation be necessary? What types of soil are located there, and what is the soil's condition? Are toxins that might affect future

Figure 3.88: Fitness cluster along a bike trail in Anchorage, Alaska.

Photo: Clark James Mishler

The Trail Edge

You need to address what will be planted along the trail's edges. Urban trails should include a mowed shoulder (at least 2 feet wide) on each side of the trail. This groomed look offers better visibility and a "lane" for joggers, equestrians, and others who prefer not to use the trail surface, especially if it is paved. Trees and large shrubs should be set back at least 5 feet from the trail's edge to reduce possible damage to the trail from root growth. Keep in mind that a tree's root system often equals the width of its branches.

The Roles of Plants and Trees

Plants and trees can play various roles along your multi-use trail. When developing your landscaping plan, consider the following:

■ Trees and Large Shrubs

Different varieties of trees and shrubs create shade and define spaces visually. Large plants also can direct trail traffic if they are planted to form corridors. Additionally, trees and shrubs serve as screening for adjacent property, help block the wind, frame important views, and provide shade.

landscape plantings present in the area? Can disturbed areas be made suitable for landscaping without compromising the quality of the surrounding environment?

Ongoing maintenance is a major factor in a multi-use trail's landscape plan. Even "natural" landscape along a trail requires maintenance, if only to manage weeds and remove overhanging tree limbs. Therefore, you need to make a realistic assessment of your financial ability to maintain different types of landscaping improvements.

After assessing your landscape opportunities and constraints, you are ready to prepare a landscape plan that addresses the following items. You may want to seek the assistance of a landscape architect who has experience in planning public spaces.

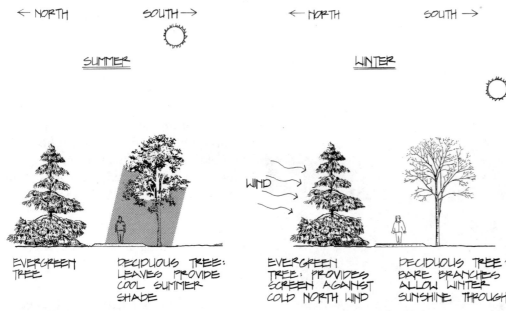

← NORTH   SOUTH →

SUMMER

← NORTH   SOUTH →

WINTER

WIND

EVERGREEN TREE

DECIDUOUS TREE: LEAVES PROVIDE COOL SUMMER SHADE

EVERGREEN TREE: PROVIDES SCREEN AGAINST COLD NORTH WIND

DECIDUOUS TREE: BARE BRANCHES ALLOW WINTER SUNSHINE THROUGH

Figure 3.89: Planting for sun and wind.

Your landscaping plan should consider a variety of trees and shrubs. Visualize the corridor in each of the seasons and try to offer attractive settings year-round through careful selection of species. Select plant and tree species that are native to your area and suitable for your climate zone, especially in a drought-prone area. Also, try to avoid trees with invasive roots.

Keep in mind the effects of tree type and placement. Evergreens on the south side of the trail, for example, may promote ice buildup in winter, while a row of evergreens on the north side can help block cold winter winds. A row of trees in the right location can serve as a "snow fence," reducing snow buildup on the trail. Deciduous trees are appropriate on the south side of a trail. They provide cooling shade during summer, but they drop their leaves in winter, letting sunlight warm the trail (figure 3.89). Trees and shrubs play an important role in creating spaces and breaking up monotony along the trail corridor. Plant them in clusters and groves rather than in single straight lines. For planting detail, see figure 3.90. If a more formal look is desired in some areas, consider planting trees in double rows on each side of the trail, in a staggered pattern, to create a more exciting passageway. In some areas, groups of trees might be planted close to the trail and others farther away to create outdoor "rooms" and meadows.

■ Understory

Formed by small shrubs and various woody plants, the understory adds visual interest to the landscape and helps crowd out weeds. The understory should include a variety of species and groupings, among them plants that provide food and shelter for birds, mammals, and other wildlife. The understory can also include special small plants of interest that slower-traveling trail users will enjoy. In urban areas, dense understory should be avoided to promote better visibility, which in turn will increase personal safety.

■ Ground Cover

Different types of ground covers—grasses, wildflowers, vines, and other surface plantings—can form the "floor" or "carpet" of your corridor. Ground cover can also provide food and cover for wildlife. Your maintenance plan should include provisions for some mowing in the corridor, especially on the trail shoulders and around rest areas. Selective mowing can help shape ground cover and create a groomed look without the use of formal landscaping. In dry climates, consider native soil, decomposed granite, or gravel "ground covers" to minimize maintenance and water consumption.

Safety and Security

Your landscape plan must address user safety and security. The design needs to create both genuine security as well as perceived security. Start with good visibility. Trail users should have at least 100 feet of both forward and rear visibility on a level grade. Sight distances are particularly important at approaches to tunnels, bridge underpasses, and intersections; the user should be able to see all the way through before entering the area.

Do not allow dense understory to grow next to the trail since it can create shadows or blind areas where some-

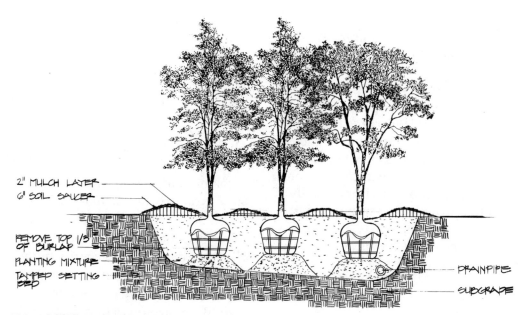

one could hide. In urban or crime-prone areas, plan to keep the trail edge groomed to create an open view and a maintained look. Ideally, dense understory growth should be cleared at least 5 feet back from the trail's edge.

Your design should provide occasional "escape routes"—ways to retreat from any problems. There should be no "box canyons," areas where the trail corridor is fully enclosed by dense vegetation, walls, backs of buildings, or other barriers. To minimize the

Figure 3.90: Tree-planting detail.

2" MULCH LAYER
6' SOIL SAUCER
REMOVE TOP 1/3 OF BURLAP
PLANTING MIXTURE
TAMPED SETTING BED
DRAINPIPE
SUBGRADE

sense of isolation, your plantings should be placed so as to maintain visibility between the trail and adjoining residences, shops, and businesses. Trees and shrubs planted in groups can help break up the imposing look of long walls. Work with owners of adjoining buildings to pursue appealing landscaping.

Service and Access

Your plan should describe how the landscape will be serviced—how maintenance personnel will mow, trim, and care for plants; what equipment will be used; and when. Consult personnel to be sure there is adequate room to mow and groom around plants. If irrigation is required, determine where the water supply will come from and how the irrigation lines will be laid.

It is best to use a variety of plants that do not require chemical pest control or fertilization. Environmentally sensitive areas, and areas near drinking water reservoirs, may have restrictions on the use of chemicals. If that is the case in your corridor, be especially careful not to plant species that are prone to pests or require fertilizers.

Addressing Odor and Noise

Some multi-use trails pass by facilities such as stockyards and sewage plants that create unpleasant odors. While you probably cannot eliminate the problem, you may be able to diminish its effect. One option is to screen with fragrant plants such as evergreens. Another is to develop a series of interpretive signs to explain the source of the pungent smell. A sign explaining that the purpose of a sewage plant is to protect public health and water quality, for example, may help

mitigate the public's reaction to the odor. Some odors can be interesting. For example, just north of Baltimore, for example, a rail-trail passes near a spice factory. An interpretive sign could give special meaning to the mysterious aroma.

If a road is the primary source of noise, the problem will vary with traffic volume and speed. In some instances you may decide that a solid fence is necessary, although this may look rather unappealing. In addition, a solid fence could create security problems, especially in urban areas, as a trail user would have no "escape route" if a dangerous situation arose. More desirable is a landscaped buffer

zone between the trail and the source of the noise. Even a narrow band of vegetation—5 or 6 feet wide—will help. Although the actual noise-dampening effect of trees and shrubs may be marginal, the psychological effect is significant (figure 3.91).

Timing and Spacing

Your landscape plan must anticipate the growth and maturity of plants over time. Trees take time to grow and in the early years can look quite scruffy (figure 3.92). Just after trail construction, when the ground is disturbed, weeds are likely to invade in full force. Therefore, plan to prepare disturbed areas and seed them as soon as possi-

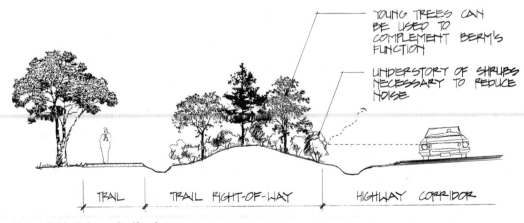

Figure 3.91: Noise reduction berm.

ble after construction. Also schedule time to remove thorny and noxious weeds so that desirable plants can take over.

Make sure there is enough space between plants to allow for future growth, and be sure to plan (and budget) for plant mortality. It is not unusual to lose 10 to 20 percent of new plantings, and other plants will eventually die of natural causes. Plant a variety of species and types to avoid a sudden die-off in the landscape because of age or disease.

Remember, too, that plants live in communities with other plants. Some live together better than others. Note each plant's special needs for sun, shade, room to grow, and other factors and group compatible plants together.

Cost and Implementation

Costs of trail landscaping vary, depending on the region of the country, the preexisting landscape along the corridor, and the goals of your trail-building effort. Urban trails often require more landscaping than rural trails.

Typical landscaping costs are difficult to gauge because prices vary widely. Trees between 5 and 10 feet tall cost about $150 to $250 each; 1- to 5-gallon shrubs range from $50 to $75

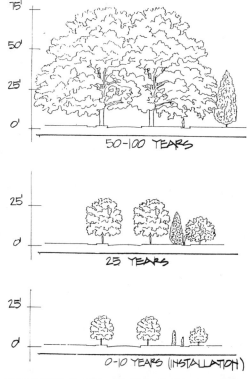

Figure 3.92: Growth of trail landscape over time.

each. Costs will be about 50 percent higher if irrigation is required.

With a little resourcefulness, you can reduce these costs. Use volunteers for trail landscaping and maintenance—tree and shrub plantings are increasingly popular community projects. Get contributions from local businesses and service clubs. In Den-

ver, a group called Volunteers for Outdoor Colorado recently planted more than 2,500 trees and shrubs along a trail in a single day as part of a three-year volunteer program called "10,000 Trees." Also, ask local nurseries to donate surplus stock as a tax write-off.

Develop an "Adopt a Trail" program is popular for landscape maintenance. Dozens of individuals and groups help maintain the landscaping along the 44-mile Washington and Old Dominion Trail in northern Virginia. Boy Scouts, Girl Scouts, and senior citizens can make ideal tree and plant custodians if they are properly trained and monitored by professional maintenance personnel.

Finally, work with the resources you already have along the corridor. Can simple grooming, trimming, and spot plantings meet your trail's landscaping needs? Can you phase in projects over time? Trail landscaping offers many opportunities to be resourceful and creative.

CHAPTER

4

Managing Your Trail

149

WHO SHOULD MANAGE YOUR MULTI-USE TRAIL?

Determining which agency (or agencies) should manage your multi-use trail is a critical step in developing a successful project. Possibilities include local, county, state, and federal agencies as well as a regional park authority. Often the choice is obvious; other times it seems as if every possible managing agency has a dozen reasons for not taking on the task. Generally, determining the management agency for short trails is easier than for long ones passing through many towns and counties and those crossing state lines.

Generally speaking, it is preferable to have one agency, rather than a group of small agencies, manage a multi-use trail. When managed by a single agency, the trail is likely to have a homogeneous look and feel—a comprehensive design, a uniform trail surface, a single set of trail regulations, and a consistent level of maintenance along its entire length. For users, the trail experience will vary less from one community to another, and trail neighbors will be less confused about where to report problems or concerns. A single agency responsible for a trail's management can develop a clear vision of how the facility should be developed.

Of course, who manages the trail depends primarily on where the corridor runs and how many jurisdictions it crosses. Large agencies such as state park systems, with their advantages of size and scale, are better able to take on long corridors that might otherwise be fragmented or only partly developed if managed by small agencies with fewer resources and a more limited mandate. On the other hand, local agencies may have better rapport with local residents.

Local Management

If a trail corridor is confined to one community, it is most appropriately managed by a local entity such as a city or town department of parks, recreation, public works, or conservation, or even a board of supervisors or the town clerk's office. Choosing among these options is generally a matter of resources, orientation, and connection with other managed lands.

If the corridor extends beyond the confines of one town, a county or state managing entity is preferable; however, if no such agency is feasible, it may be necessary to string together several local management agencies. An example of this is the Mohawk-Hudson Bikeway near Albany, New York, where three towns and two counties cooperatively—but independently—manage the 41-mile facility. Under this kind of scheme, trails usually change complexion—different signs, rules, surfaces, landscaping materials, and levels of upkeep — at each community's border.

County Management

According to a 1992 survey conducted by the Rails-to-Trails Conservancy, almost 25 percent of rail-trails are managed at the county level.[1] Generally speaking, if a corridor traverses several localities within one county, it is best managed at the county level. A county parks department (or an equivalent agency, such as forest preserve districts in some Illinois counties and county conservation boards in Iowa) may be the most logical managing agency. If there is no county park or conservation agency in your county (as is the case in many rural areas), perhaps the county's transportation department or a county water district can manage the trail. In some cases, a county transportation or public works department develops the trail and then turns it over to a parks department for management.

State Management

Corridors that traverse more than one county tend to be managed best on the state level, usually as state parks. Joining a state park system brings many advantages, including economy of scale, a large planning staff, diversified personnel, and often a consistent budget. The state can ensure uniformity of signs, amenities, and maintenance across county borders. Moreover, the state can plan for and develop trail extensions.

Particularly in less-affluent rural areas, a state agency may more effectively preserve a unique state resource than local municipalities trying to work together. For instance, the 57-mile New River Trail State Park in the mountains of southwestern Virginia may never have been developed without the state's involvement; the small jurisdictions through which the trail passes did not have the resources to take on the project by themselves.

Of course, some people are skeptical of projects coming out of the state capi-

tal. State managing agencies may find it difficult to build a local support network. Often landowners and potential users feel more comfortable with a smaller, closer-to-home agency. For this reason, state-level trail managers should set up a local advisory committee to foster community support and iron out problems at the point of conflict.

State trails don't work in every situation. Some state park systems are in such bad financial shape that they have placed a moratorium on the creation of new parks. Or your area may already have an abundance of state parks. If this is the case, a multicounty or regional park authority may be the answer.

A solution that is rapidly becoming popular is a partnership formed by different levels of government. Under one such scenario a state transportation or natural resource agency purchases an abandoned railroad corridor with the understanding that the county or locality will develop and maintain it as a multi-use trail. Sometimes state departments of transportation purchase corridors for future road or rail use but allow them to be utilized as "interim" trails for ten, twenty, or more years. Although transportation departments typically do not

want to develop and operate trails, they sometimes are willing to lease the corridors to local park agencies.

Federal Management

Federal-level management is not very common for multi-use trails, although the U.S. Forest Service does manage about seventy-five trails within national forests that were developed from former logging railroads. Other federal multi-use trail managers include the National Park Service, the Army Corps of Engineers, and the Bureau of Land Management.

If your corridor runs across federal land, one of these agencies may well be the obvious manager. If the corridor is not on public land, however, it is unlikely that a federal agency will become active as a trail manager.

A Regional Park (or Trail) Authority

If your corridor traverses several counties but your state park agency is unable or unwilling to undertake the project, consider utilizing or forming a regional authority to manage the trail. The authority can be an existing agency, such as a council of governments, a metropolitan planning organization, or a regional park authority. Or you may want to establish a new one specifically for the trail. Two highly successful agencies that manage multi-use trails are the two-county East Bay Regional Park District, near San Francisco, and the two-county, three-city Northern Virginia Regional Park Authority, near Washington, D.C. A third, which manages an automobile parkway but not a multi-use trail, is the two-state Palisades Interstate Park Commission near New York City.

Regionally managed trails have all the advantages of state trails: comprehensive development, a uniform set of standards, continuity of maintenance, and greater likelihood of extension beyond the county line. Additionally, the trail will be perceived as a regional rather than just a local facility, which can build public support over a broader political and geographic area. And with that support, the trail may generate higher levels of funding.

Nongovernmental Management

Other management possibilities include nongovernmental solutions—private foundations, land trusts, and local citizens' associations—although this form of management is rare for a multi-use trail. While many single-use trails (hiking, equestrian, and snowmobiling trails, for example) are run by private groups, the heavy use and complex dynamics of multi-use trails, particularly river and rail corridors, make them difficult to manage on a low budget and volunteer basis. Generally, the nongovernmental route is chosen only if no government entity can be found for the task.

When a Single Agency Is Not Possible

If your trail passes through several jurisdictions but you are nevertheless unable to find or create a single managing agency, try to develop at least a cooperative management strategy for the trail. This will promote some consistency and will also establish guidelines and expectations for each agency. Some other tips to help unify the trail:

▶ Make sure the trail has a consistent name throughout its length. (If local pride makes it necessary, individual sections can have subnames such as "Iron Horse Trail, Montgomery County Section.")

▶ Make sure your trail map covers the entire length of the trail, not just the portion in your jurisdiction. (Or at least make sure all the maps of the trail are made available as a packet.)

▶ Support the formation of a "Friends of the Trail" organization that covers the entire facility, not just one section of it. The Friends can work to pull together bureaucracies that otherwise would not communicate (see "'Friends of the Trail Groups'" in chapter 5).

▶ Periodically visit sections of the trail that are not in your jurisdiction to see and feel what average trail users experience and to get ideas of what (or what not) to do in your section. Even better, jointly sponsor a group hike, bike, or equestrian ride along the entire trail with all the other trail managers and follow that up with a half-day discussion of all the issues affecting the trail.

❖

TRAIL MAINTENANCE AND SAFETY

Comprehensive planning minimizes safety and maintenance problems later, so you need to develop a thorough maintenance and safety plan, including a budget, before construction begins on the trail facility. If you have not developed a plan, do so now (see "Developing a Comprehensive Budget and Management Plan" in chapter 2). And remember that neglected facilities can be unsafe and will become a liability.

Maintenance

A successful maintenance program requires continuity and a high level of citizen involvement. Regular, routine maintenance on a year-to-year basis not only ensures trail safety (and reduces potential legal liability) but also prolongs the life of the trail.

Maintenance activities required for safe trail operation should always receive top priority. The following tasks should be part of a maintenance schedule:[2]

▶ **Signs and Traffic Markings** Inspect signs for both motorists and trail users and keep them in good condition. Make sure any pavement markings are clear and prominent.

▶ **Sight Distance and Clearance** Do not allow sight distances, especially those leading up to crossings and curves, to be impaired by vegetation. Trim trees, shrubs, and tall grass to meet sight-distance requirements based on a 20-mile-per-hour trail design speed. Also, maintain adequate clearances on the sides of the trail and overhead. Trim tree branches to allow room for seasonal growth.

▶ **Surface Repair** Patch or grade the trail surface on a regular basis. Ensure that finished patches are flush with the trail surface. Remove ruts and take steps to avoid their recurrence.

▶ **Drainage** Repair any trail damage from seasonal washouts and silt or gravel washes. Identify the source of the drainage problem and take steps to remedy it. Clean all culverts, catch basins, and other drainage structures at least once a year.

▶ **Sweeping and Cleaning** Keep the trail free of debris, including broken glass and other sharp objects, loose gravel, leaves, and stray branches. If nearby roads are swept mechanically, make sure material is not thrown onto the trail. Frequently sweep trail edges, especially if they are made of loose material like bark or gravel.

▶ **Structural Deterioration** Inspect structures annually to ensure they are in good condition. Pay special attention to wood foundations and posts to determine whether rot or termites are present.

▶ **Illumination** Make necessary lighting improvements, especially at busy road crossings and in tunnels. Keep lights clean and replace fixtures as required to maintain desired luminescence.

A few other items to consider for your maintenance schedule:

▶ Mow trail shoulders and other selected areas (figure 4.1).

▶ Spot prune and remove encroaching vegetation.

▶ Pick up litter and empty trashcans.

▶ Maintain furniture and other support facilities.

▶ Remove any fallen trees.

Photo: Leona K. Jensen

Figure 4.1: Trailside maintenance along the Outlet Trail in New York State.

mer youth program, which would provide young adults with work opportunities and expose them to the trail while providing you with a source of seasonal, temporary labor. Some communities have even used low-risk inmates from local correctional facilities to maintain their trails.

You should establish a mechanism for tracking citizen complaints and maintenance requests. From a liability standpoint, this is critical. Once an agency has been "put on notice" concerning a particular safety-related maintenance problem, it must correct the problem within a reasonable period of time or else it will be considered negligent. Develop a complaint/request form that includes a place for the date, the person's name and daytime telephone number, and the location and nature of the problem. Field crews will use these forms to investigate potential maintenance problems.

Encourage trail users and neighbors to monitor and report maintenance problems and requests along the corridor. "Improvement Request Forms" should be available at trailheads, through user organizations, and at bicycle shops. Request forms should in-

▶ Improve trail/road intersections.

Invite trail user organizations, community groups, civic organizations, and businesses to provide periodic maintenance work along the trail corridor as a means of improving trail safety, keeping maintenance costs down, and building goodwill with people living adjacent to the trail. An "Adopt a Trail" program could be established to encourage groups to improve certain areas along the trail.

Also explore the possibility of using a local conservation corps to help out with maintenance, or sponsor a sum-

clude the same maintenance items that are covered in the routine maintenance schedule.

Risk Management

In the current litigious atmosphere, trail users may be tempted to sue the managing agency for any accident that happens along the trail—regardless of fault.[3] Although every case is different and is dependent on the specific circumstances surrounding the accident, negligence will play a key role. The law requires that the managing agency provide a reasonably safe facility. Therefore, the best solution to the liability problem is prevention: Eliminate hazardous situations before an accident occurs.

It is in your best interest to establish a risk management program that will aid you in discovering problem areas before anyone is injured and decides to sue. Risk management diminishes the potential for lawsuits, reduces insurance costs and claims, and enhances the safety of your facility.[4]

Although many risk management strategies are quite simple, they are often overlooked. First, develop procedures for periodic inspection and maintenance of the trail and any sup-

Figure 4.2: A smart risk-management sign.

port facilities. Negligence is predicated on the knowledge of a dangerous condition; governmental agencies are generally not held liable for a hazard unless they knew about it long enough before an accident occurred to have made repairs or posted warnings. For example, if a large branch has fallen across your trail and a bicyclist is injured, your agency is unlikely to be

negligent if it can be proven that the branch fell a short time before the accident. However, if the branch had fallen the day before and several trail users reported the hazard, then the agency would be negligent. Furthermore, if the branch had fallen several weeks earlier—even if no one reported it—the agency may be held negligent because it *should have known* about the hazard.

A second risk management principle is to provide adequate warning of risks. On multi-use trails, signs can play a key role in warning users of hazards. Place signs such as "Walk Bicycle through Underpass" or "Dismount Horse Before Crossing Bridge" in appropriate locations along your trail (figure 4.2).

Proper handling of a medical emergency is another important element in risk management. If someone is injured, a staff member should watch over the person while another calls for immediate help. It is wise to have staff properly trained in basic first aid and CPR, but if this is not the case, they should not attempt to "play doctor" on the injured person as they may inflict more harm. Be sure to follow up any accident with an accurate and thorough report. Failure to do so could have serious repercussions if the injured party sues.

A final risk management principle is documentation. Documenting regular inspections of your trail, its signs, and its support facilities can prove adherence to legal duties, which could make the difference in winning or losing a case. Use this common-sense procedure (along with the other risk management principles), and you can significantly reduce your overall chances of liability problems.

Personal Safety

Ideally, your trail was designed with personal safety in mind. Good design prevents many security problems. As in most parks, many security problems on trails occur in parking lots. To increase security, erect a fence, with one entrance, around the lot. This allows for easy surveillance and patrol, and allows the lot to be closed if necessary.

Consider providing emergency telephones or call-box systems with direct connections to the local 911 network. The calling system may be installed at measured points along a trail and is particularly important in remote sections.

You might think about installing night security lights at trailheads and major road crossings or activity areas if there are problems at those locations. Providing security lighting along the entire length of the trail is not recommended. Lights are expensive to install and operate, and they often generate opposition from local homeowners adjacent to the trail. In addition, their effectiveness in reducing crime is questionable. Some studies have shown that lights simply expose a potential victim, while providing shadow in which would-be criminals can hide.

Landscaping is also a factor in personal safety; vegetation adjacent to the trail can easily serve to hide potential offenders. Plantings should be limited to low shrubs. Branches should be cropped close to the trunk, at least 10 feet from the ground. (For more information, see "Landscaping" in chapter 3.)

Your trail corridor should be able to accommodate security, safety, and other emergency equipment, including fire trucks and ambulances. If you have installed motorized vehicle barriers at access points and road crossings, they should be the type that emergency vehicles can knock down or security or

safety personnel can unlock and remove during an emergency response.

■ Trail Patrols

If trail security is perceived as a problem, you may want to set up a trail patrol. Although most multi-use trails do not have them, regular patrols can serve some useful functions and should at least be considered. A trail patrol's primary function is to provide assistance and information, not to apprehend criminals. If a serious crime does occur, members of the patrol can contact the emergency 911 network or police radios.

Patrol personnel should perform positive trail functions as much as possible—distributing maps and brochures, providing information, offering bicycle safety checks, and performing other service-oriented activities. Security personnel should use a bicycle or horse to patrol a trail, not a motorized vehicle. Users tend to respond favorably to someone who appears more like a trail user than a law-enforcement officer.

At the beginning and end of each season, the trail patrol should conduct a field survey to measure its effectiveness and to identify potential enforcement problems. The survey, which could be done with volunteer assistance, also provides an opportunity for a count of trail users.

Trail patrols can fill another positive role: filing accident report forms for any incidents that occur on the trail. The reports should be compiled and analyzed yearly to determine any necessary improvements in traffic-control systems and patrol methods.

Where security is of particular concern, it may be advisable to form a technical security group made up of representatives from the police and fire departments, the emergency aid service, and the trail's managing agency. The security group should coordinate their trail safety roles and establish procedures for responding to emergencies. The group should also determine how they will work together to coordinate security for special events.

Trail User Conflicts

Because they are used for a variety of purposes, multi-use trails are prone to a certain level of conflict among users, which in turn can lead to safety problems. Typically, conflicts occur on heavily used urban and suburban

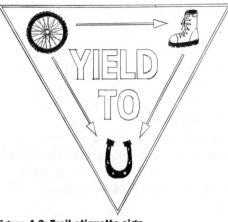

Figure 4.3: Trail etiquette sign.

trails. While they may be difficult to solve, conflicts should be viewed as problems of success—an indication of the trail's popularity.

■ Regulations

An important step in preventing user conflicts is the creation and adoption of trail user regulations. The regulations, developed in conjunction with trail user groups, should spell out the rules governing public conduct on the trail. They should also state the methods by which they will be enforced and the civil penalties imposed for noncompliance. Post the regulations at trailheads and include them on all trail brochures and maps.

The most common regulation for multiple-use trails is "wheels yield to heels." The self-explanatory sign shown in figure 4.3 illustrates protocol for yielding right-of-way: bicyclists yield to all trail users, and pedestrians yield to equestrians. In addition, consider including these regulations:

▶ Stay to the right except when passing.

▶ Travel at a reasonable speed in a consistent and predictable manner.

▶ Always look ahead and behind before passing.

▶ Pass slower traffic on their left; yield to oncoming traffic when passing.

▶ Give a clear warning signal before passing.

▶ Keep all pets on a short leash.

▶ As a courtesy to trail neighbors, refrain from loitering near adjacent homes.

▶ Move off the trail when stopped to allow others to pass.

▶ Yield to other users when entering and crossing the trail.

▶ Motorized vehicles are prohibited (except electric wheelchairs).

▶ Alcoholic beverages and illegal drugs are not permitted on the trail.

▶ Firearms, fireworks, and fires are not permitted on the trail.

▶ All trail users should use a light and reflectors after dusk and before dawn.

You may also opt to establish times when the trail is closed, such as from midnight to 5 a.m.

■ Speed Limits

A common complaint on multi-use trails is "speeding" bicyclists. But establishing a formal speed limit on trails to reduce user conflicts is a strategy of last resort and should be implemented only when all else fails. An effective speed limit requires consistent, ongoing enforcement, and it is unclear whether reducing the speed actually improves the real or perceived safety of the trail. Pedestrians using a trail may feel just as uncomfortable with a bicyclist passing at 12 miles per hour as 15 miles per hour. Speed limits

also may discourage those who use the trail to commute by bicycle. Finally, few bicyclists actually know the speed they are traveling. Although several multi-use trails have used speed limits effectively, consider all of these factors prior to establishing a speed limit because it may not solve user conflicts on your trail.

■ Enforcement

Enforcement of the regulations is critical to trail safety, particularly when the trail first opens. At that time, many users of the trail are unfamiliar with the rules. Early enforcement establishes the proper operation of the trail.

Plan to set up a system for penalizing violators of the rules. It can include fines or special duties such as trail maintenance work or other trail support activities. Reserve the stiffest penalties for safety infractions, such as speeding, failure to obey stop signs, not yielding the right-of-way, or blocking the trail. In lieu of a citation, consider offering a monthly trail safety class for violators.

However, do not assume that all trail users instinctively know the rules of the trail—or the outcome if the rules

are not followed. To promote goodwill on the trail, consider issuing verbal warnings to first-time offenders who may be unfamiliar with the regulations. Take time to explain why the rules were created (for example, to avoid collisions) because users will be more apt to comply with them.

Promoting Trail User Etiquette

Many managers of successful multi-use trails have developed an ethic of trail-use etiquette as a way to encourage compliance with regulations and cooperation among users. One of your critical roles as a trail manager will be to promote courtesy on the trail. An etiquette ethic will not only create a more enjoyable trail experience but also will facilitate efficient and safe circulation on the trail.

Trail safety and etiquette are responsibilities shared by everyone. You should seek to develop an education campaign that instills an etiquette ethic in all trail users. There are several educational methods you can employ:

■ Signs

Trail safety signs are one of the simplest and most effective ways to promote trail etiquette because they convey important information quickly. Develop a uniform system of trail operating and advisory signs and post them at regular intervals along the trail. Present only one idea on each sign. Keep the message as simple as possible and portray it so both children and adults will understand it (figure 4.4). The signs should repeat basic trail safety and operating rules such as "Bicyclists Use Bell or Voice When Passing," "All Users Keep Right," and "Bicyclists Yield to Pedestrians."

■ Printed Materials

Brochures, pamphlets, and newsletters displayed along the trail route, at trailheads, and at ranger stations can help cultivate a positive user ethic. Trail regulations should be printed in all publications to reinforce the user ethic. Be sure to post a copy of the trail user regulations at each trailhead and major rest stop to inform all users of trail rules.

Trail maps can be a tool for encouraging etiquette in a different way. Maps should include alternate routes (on parallel roads) and should suggest that fast bicyclists may have "outgrown" the trail and will find riding

Photo: Northern Virginia Regional Park Authority

Figure 4.4: An innovative "Share the Trail" sign along the Washington and Old Dominion Railroad Regional Park.

on the streets faster and more satisfying. Maps can be posted at trail intersections, directing fast bicyclists to alternate routes. The focus should always be on speed, not on the type of bicyclist.

■ Safety Days

Trail safety days are an enjoyable way to promote safety and etiquette.

Have volunteers set up a trailside stand once a month during the trail's busiest season to provide free refreshments, safety literature, copies of the trail user regulations, brochures on helmet safety, and information concerning membership in area bicycle, equestrian, hiking, and walking organizations. During safety day, local law-enforcement officers can perform radar-gun checks to provide riders with their actual speeds and can help them with bicycle safety checks and maintenance assistance (figure 4.5). Generally, the program requires volunteers with safety and equipment experience, printed safety materials, and a modest service and refreshment budget.

■ Presentations

Recreation clubs, schools, civic groups, and religious and service organizations typically hold regular meetings and often seek interesting speakers. Consider making presentations to local clubs and schools as a way to reach out to potential trail users. The presentations allow you to introduce the trail to many people while educating them about trail use. You can foster the etiquette ethic even before trail users get on the trail.

Make presentations compelling by tailoring them to your audience. Particularly for children, use innovative instruction methods. For example, set up a mock trail on the school playground—complete with lines, obstructions, and signs—and then invite

Figure 4.5: A local sheriff instructs a young bicyclist in proper trail use during a "Trail Safety Day" on the Wood River Trails in Idaho.

Photo: Jonathan Stoke

students to help demonstrate safe riding and walking practices. Set up a few conflicts to illustrate why the regulations were established, and then discuss how the conflicts could have been avoided.

School-aged children make up a large percentage of potential trail users. If they are excited by your presentation, they will no doubt share the information with their families and friends.

■ Public Hearings

Hearings regarding trail policy changes or budget needs should be viewed as opportunities for a two-way exchange. Encourage individuals to voice concerns about user conflicts in a constructive way, and, as the manager, take the opportunity to explain conflict-prevention techniques and encourage etiquette.

■ Mass Media

Use the media to promote your etiquette ethic. Radio, television, cable, and newspaper features can provide an effective, legitimate means of disseminating information to large numbers of people. Every publicity opportunity or media story should include proper trail-use information, so show people riding and walking safely and courteously along the trail. Also, don't forget that many local recreation clubs and civic groups have newsletters and other publications that could serve as an outlet for trail information.

❖

MAINTAINING GOOD RELATIONS WITH ADJACENT LANDOWNERS

If you followed some of the techniques to involve adjacent landowners in the trail-planning process, you should not have much difficulty in maintaining good relations with them now (see "Meeting the Needs of Adjacent Landowners" in chapter 2). If you did not use these techniques or you still have considerable opposition, managing the trail properly and working with the landowners from now on will likely neutralize opposition and may even turn opponents into supporters.

Once a trail is open, many ardent opponents realize that their fears are unfounded and begin to recognize that the trail is a good neighbor, not to mention a nice amenity. In addition, some

Trails lead to profits for shops on the way

BRANDON, IA. — Health-conscious bikers choose the low-cal plate, with chicken breast, cole slaw and cottage cheese. Really hungry cyclists can't resist a brownie sundae, blueberry pie or a chocolate malt.

"Our food is good enough that when they get in here, they order something whether they had planned to or not," boasts Jan Bland, manager of the Homestyle Cafe in Brandon.

The cafe, located in the 74-year-old Farmers Savings Bank building just two blocks north of the Cedar Valley Nature Trail, is an oasis for trail users.

It's a mutually beneficial relationship. The trail brings at least one-third of the cafe's summer sales, says owner Kent Miller.

To accommodate the visitors, Miller has installed a bike rack, a picnic table and an outdoor water faucet. Bland added the low-cal special and a children's menu in response to **trail users'**

When Iowa moved to develop a recreation trail on a rail line between Cedar Rapids and Waterloo, residents along the route united in opposition. Six years later, the same folks are singing the praises of the trail and those who use it.

CONVERTING RAILS TO TRAILS

Program paves way to recreation

By Rachel Alexander
USA TODAY

About 150,000 miles of railroad track in the USA have been abandoned. David Burwell and Peter Harnik want to buy it all.

but also a message that rail-trails can be the solution to so many problems, from transportation to recreation to preservation," said Burwell, RTC executive director. "After all, how many people drive somewhere just to be able to walk or bike? This project puts the trails right in your backyard."

RTC has helped lay more than 5,000 miles of trail to date by working with local organizations and governments and serving as an exchange of information and ideas.

"We make it so that each group does not have to reinvent the wheel," Burwell said. "Before we formed, nine out of 10 projects were failing. Now 90 percent succeed, because we can give the local organizations solutions to their problems that other groups have used when dealing with the same thing."

Almost every state has at least one rail-trail. Pennsylvania, Iowa, Michigan, Wisconsin and California each has more than 30.

Police say crime on trail notable for its scarcity

By MICHAEL FAY
Tribune Staff Writer

LARGO — Since The Pinellas Trail's inception, law enforcement and county officials have taken crime along the linear park seriously.

Some police agencies use bicycle patrols to cover The Trail, and a security task force composed of police and county representatives meets quarterly to discuss crime problems.

Land owners now hail scenic courses

Rick and Diana Spence's farm in La Port City, Iowa, used to be pretty quiet. Now, 15,000 people travel through it every year.

The Spences live along the Cedar Valley Nature Trail, a limestone-paved trail that was converted from an abandoned railroad track. Now, they love having the trail run through their land and they use it often. But it wasn't always that way.

When they first heard about plans for the trail, the Spences, like many others who own land adjoining Rails

"But when it's all said and done, they become the biggest advocates of the trails. One guy in Iowa who had vehemently opposed a rail-trail later had such a change of heart that he opened up a bed and breakfast on his land for trail users."

Farmers worry about hikers and bikers stealing their livestock or vandalizing their crops, while others worry about excess noise and the prospect of strangers wandering onto their land. The Spences spearheaded a group of farmers that took

Most who live near trails give the projects favorable ratings, and a new National Park Service study of the rail-trails is very positive. It estimates that, in addition to the obvious entertainment and fitness benefits the trails give, those who live along the trails see marked economic benefits as well.

The Park Service Commission found that trail users spend an average of $8 a person a day. This results in a total economic impact of $1.2 million a trail, including an average

Figure 4.6: Favorable press clips.

---

adjacent landowners may gain unanticipated social and economic benefits from the trail and suddenly become avid supporters. The owner of a bed-and-breakfast along Missouri's Katy Trail State Park, who was nervous about the trail's opening, now supports it, particularly since her business has doubled since the trail's development. As shown in figure 4.6, newspapers have published numerous articles quoting converted landowners.

Landowners can be good allies, so it is critical to sustain and cultivate your relationships with them. They can become the "eyes and ears" of the trail and should be encouraged to play this role.

An important first step is to be sure that all adjacent owners know whom to contact about specific problems. Provide them with appropriate names and phone numbers at the trail's managing agency so they can more readily report a problem or make a suggestion.

Next, make sure the trail is maintained on a regular basis. The issues most likely to cause continuing concerns for adjacent residents are maintenance related—overgrown weeds, fallen and overhanging trees, and insufficient vegetative screening to buffer homes from the trail. Most of these problems can be solved through routine maintenance. If you do not already have a regular maintenance schedule in place, take steps to establish one (see "Trail Maintenance and Safety" earlier in this chapter). It should include a timetable for performing all aspects of trail maintenance, ranging from trash pickup to tree pruning. If possible, print the schedule and distribute it to trail neighbors.

There may be lingering problems such as unauthorized motorized vehicle use and vandalism, theft of trail-re-lated signs, or graffiti on the trail corridor. Respond to these problems promptly. Consistent, quality upkeep of the trail corridor will build trail neighbors' confidence in your agency's ability to manage the trail. You can also build landowners' confidence by scheduling periodic meetings with them to provide an outlet for any continuing concerns. Frequent communication is the cornerstone of successful relations with landowners. Make sure you listen to their comments, involve them in any new trail developments, respond to their needs, and maintain consistency in your discussions with them.

Establish a mechanism for regular input from users and landowners. For example, the Baltimore and Annapolis Trail in urban/suburban Anne Arundel County, Maryland, developed a "Good Neighbor Program" to encourage landowners to point out problems and make requests to the managing agency. The Anne Arundel County Department of Parks and Recreation staff makes periodic personal contact with each landowner. This visit is followed up with a mailing that includes general trail information (including the department's mailing address and phone

number) as well as a pamphlet explaining the department's commitment to excellence and desire to be a good neighbor. The county asks the landowners to reciprocate the good-neighbor policy.

The department's staff members, who are committed to listening to every comment, build landowners' confidence by responding promptly and fairly. Although the department cannot accommodate every request, it does its best to reach a mutually acceptable solution. One of the trail's rangers has said, "Through the use of this program, landowners who were initially against the trail's construction are now our most ardent fans."

Another approach is to invite the landowners on a trail tour led by a park ranger. This gives the adjacent residents a firsthand opportunity to point out any continuing problem areas, while providing your agency with a chance to showcase the wonderful facility landowners have in their own backyards. If they have not previously been on the trail, the tour may improve their view of it. They will be able to see the types of people who use the trail, and they will also view improvements that have been made along the corridor.

Still another way to win the support of landowners is to write personal letters, particularly to those residents not yet convinced of the trail's benefits. If you have received letters from local citizens supporting the trail, you might enclose a copy of one. Also, if time and money permit, send them invitations to any special events along the corridor, including trail extensions, dedications of trail support facilities, and trail festivals. These small gestures can go a long way toward maintaining good relations with adjacent landowners. The manager of the Cannon Valley Trail in southeastern Minnesota sends holiday greeting cards to residents living along his 19-mile trail.

In addition to dealing with the concerns of adjacent landowners and working to maintain good relations, you may encounter problems *caused by* adjacent residents. You will need to handle these in a consistent and efficient manner to prevent them from getting out of control.

The main problems you will likely face are encroachment and damage—for example, landowners dumping lawn clippings on trail property, ille-

gally using the corridor for private access, and making cuts in fences to gain trail access. The best way to overcome these problems is to set clear boundaries between the trail and private property and to make these borders known to all landowners. Take time to use some of the previously mentioned strategies (letter writing, personal visits) to encourage landowners to comply with rules and regulations of the trail. In addition, instruct patrols to watch problem areas and enforce the boundaries.

If you are unable to work out an agreement informally, you may opt to develop a lease arrangement for nontrail uses. In this arrangement the landowner is allowed continued encroachment, but he or she is charged a fee for this private use of the corridor. The lease should be a one-year, renewable agreement including a set fee. This fee would be used to cover maintenance costs or any minor damage caused by the landowner.

If this is not appropriate in your situation or if the problems persist, you may need to take a stronger stance to protect the trail. If issuing fines to violators does not alleviate the problem, you may need to consider legal action. Whatever the case, make it public knowledge—

through the media, if possible—that you will not condone any inappropriate activities and that you will take serious action against illegal activities.

DEVELOPING A FEE STRUCTURE

One management issue you should consider is whether to charge fees for the use of your multi-use trail. You need to weigh the revenue possibilities with the time and effort involved in administering fees. And don't forget that fees are potentially applicable not only to trail users, but also to nontrail uses within the corridor.

Trail Users: To Fee or Not to Fee?

Before you decide whether or not to charge a fee for use of the trail, you should consider the advantages and disadvantages of doing so. On the positive side, fees can generate income for trail maintenance or additional trail development. Also, by paying a fee, users may develop a stronger commitment or sense of stewardship to the trail. And, depending on how you set up your fee collection system, you may collect thousands of trail users' names, which could be used in a trail-activist mailing list or possibly a fundraising list.

On the other hand, it may cost more money to administer a fee program than it raises, and payment may be difficult to enforce, especially if the trail has many access points. In addition, if the trail was built with taxpayers' money, local residents may protest against paying for what they perceive is a public facility.

If your trail is part of a large managing agency, you may have little choice about fees. The Little Miami Scenic State Park Trail, for example, is part of the Ohio State Park system, and state law prohibits user fees in any Ohio state park. In contrast, several multi-use trails in Wisconsin are required by law to charge a user fee as part of that state's park system.

The following are some issues you need to work out when setting up a fee structure and developing a trail-use permit.

■ Sample Fee Structure

It is best to offer several fee options for trail users, such as $2 per day for an individual, $5 per day for a family, $8 per year for an individual, and $20 per year for a family. An annual-pass option allows local trail users to enjoy the trail as often as they like for a low cost and encourages visitors to return. (These prices are the average charged by several rail-trails.)

Some fee structures include a higher rate for out-of-state users. The trails in Wisconsin had such an arrangement for several years, but the state recently decided that all users would pay the same fees to make enforcement and administration easier.

In 1991, the state of Wisconsin, which manages about ten rail-trails, raised almost $150,000 through trail-pass sales. Administration costs to collect these fees are estimated at approximately $45,000, or 30 percent of the income.

If you do offer an annual trail pass, decide whether it is valid for one year from the date purchased or only for the calendar year. First-time trail users and visitors are more likely to buy an annual pass if they can use it for an entire year beginning on the purchase date.

■ Whom to Charge?

Different trail managers have made different decisions about who should pay a fee. On some trails, all users pay. On others, only bicyclists pay. And in some cases all users except pedestrians (hikers, walkers, joggers, and people in wheelchairs) pay to use the trail. In many cases, winter users such as snowmobilers are not charged a trail-use fee because they are required to pay a registration fee that entitles them to free access to trails. Some managers base their decisions on who has the greatest impact on the trail. In Wisconsin, one trail manager says only bicyclists pay because they require a more developed (and costly) trail surface than hikers or walkers do.

Managers of Iowa's Heritage Trail provided free trail passes to adjacent landowners for the first two years to build good relations with them.

■ Selling Trail Permits

If you do opt for a fee structure, you need to develop a system whereby trail users can prove they paid to use the trail. The best option is to develop a "permit," a pass sold at various locations that represents payment of the fee. Make it as easy as possible for trail users to pay for user permits. They should be available for purchase at trailheads, such as the self-service station depicted in figure 4.7, and at managing agency offices.

Encourage local businesses (including restaurants, bicycle stores, chambers of commerce, visitors' centers, and grocery stores) to sell trail passes. Most merchants are happy to offer this service because it brings in customers. In addition, trail rangers and people patrolling the trail should carry passes with them and offer them for sale to anyone who failed to buy one. Also, you can make trail passes available through the mail. The state of Wisconsin set up a telephone and mail-order system so people can buy them in advance of their visit to a trail—and use a credit card to pay.

■ Making Trail Users Aware of the Fee

Trail users (particularly first-time visitors) will not necessarily know that they need to obtain a trail user permit, so you need to inform them that a fee is required. You should post signs or notices at every trail access point. Post the daily fee as well as any annual fee, and include a list of locations where users can purchase permits. Also, setting up self-service registration stations at trail access points forces people to take

Photo: Bruce Blair

Figure 4.7: A simple yet effective self-purchase permit station along Minnesota's Cannon Valley Trail.

notice. Fees should be listed in any trail-related literature.

To broaden awareness, undertake additional promotion. Have local stores, restaurants, and chambers of commerce post signs like "Get Your Trail Pass Here!" The signs will remind people that they need a permit before they get onto the trail.

■ Enforcement

If you really want your fee structure to succeed, you will have to enforce it, although there is no need to be heavy handed, particularly with first-time violators. Most users who do not purchase a trail pass probably do not know one is necessary. Anyone who patrols the trail (or maintains it) can periodically ask to see trail user permits and can sell permits to those who lack one. If someone repeatedly uses the trail without a pass, you may need to issue a citation.

Fees for Nontrail Users

In the course of developing and managing your multi-use trail, you will likely encounter agencies, companies, and individuals who are interested in your trail for nontrail purposes—for example, as a right-of-way for utility lines, fiber-optic cables, sewer pipelines, or cable television wires. Many of these uses may be compatible with trail use; however, you should set up a fee system whereby nontrail users compensate your agency in exchange for use of and access to the right-of-way (see "Joint Ventures within Your Multi-Use Trail Corridor" in chapter 2). Ideally, you should receive fees based on the fair market value of the property as well as any expenses you incur (including staff time) in setting up the arrangement with the nontrail user.

The Ojai Valley Trail in southern California charges fees according to the total square footage required for a nontrail use multiplied by the fair market value of the property. The local park agency administers the fee program and assesses fees on a yearly basis.

The Northern Virginia Regional Park Authority has developed an extensive fee system based on the impact that the nontrail use will have on park property, park use, park patrons, and land values. Fees are typically set up as annual rentals. The authority also reserves the right to charge for "damages" caused by the nontrail user, including physical or aesthetic damage, permanent inconvenience to trail users, and new legal or operating liabilities that are imposed on the park authority.[6]

It is critical to develop some type of standard fee structure to safeguard your trail. While nontrail uses can be compatible and potentially profitable, you need to ensure that they do not interfere with the trail's primary functions of transportation and recreation.

❖

TRAIL PROTECTION

If your trail is located in an area of rapid growth, public support for the trail facility may be overshadowed by pressure to accommodate development. Sewer systems, roads, mass transit lines, electric power lines, and other components of a community's infrastructure require rights-of-way to serve newly developed areas. Any or all of these systems may compete with your trail. Unless their development is carefully managed, they may ultimately destroy the trail's character or displace it completely.

Uses within the Trail Corridor

The entire right-of-way in which your trail lies may be only 100 feet wide or less, making it vulnerable to the negative impacts of surrounding development. A single highway crossing can sever a trail's continuity; a mass transit line can displace a trail altogether. Even smaller encroachments, such as adjacent buildings overlapping a corridor's boundary or private driveways bisecting the trail, can add up to an overall degradation of the trail experience. Inappropriate uses of your corridor can create safety hazards, increase maintenance needs, decrease aesthetic appeal, diminish land values, add legal liabilities, and limit future management options.

You cannot stop development, but you can prevent it from damaging your corridor by establishing a strong trail protection policy. The policy must set forth the "paramount," or primary, use of the corridor—recreation, transportation, or historic preservation. Any use of the trail corridor deemed incompatible with its paramount use will be denied; those that are compatible with the primary use will be considered and, if approved, carefully regulated.

Fiber-optic cables, sewer pipes, and water lines, for example, are well suited for placement along a recreational or commuter trail because they are underground and do not impede activities along it. But constructing a four-lane highway across a trail with no grade separation would bisect a trail, destroying its linear continuity. This would not be a compatible use if the trail's primary function is transportation.

You should take steps as soon as possible to set up a truly comprehensive trail protection policy that will provide you with the authority to do the following:

▶ Regulate all nonparamount uses of the trail corridor in a fair and consistent manner.

▶ Minimize inconvenience to trail patrons, and assure protection of wildlife habitat and natural and historic resources within the trail corridor.

▶ Minimize damage to the trail corridor at all times.

▶ Establish uniform standards for construction and restoration of the trail corridor if it is damaged by a nonparamount use.

▶ Ensure that your agency recovers all its administrative costs and receives appropriate compensation for use of, or damage to, the trail corridor by nonparamount uses.

▶ Inform all public and private interests of the expectations and intentions of the trail managing agency with respect to nonparamount uses.

▶ Issue permits and licenses for nonparamount uses; prohibit the transfer of ownership rights through the use of easements or other mechanisms.

If your agency is authorized to collect fees, your trail protection policy should stipulate that financial compensation is required for all approved, nonparamount uses of the corridor. Your policy should also require that all entities using the trail corridor for non-designated purposes pay for damages and, if appropriate, improvements to trail facilities.

If you include each of the points listed above, you will have crafted a trail protection policy that is strong enough to deny harmful nonprimary uses but flexible enough to allow compatible—or even beneficial—uses. For example, you might oppose a transportation department's proposal to build a road within the corridor if you have determined that it would have a damaging effect on your trail's uses. However, you might approve the telephone company's proposal to pay your agency an annual fee for the right to bury and maintain a fiber-optics cable under the trail. While a fiber-optics cable does not necessarily enhance a multi-use trail, it may benefit it by providing a steady source of funding for trail-related costs.

If your agency does not hold full title to your trail corridor, your trail protection options may be more limited. If, for instance, your agency has a recreational easement over adjacent, privately owned land, you may not have the legal right to control other uses of that land even if it extends into the corridor.

In any event, you should communicate with all parties who have an interest in the trail corridor. You should know who holds limited title to the corridor, including individuals, local planning commission members, the department of transportation, area developers, elected officials, and recreational and environmental groups. By developing a relationship with each of these parties you will be in a better position to discover and defuse proposed actions that may negatively impact the integrity of your trail corridor.

Regardless of the status of your agency's ownership in the corridor, a supportive citizen-based "Friends of the Trail" group may ultimately be your trail corridor's best protection. Even with a strong trail protection policy in place, your agency is probably susceptible to the political pressures that developers and commercial interests can put on elected officials. Widespread, organized citizen opposition to proposals that would negatively impact the trail is the most effective way to protect it (see "Friends of the Trail Groups'" in chapter 5).

Land Uses Adjacent to the Trail Corridor

Regulation of uses outside the corridor that adversely affect the trail's integrity is important but difficult to achieve. Problems include runoff from construction activities, deterioration of scenic vistas and viewsheds because of encroaching development, noise from development and traffic, and deterioration of wildlife habitat stemming from the loss of adjoining natural areas and open space. Some of these problems can be addressed through local planning processes and permit-approval procedures for residential and commercial development. By monitoring proposals for development adjacent to the trail corridor you may be able to

work effectively with developers or with other government officials. You can also make requests for license and permit conditions that will ameliorate many of the harmful effects of a proposed development on the trail corridor.

Protection of scenic vistas and viewsheds and adjoining open space and wildlife habitat poses special and often complex problems. Two approaches are possible: Seek to protect an entire viewshed or whatever can be seen from a particular vantage point; or protect discrete ecological units, such as the area between your trail corridor and a river or a wetland adjacent to the trail corridor.

You may be able to gain some viewshed protection through federally financed or approved projects under statutes like section 102 of the National Environmental Protection Act and section 106 of the National Historic Preservation Act. However, most protection of vistas and adjoining open space, especially when related to private development, is a matter of state and local law. Thus, whatever your goal—preserving scenic vistas, maintaining a buffer zone, or safeguarding an ecological unit—you need to work within applicable laws.

Two basic legal mechanisms are available. One is zoning and land-use regulation to preserve open space. The other consists of programs to acquire or encourage the donation of development easements that restrict adjoining property to such uses as farmland, woodland, and low-density residential areas (see "Acquiring More Land" in chapter 5).

Protect Your Trail in the Face of Change

Changes in land-use patterns along your trail corridor are probably inevitable. Some, such as the creation of new parks or adjoining trails, may enhance the trail experience. Others, such as construction of new highway crossings or adjacent industrial sites, may significantly degrade it. Regardless of the type of change, if you are armed with a protection strategy and a base of public support for the trail, you will be better equipped to anticipate and manage change in a way that protects your trail's special qualities for present and future generations.

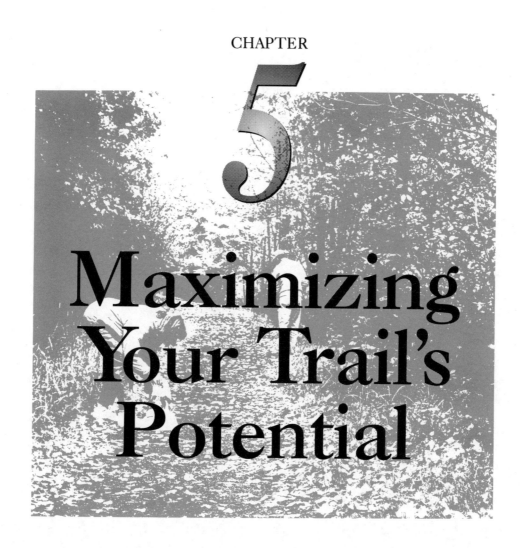

CHAPTER

5

Maximizing Your Trail's Potential

PROMOTING AND MARKETING YOUR TRAIL

With so much time devoted to planning, designing, and managing your trail, you probably have not thought about how to promote and market it. But promotion and marketing are key ingredients of a successful multi-use trail. Developing an effective promotion campaign will take time and thought, but you may be surprised to learn how much you enjoy spreading the word about your trail.

Why Publicity Is Important

Multi-use trail planners and managers commonly decry their lack of money. Yet often the real problem is lack of public support, which usually stems from the public's lack of knowledge about the trail or trail project. Therefore, public awareness, which can be increased through the media, is critical.

Your initial task is to determine how much publicity you want, because it is possible to get too much. For example, a national magazine article highlighting your trail could bring more trail users than you can handle. If your trail is in a rural area that shuns outsiders, you may want to curb your exposure. On the other hand, if you want to attract tourists to your area, widespread press may be a big benefit.

To determine the amount and type of exposure your trail needs, decide what audience you want to reach. People living in towns near the trail? Regional residents? Potential users throughout the state or nation? If your trail is still in its infancy, your audience will be pretty close to home. Consider the following reasons that it is important to publicize your trail:

▶ **Your trail is not completed and needs increased support to get funding and visibility**. Often, when a trail project gets under way, the public assumes that it will be completed. Be sure people are aware that the trail is a "work in progress." Use the press to provide periodic updates that will keep the public excited about day-to-day or month-to-month operations of the project.

▶ **Your trail is complete and you want to celebrate its opening**. All the hard work finally pays off when a trail is complete, and you should call attention to this milestone. Be sure that all the communities along the trail (including any remaining opponents) are aware of any festivities, so that they assume a sense of trail "ownership" from the outset.

▶ **Your trail is open but not well known or used and you want to increase its level of activity.** If your trail does not get much use, it is probably because few people know about it. You have to tell the public about the opportunities your trail offers. A trail also may not be used because it is in an out-of-the-way location or because it passes through unattractive terrain. In these cases, request ideas for improvement from the public while pointing out the trail's positive aspects.

▶ **Your trail is open but "misused."** Misuse can range from litter to graffiti and from speeding bicyclists to unauthorized vehicles on the trail. Publicizing "proper" trail use can go a long way toward preventing these problems. People respond better to explanations than to scolding: Litter detracts from the trail and can damage the environment; speeding cyclists can frighten senior citizens or injure an unsuspecting child; certain vehicles are prohibited because they pose a safety problem and may cause costly damage to the trail. The public needs to be told how they can be better stewards of their trail. When informed, they respond.

▶ **You want to attract tourists to your area.** Tourists can add dollars to the local economy, particularly if your multi-use trail has features that will attract them. But tourists will not know what your trail has to offer unless you inform them. Attracting visitors typically requires a broad level of promotion.

Of course, if your trail is too crowded or not ready for visitors, do not publicize it. Too much publicity may damage the character of your trail, particularly if you cannot accommodate more users. Too many people on a trail can cause accidents and make the trail experience unpleasant.

How to Get Publicity

If you are lucky, someone in the media will hear about your trail and de-

Figure 5.1: Volunteers picking up trash during a trail workday.

cide to do a story about it. More often you will need to contact a reporter and encourage him or her to do a story. Try to offer reporters a variety of ways in which to write about the trail.

One of the best ways to get media coverage, while also raising trail awareness, is to hold an event. It should be all-inclusive, giving as many people as possible the opportunity to participate.

Events Before Your Trail Is Complete

Some events work best prior to the trail's completion. Here are a few ideas:

■ Trail Corridor Tours

Host walking or bicycling tours of the trail corridor for donors, press, or politicians, or if necessary, drive them along your trail route. A firsthand view can go a long way toward making a nonbeliever into a convert. Also, consider a tour to another established multi-use trail nearby.

■ "Name the Trail" Contest

If the trail does not have a name (or if you want to improve the current name), hold a contest with a trail-related prize for the winner and make an event out of announcing the name.

■ Trail Work Day

Encourage volunteers to spend a day cleaning or grooming the trail (figure 5.1) or helping build trail facilities along the route. People enjoy working with others to help "get the trail on the ground." Arrange shifts if volunteers cannot put in a full day, and include chores for people of all ages and abilities.

■ Photo Competition

To document the "before" and "after" scenarios of your trail corridor, stage a photo competition. Some older residents may even have pictures depicting former uses of the corridor. Offer prizes for various photo categories and display the winning photos in a public place.

■ Poster Contest

Get children interested in the trail by staging a children's poster contest. Children can be awarded prizes for their trail drawings, and the best one could be developed into a poster for distribution to local businesses. If you want more sophisticated art, sponsor an adults' contest for the best logo or natural rendering of the trail.

Events on Opening Day

Other events are ideal for the day the trail opens:

■ "Thank You for Giving" Event

As you celebrate the trail's opening, throw a party to thank the donors who made the project possible. Ask local restaurants or grocery stores to donate food for the event. Hold the party in an interesting spot along the route, perhaps at a former train station or an old canal lock.

■ Trail-athalon

Host a race that spans the length of the trail and involves several trail user groups. A horseback rider passes a baton to a jogger who passes it to someone in a wheelchair who passes it to a bicyclist. The winning composite team can be photographed for the local newspaper.

■ Decorated Bicycle Parade

Have children and adults decorate their bicycles for the opening celebration, perhaps following the color scheme of the trail's logo; offer prizes. The participants should demonstrate proper bicycle safety, such as wearing helmets and following trail rules.

■ Float Competition

Encourage people to decorate floats for a trail parade. Give out prizes for the most creative floats.

Events When the Trail Is Extended

Your trail may open in phases, or it may be extended beyond its original length. Whenever you open a new section, take time to publicize it with an interesting event:

■ Walk-a-Thon

Participants can walk the length of the existing trail and use other means where the extension is not yet passable on foot. For instance, horses can transport people through shallow water in the absence of a bridge. Thus, obstacles can be made into photo opportunities for the media.

■ Nature Walk

Schedule a hike with a naturalist on the proposed extension to identify fauna and flora. This could launch an interpretive sign program for the entire trail.

■ "Burma Shave" Signs

You may remember the "Burma Shave" highway signs that used to be placed in series along highways. Each one contained a line from a rhyme, and the last one read "Burma Shave." Develop your own set of trail rhymes and post them along the trail extension to promote it. The last sign could read "Support the Trail."

Ongoing Events

There are various ways to gain publicity for your trail throughout the year:

■ Special-Features Tour

Organize a trail tour that highlights interesting sights along the route, including historic houses, old railroad stations, gardens, and barns. This is similar to a house tour except that the "rooms" are adjacent to the trail.

■ Contests

You can hold a competition to find the "best" of just about anything relating to your trail. You can have writing, art, or photo contests; bicycle or foot races; and even children's tricycle contests. Anything that brings more people to the trail and draws attention to it can be effective.

■ Newspaper Column

Initiate and write a regular column in the local newspaper featuring interesting tidbits about the multi-use trail.

■ Awards

Gain national recognition by going after awards such as "Take Pride in America," "A Thousand Points of Light," "Keep America Beautiful," and "Enjoy America's Outdoors." All of these awards can generate significant trail pride and publicity (figure 5.2).

■ Holidays

Use holidays as the catalyst for decorating the trail and planning events. Encourage children to place ghosts and scarecrows along the trail around Halloween or host an "egg hunt" around Easter.

Working with the Media

Once you know the level and type of publicity you want for your trail and the kind of events you want to hold, the next step is to work with the media. You will need to learn the nuts and bolts of getting the newspaper, television, and radio coverage that you want.

■ Newspapers

One of the best (and simplest) ways to get a story into a newspaper is to is-

Photo: Northern Virginia Regional Park Authority

Figure 5.2: Officials and volunteers of the Washington and Old Dominion Railroad Regional Park cut a ribbon after receiving an "Enjoy America's Outdoors" award.

sue a "news release." The form of a news release is fairly universal—one or two double-spaced, typed pages of text with a contact person and phone number listed in the upper-left corner. The release should be neat and grammatically correct and should be sent early but not too early. Ideally, it should be addressed to a specific reporter with an interest in the trail.

You catch the reporter's attention by putting *news* in the first paragraph of the news release. Most reporters are looking for something new, current, and interesting to the public. If you do not have any specific "news," create something. Hold an event, stage a race, urge the county council to pass a bill, invite landowners to donate parcels of land. In other words, give the reporter some news to cover. And be sure to phone the reporter to ensure that your release was received and to offer any additional information he or she may need. A follow-up call from you will increase the chances that a reporter will pay attention to and act on your release.

Generally, it is much easier to get coverage in small, local newspapers than large metropolitan ones, but send your news releases to all press in the

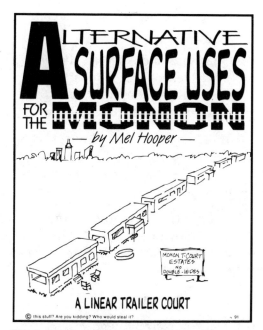

Figure 5.3: An Indiana cartoonist uses humor to gain publicity for converting the abandoned Monon Line into a trail.

area. Often when a story appears consistently in local papers, the larger ones realize it is newsworthy and may opt to write their own articles.

To expand your chances of coverage and readership, reach out to different sections of the newspaper. In addition to the main news section, send press releases to the editorial board, sports section, society page, and features editor. As your trail improves, seek coverage

in national magazines and newspapers, particularly travel sections. This coverage can increase local use and promote tourism.

Multi-use trails lend themselves to photographs. Pictures of beautiful landscapes, smiling children, and an interesting mix of users can quickly catch a reporter's eye. You could prepare a news release based on a unique photo. This also works well if you are planning to take local dignitaries on a trail tour. And, if the media do not cover your event, send them a photograph after the fact.

Photos are not the only graphics that can bring publicity to your trail. A cartoon could highlight some interesting or humorous aspect of the trail (Figure 5.3). You might invite local sporting goods stores to take their advertising photos on the trail.

■ Television and Radio

Sending news releases and photographs to television and radio stations may encourage them to cover a trail-related story. As with newspapers, you need news to attract the cameras and tape recorders.

Television and radio also offer opportunities for public-service announcements (PSAs). These usually can be made on low budgets with volunteer professionals. Most PSAs consist of thirty seconds of prerecorded commentary. Some radio stations have their disc jockeys read short PSAs on the air.

Before you invest time and money in preparing a PSA, consider your market and what you want to say. Are you trying to raise money? Do you want to publicize an event for young people? Are you looking for volunteers? What impact do you want to make with a PSA?

News Release (or PSA) Topics

Consider these creative ideas for generating media coverage for your trail:

▶ **Trail Statistics** Offer data about your project: How many users are there? How long is the trail? What population base does it serve? How many community resources does it connect?

▶ **Success Stories in Other Communities** Profile a trail with characteristics similar to yours. Include quotes from converted opponents to show that similar projects have had positive results in other communities.

▶ **Questions and Answers** Prepare a fact sheet of the ten most commonly asked questions about the trail, and provide the answers.

▶ **Trail Survey** Have volunteers conduct a survey of trail users and neighbors, and provide the results to the media.

▶ **Interview a Favorable Politician or Landowner** Include interesting quotes and favorite trail anecdotes.

"Sound Bites"

When you work with reporters, they will take notes as you talk. Prior to talking with a reporter, know the points you want to get across. You might also think of some short, interesting quotes. The media are often searching for "sound bites," catchy one-liners that convey a lot of meaning in just a few words. These are different from a motto or a mission statement that guides your agency or trail organization. An example of a sound bite is "Invest in land, they ain't making any more of it." Will Rogers said this to convey the idea that land should be

conserved because it is not in unlimited supply. Perhaps you can adapt a memorable line for your project. The line, "If we build it, they will come" from the movie *Field of Dreams* has been used by several managers in promoting their multi-use trails. If you can invent your own "sound bite," you may grab the attention of a reporter and the interest of many potential trail users.

Trail Marketing Tools

Another way to spread the word about your trail is through a series of trail marketing tools that can be distributed at various locations near the trail.

■ Posters

These should be developed and posted in the area to herald a special event, call attention to a meeting, or just to focus on the special community value of the trail. Hang posters on bulletin boards at grocery stores and restaurants; at dry cleaners' counters; in waiting rooms at gas stations, in drugstore windows, school lobbies, office lunchrooms, and town halls.

■ Bumper Stickers

Bumper stickers may be small, but they can convey key information. They are especially useful in generating support when a trail-related issue will be on the ballot. If there is an upcoming vote to fund a trail extension, your bumper sticker could say, "Vote *Yes* for the Trail." Ask local businesses to sell the stickers and to post them in prominent locations.

■ Fact Sheet

You may want to develop a single page outlining basic facts about your trail: its length, its endpoints, interesting community resources along the route, the number of users each year, and other information. The fact sheet should be posted at trailheads and in local businesses to encourage people to experience the trail.

■ School Flyers

Ask a local school to distribute an informational flyer about the trail. Children can take flyers home to parents after school. If you have had a drawing contest for children, perhaps you can use some of their art in your flyer.

■ Sunday Supplements

Many local newspapers allow supplements to be inserted into their papers. You could prepare a simple, single sheet with a headline, some news about the trail, and perhaps a photo.

■ Brochures and Newsletters

Every trail should have a general information brochure as a basic marketing tool. Many trails publish a periodic newsletter to keep trail users and neighbors up-to-date on trail news (see "Publications," following).

❖

PUBLICATIONS

Printed materials are essential in promoting and marketing a multi-use trail. In addition to spreading the word about your trail, publications provide trail users with important information, direct them to sites of interest along the corridor (and in neighboring communities), highlight the area's history, and foster an appreciation of nature.

General Information Brochure

An attractive trail information brochure is a must. It should include the trail's length, permitted uses, rules and regulations, the fee schedule (if any), a trail map, a brief description and history of the trail, and the managing agency's address and telephone number. You could also include photographs or drawings showing nearby points of interest. Figure 5.4 depicts several attractive brochures.

Make copies of the brochure available at the trail's office and post them on kiosks at all trail access points. Brochures should also be placed at local chambers of commerce and visitor centers and at nearby motels, restaurants, and other commercial establishments. They can also be distributed to local recreation clubs and civic groups and to your state or regional division of tourism. Be sure to print plenty of copies because the brochure will be a popular item.

Trail Map

You may decide to produce a separate, detailed map of the trail showing the facility's relation to surrounding streets and communities, especially if your trail is long, is used by bicycle commuters, or has many access points that cannot be depicted accurately in a brochure. The map should show the trail in relation to the existing road system and should highlight points of interest along the corridor. Make it a

Figure 5.4: Examples of trail brochures.

"foldable" publication that fits easily into a pocket, fannypack, or pannier.

Visitor's Guide

Another popular piece of literature for trail users is a brochure detailing attractions, restaurants, accommodations, and trail-related facilities located near the trail. This brochure, which is particularly helpful if you are trying to promote tourism along the corridor, can provide information on everything from motels, bed-and-breakfasts, and campgrounds to bike shops, museums, and historic sites. Several of Wisconsin's state-managed trails include a tourist guide as an insert within their general information brochures.

One effective guide is the 32-page, 5-by-9-inch color booklet describing the Northern Central Rail-Trail in Maryland. The guide combines general trail information with detailed maps that include historical information, points of interest, restrooms, stores and boating access. Copies of the guide are sold at the area's commercial outlets and through the managing agency, with profits going toward trail maintenance.

Newsletter

You may also want to publish a newsletter to inform trail users of any changes and improvements along the trail. Copies can be posted at kiosks at trail access points and along the corridor; additional copies may be made available at trail visitor centers. The Washington and Old Dominion Railroad Regional Park produces a simple quarterly newsletter highlighting trail etiquette, safety, and trail events. Each newsletter includes telephone numbers and an address where trail users can ask questions, make suggestions, and report any problems.

Nature Guides

A nature guide describing and illustrating plants, trees, birds, and mammals located within the corridor will interest many trail users. Minnesota's Heartland Trail publishes an excellent illustrated nature guide (figure 5.5) that includes harmful plants to avoid (poison ivy, stinging nettle), wildflowers listed by color, nonflowering plants (mosses, mushrooms), common trees, and birds and mammals. The Military Ridge State Trail in Wisconsin and the Illinois Prairie Path offer nature guides, both of which weave in the history associated with the trail route.

Local History Guide

Some multi-use trails are steeped in history because of former uses within the corridor. Boston's Minuteman Trail parallels the route of Paul Revere's famous ride during the Revolutionary Era. And a rail corridor in York County, Pennsylvania (soon to be converted to a trail), transported President Lincoln to Gettysburg, where he delivered his famous address. A local history guide is a good place to feature the interesting history and lore of your trail.

The Illinois Prairie Path's support organization developed a publication to celebrate the 150th anniversary of one of the counties through which the trail

ALONG THE TRAIL

a guide to nature on the Heartland trail

Minnesota Department of Natural Resources

Figure 5.5: Cover of the Heartland Trail's guide.

runs. Called "History Treasure Hunt," it points out historical features beginning 150 *centuries* ago, including information on 11,000-year-old elephant bones (on display at a college three blocks from the trail), Native American burial mounds dating from 300 B.C., and an 18th-century trading post.

Regardless of which publications you decide to develop, make sure all trail-related literature includes the name of the managing agency with its address and telephone number. Each publication should be attractive, concise, and an appropriate size for its use; dull brochures or oversized trail guides will not be effective. Be sure to consider the many types of users your trail will attract—children, senior citizens, the disabled, and foreign visitors.

❖

"FRIENDS OF THE TRAIL" GROUPS

The formation of a private, nonprofit "Friends of the Trail" organization can be critical to the long-term success of your trail. No matter how competent and savvy the governmental agency that manages the trail, there will always be times when a group of active volunteers can provide the kind of assistance—whether through muscle power or political power—that will noticeably improve your trail. The single most important function of a Friends organization is to act as an advocate for the trail, defending it when

181

necessary and promoting it the rest of the time.

Ideally, whenever there is a public hearing on anything remotely related to the trail facility—a nearby road project, your state's policy on parks, local open space preservation, bicycle policies, or air pollution reduction—a Friends of the Trail representative should testify and speak on behalf of the trail. If this is not possible, members of the Friends group should at least attend any meeting or hearing dealing with funding for the trail. Funding decisions often depend on to public pressure, and money is generally allocated to projects with high public visibility.

Friends groups provide many other services to trails around the country. For example:

▶ Physical labor performed through an "Adopt a Trail" program—litter cleanup, sweeping, brush cutting, painting, minor bridge repair, and even construction of support facilities such as benches, picnic tables, and kiosks

▶ "Eyes and ears" surveillance and reporting of any problems, dan-

gers, or inappropriate activities taking place on or near the trail

▶ Fundraising to pay for trail structures (like bridges), amenities (such as trailside rest areas), or threatened adjacent properties of environmental significance that are not included in the regular budget for the trail

▶ Developing maps, newsletters, and other publications to educate users and improve the quality of their experience on the trail

▶ Promoting the trail as a tourist destination throughout the state and region

The trail managing agency should be careful to maintain legal separation from a Friends group. The trail manager, for instance, should not be an officer or a board member of the Friends. However, there is no reason that the two entities cannot communicate closely and freely. In fact, they should coordinate activities and programs to avoid making duplicate efforts or pursuing divergent goals.

Often a Friends group grows out of the original citizen organization that promoted the creation of the trail. Mak-

ing this transition often requires the gradual replacement of the trail's original advocates and activists by a broad-based leadership composed of people from mainstream tourism, corporate, financial, and service agency communities. Sometimes changing the group's mission from "creating" the trail to "supporting" it can be painful for the original members, so it should be handled gradually and diplomatically.

If an effective citizen organization never formed during the trail creation period, a Friends group should be defined and set up from scratch. In this case, active members should be drawn from trail users and adjacent landowners. It is important to specify clearly the purpose and mission of the group.

❖

ACQUIRING MORE LAND

In most trail systems, acquisition of additional right-of-way continues long after trail development is complete. In some cases the right-of-way can be expanded to include an adjacent "buffer zone," nearby wetlands or other sensitive lands, undeveloped wooded areas, and open space that offers important viewsheds. And opportunities to extend the trail often occur. Many trails are actually built in segments, as additional rights-of-way become available. If the local or state agency managing the trail adopts a comprehensive trail plan, there will probably be a need to connect existing trails to complete the plan.

Citizen Support

Once a trail is open, the community begins to develop a tremendous sense of "ownership" toward the trail. Individuals develop strong personal attachments to a trail as it becomes part of their daily or weekly routines. Consequently, citizens frequently will be the first to recognize opportunities to expand the trail corridor and possible threats to the existing corridor.

As previously discussed, a Friends of the Trail group can be vital to a trail's future expansion. The Friends of the M-K-T Parkway in Columbia, Missouri, formed specifically to protect their rail-trail corridor and to expand its boundaries, making the trail a true linear park.

It is critical that you work with citizens who feel some "ownership" of the trail if it is to be expanded. They have the interest and energy to work with elected officials and other decision makers. Help citizens focus their energy on specific tasks related to acquiring more property. And provide them with information that allows them to act in a timely way.

Citizens can be very helpful with environmental impact studies and environmental assessments, for example. By keeping a mailing list of interested and supportive citizens, you can alert them to comment-period deadlines and provide summaries of relevant trail issues. Another effective way to involve interested citizens is to have them help identify and prioritize property that should be acquired. With their help you can develop a strategy to secure funding.

Do not underestimate the ability of local citizens' groups! The Friends of the M-K-T Parkway worked successfully to pass a $1.3 million local bond issue to purchase parcels of land along the parkway. No agency would have had the leverage to accomplish such a goal without citizen support.

Zoning

Zoning can effectively protect trail corridors from development adjacent to the trail that might block views, destroy sensitive habitat, create traffic problems, and generally diminish a trail experience. Zoning is different in every community. Explore such zoning categories as shoreline, floodplains, park, open space and residential. Keep in mind, however, that "down zoning" (changing zoning from high- density to low-density use) can be a political hot potato and should not be pursued without neighborhood and property owner support. Zoning must reflect an area's character and should not be done arbitrarily. For example, a trail through an industrially zoned area should not be zoned as parkland if it limits the ability of adjacent property owners to conduct their business.

Funding

Most trail projects require money for additional right-of-way acquisition. The three ingredients to successful fundraising are a sound idea, popular support, and aggressive pursuit of every opportunity. Fundraising is an ongoing process in which support for trails and open space is nurtured over the long term.

■ Donations

Before paying cash for additional property, always ask for donations. Experience has shown that a significant number of adjacent property owners (up to 30 percent) are willing to transfer property interests to their portions of former railroad rights-of-way for the development of trails and preservation of open space. The agency managing the ongoing development of a multi-use trail should set up a property donation function to deal with property owners who are interested in making donations. This strategy should be implemented once there is broad-based public support for the trail. People want to be part of a successful, high-profile project. And a donation option represents an important opportunity for citizens to be involved in the trail and their community.

■ Federal-Aid Highway Funds

The Intermodal Surface Transportation Efficiency Act of 1991 (ISTEA) has several programs that will fund multi-use trails. The Surface Transportation Program calls for more than $3.3 bil-

lion to be spent over the six-year life of the law for ten specific "transportation enhancements." These nonhighway activities include the development of rail-trails greenways and other bicycle and pedestrian facilities. The funds,

Photo: Henri Bartholomot

Figure 5.6: A spokesperson for Montgomery County, Maryland, accepts a large check from the Maryland Department of Transportation to develop the Capital Crescent Trail.

which may be used for acquisition as well as development, are channeled through every state's department of transportation, with the apportionment of funds based on a state's population and size.

Another program under ISTEA is the Congestion Mitigation and Air Quality Improvement fund (CMAQ), which makes money available for transportation projects that will contribute to improved air quality. The Scenic Byways Program calls for the construction of pedestrian and bicycle facilities along scenic highways. Another program, the Federal Lands Highway Program, makes funds available only at the request of a federal agency for projects located on or providing access to federal lands. These funds can be used to acquire scenic easements and scenic or historic sites and to develop bicycle and pedestrian facilities.

Federal-aid highway funds cover 80 percent of a project; the remaining 20 percent comes from the state. Federal land projects are completely financed by federal funds. Projects must be principally for transportation rather than recreational purposes. The facilities must be included in an overall plan developed by a metropolitan planning organization or the state.

Maryland State Department of Transportation was one of the first agencies to disperse its ISTEA funds in 1992. The Capital Crescent Trail project received more than $850,000 for trail development (figure 5.6).

■ National Recreational Trails Trust Fund

This new federal program provides funds for nonmotorized and motorized recreational trails. Administered by the U.S. Department of Transportation, the program makes trail grants to private individuals, organizations, and government entities, with funding divided between nonmotorized and motorized interests. Congress can approve up to $30 million annually for the fund, to be distributed among the fifty states. In the 1993 fiscal year, Congress appropriated only $7.5 million.

■ Open Space Special-Benefit Assessments

Many states are offering tax breaks to property owners who preserve open space. Under Washington state law, for example, property owners may reduce their property taxes by as much as 50 percent by agreeing to preserve their lands as open space for ten-year periods. This approach can be used to conserve open space and agricultural and timberland areas that may adjoin trail corridors.

■ Railroad Franchise Agreements

Wherever a railroad line crosses through a street or cuts across a street, there will usually be a franchise agreement giving the railroad the right to use the property. A franchise agreement is much like a street-use permit, in that it allows a private use in a publicly owned space. Most franchise agreements require railroads to remove tracks and restore the improved portions of the street when the tracks are no longer needed for rail purposes. Since this can be relatively expensive, especially in urban areas where long sections of track may be in street right-of-way, the railroad may be willing to exchange right-of-way property for cancellation of its obligations to restore the street. The agency then takes on the responsibility for removing the track and restoring the street when it constructs the trail. While it is not free of cost, this strategy—which has been successfully implemented by the City of Seattle—allows for quick acquisition of right-of-way with no immediate outlay of cash. This can be particularly useful when land must be purchased in a short period of time.

■ Impact Mitigation Funds

County and city subdivision policies can require residential, industrial, and commercial development projects to provide sites, improvements, and funds for developing public improvements like open space and trails. Project mitigations are usually on-site improvements but may, in special situations, include funds or other provisions for off-site projects like open space acquisition. Sometimes an off-site location can better mitigate a project's impact.

Land development projects in other areas of a county or city may allocate project mitigation funds to a particular trail if the funds flow through a set-aside account dedicated to development of a county- or city-wide system of trail projects. The initial funds could be spent where there is a pending trail opportunity, which need not be within the immediate local area of the impacting land development project. Likewise, future project impact funds could be spent wherever trail acquisition opportunities exist at the time of impact mitigation.

■ Growth-Impact Ordinances

Cities and counties may develop and adopt a growth-impact ordinance that applies to all residential, industrial, and commercial development. The ordinance estimates the impact of each development project on public park and recreational facilities within the development project's local and regional service zones. The ordinance makes provisions whereby the project developer will set aside the lands or monies necessary to offset the project's specific park and recreational impacts.

■ Bonds

Most communities use a variety of bonds (local, regional, and statewide) to raise revenues for public projects. Typically, general-obligation bonds are used to acquire and develop multi-use trails. In most cases, they must be approved by 50 or 60 percent of the voters. Mounting a successful bond campaign is like running any other political campaign. It requires money, participation by local elected officials and business leaders, and lots of hard work. The rewards, however, can be substan-

tial. The Seattle/King County area recently passed an open space bond issue that is providing $33 million for trail acquisition and development.

■ Fiber Optics/Other Utilities

Fiber-optic and utility companies often find trail corridors to be attractive alternatives to street rights-of-way for their underground cables. There are many opportunities to secure funds and improvements for trails by working with these companies. Modern underground cables generally require little maintenance. A reasonable fee can be established by determining the cost of installing a cable on an adjacent street. In large urban areas, this can cost more than $100,000 per mile. (See "Joint Ventures within Your Multi-Use Trail Corridor" in chapter 2.)

■ Real Estate Taxes

Several types of real estate taxes can be used to raise revenues for trail acquisition. A fee (possibly ½ of 1 percent of the sales price) can be assessed on all real estate transactions. The interest on earnest money can be collected into an open space fund. Or an assessment can be made on all property on an annual basis. While all three

methods have been used to raise substantial amounts of money, they should be approached with great caution. They may ignite the wrath of the real estate industry and are generally unpopular with voters. Additionally, they almost always require state enabling legislation, which can be difficult to enact.

■ Dedicated Sales Tax

A portion of the sales tax can be dedicated to acquisition of open space for trails. Action is usually required by the state legislature and possibly a vote of the people at the state or county level. A dedicated sales tax is difficult to obtain, but even a very small dedication of ¼ of 1 percent can raise millions of dollars.

■ Land and Water Conservation Funds

Land and Water Conservation Funds (LWCF) are a specialized type of federal funds distributed through the states. They are available from the National Park Service and administered by a designated state agency. The federal funds are allocated to each state and then to local communities within each state on a competitive basis. The funds are to be used for the acquisition and development of outdoor park and recreational facilities including linear parks and multi-use trails. LWCF monies are generally limited to no more than $150,000 per project on a 50 percent matching basis with another source of public or private funding. In the past few years, project awards have become quite competitive as the federal government has significantly reduced the amount of federal monies available to the National Park Service.

In addition to these sources, research the various funding opportunities that may be available within your state. Several states dedicate a portion of their lottery receipts to open space acquisition and preservation. Other states may offer community development funds for trails that help spark urban renewal. Some trails, located near rivers or lakes, may qualify for fish and wildlife funds if the trail provides access to fishing areas. The possibilities are many, so do not underestimate the diverse resources available as you seek additional acquisition and development funding.

Notes

Chapter 1

1. Roger L. Moore et al., *The Impacts of Rail-Trails: A Study of Users and Nearby Property Owners from Three Trails* (Washington, D.C.: National Park Service, 1992), III:9.

2. Jack Gray, "A Look at Visitors on Wisconsin's Elroy-Sparta Bike Trail" (Madison, Wis., 1989).

Chapter 2

1. Moore, *The Impacts of Rail-Trails*, IV:2.

2. Seattle Engineering Department and Office for Planning, *Evaluation of the Burke-Gilman Trail's Effect on Property Values and Crime* (Seattle: Seattle Engineering Department, May 1987), 3.

3. Seattle Engineering Department, *Burke-Gilman Trail*, 2.

4. James C. Kozlowski and Brett A. Wright, "The Supply of Recreational Lands and Landowner Liability: Recreational Use Statutes Revisited" (Washington, D.C.: Rails-to-Trails Conservancy, photocopy).

5. David C. Hobson, "Developing Joint Ventures," (Fairfax, Va.: Northern Virginia Regional Park Authority, 1991), 1.

6. Rails-to-Trails Conservancy, "Fiber Optics Leasing Along Rail-Trails and Active Railroad Rights-of-Way" (Washington, D.C.: Rails-to-Trails Conservancy, 1990, photocopy), 2-3.

7. Northern Virginia Regional Park Authority, *Manual on Policies and Procedures Governing Easements and Licenses and Non-Park Uses of Northern Virginia Regional Park Authority Property* (Fairfax, Va.: NVRPA, 1989), I:3.

8. American Association of State Highway and Transportation Officials, *Guide for the Development of Bicycle Facilities* (Washington, D.C.: AASHTO, 1991), 41.

Chapter 3

1. Samuel Stokes, *Saving America's Countryside: A Guide to Rural Conservation* (Baltimore: John Hopkins University Press, 1989), 81.

2. AASHTO, *Bicycle Facilities*, 25.

3. U.S. Department of Agriculture and U.S. Department of the Interior, *Design Guide for Accessible Outdoor Recreation*, interim draft (Washington, D.C.: 1990), 22.

4. USDA and USDI, *Accessible Outdoor Recreation*, 16.

5. Continental Bridge, *How to Buy a Bridge*, (Alexandria, Minn.: Continental Bridge, 1991), 8.

6. Continental Bridge, *How to Buy a Bridge*, 8.

7. AASHTO, *Bicycle Facilities*, 28.

8. AASHTO, *Bicycle Facilities*, 34.

9. AASHTO, *Bicycle Facilities*, 33.

10. Kevin Lynch, *Site Planning* (Cambridge, Mass.: MIT Press, 1973), 202.

Chapter 4

1. Rails-to-Trails Conservancy, *Trailblazer* (January-March 1992): 7.

2. AASHTO, *Bicycle Facilities*, 41.

3. "Risk Management: The Defensive Game Plan," *Parks and Recreation* (September 1988): 53.

4. "Risk Management," *Parks and Recreations*: 54.

5. Robert K. Seyried. "Bicycle Facility Design and Legal Liability," *Bicycle Forum* (Winter 11981—82): 19.

6. NVRPA, *Manual*, V:7.

Annotated Resource Directory

This annotated resource directory will guide you to additional information on trail planning, design, and management.

Although few resources relating specifically to multi-use trails exist, numerous publications discuss aspects of trail development. The first section of this directory lists general-interest references; later sections correspond to the chapters of this book. "Additional Bibliographies" provides useful reference and reading lists.

General Interest

American Trails. *Trails for All Americans: Report of the National Trails Agenda Project.* Washington, D.C.: National Park Service, Summer 1990. 21 pp.

Offers an exciting and a comprehensive vision for a nationwide system of trails that is accessible within fifteen minutes of every front door in the country. Discusses the wide-ranging benefits of multi-use trails to health, the economy, conservation, transportation, and recreation. Examines the role of local, state, and federal governments in providing trail infrastructure. Discussion of existing policy and programs and recommendations for change chart the future of an American trail system.

Association of State Wetland Managers, Association of State Floodplain Managers, and National Park Service. *A Casebook in Managing Rivers for Multiple Uses.* Philadelphia: National Park Service, Mid-Atlantic Regional Office, 1991. 79 pp. Maps, photos.

Contains eight case studies, some of which discuss multi-use trail development as a component of river management and preservation. Identifies the objectives, participants, innovative aspects, and accomplishments of each project and discusses their planning processes. Provides contacts within management agencies and bibliographic references.

Burwell, David. "Rails-To-Trails: America's Next Park System," 1987. 8 pp. "Trailblazing for Tomorrow: A National Greenway Network," 1989. 10 pp. Washington, D.C.: Rails-to-Trails Conservancy. Photocopies.

Both of these speeches communicate an exciting vision for development of greenway trails across the American landscape.

Diamant, Rolf, J. Glenn Eugster, and Christopher J. Duerksen. *A Citizen's Guide to River Conservation.* Washington, D.C.: The Conservation Foundation, 1984. 113 pp. Appendices.

An excellent source for projects near rivers. The section on "getting started" applies to river and non-river projects alike. Includes useful appendices and a bibliography.

Flink, Charles A., Robert M. Searns, Loring Schwarz ed., *Greenwyas: A Guide to Planning, Design, and Development.* Washington, D.C.: Island Press and The Conservation Fund, 1993. Illustrations.

A "how-to" guide for planning and designing greenway projects. The guide takes a step-by-step approach to greenway development and addresses many issues that face greenway planners and designers.

Grove, Noel. "Greenways: Paths for the Future." *National Geographic* (June 1990): 77-98.

Provides a well-written introduction to the greenway movement in the United States; cites examples from many greenway projects across the country.

Hoffman, Williams, Lafen & Fletcher. *Illinois Rail-Trails Developer's Handbook*. A component of the *Illinois Railbanking Study* produced for the Illinois Department of Conservation. Silver Spring, Md.: Hoffman, Williams, Lafen & Fletcher, 1990. 56 pp. Appendix.

A guidebook to rail-trail conversion prepared for state and local park planners and managers. Outlines the conversion process from beginning to end. Includes sections on assessment, feasibility studies, gathering local support, trail design, public involvement, and the railroad abandonment process; discusses issues involved in managing public review.

Little, Charles E. *Greenways for America*. Baltimore: Johns Hopkins University Press, 1990. 237 pp. Color photos.

Traces the history of the greenway movement and its efforts to preserve and restore linear open space. Describes many benefits of greenways, particularly those used as bicycle and pedestrian trails, and includes a valuable bibliography of published and unpublished sources.

Lowe, Marcia D. "Alternatives to the Automobile: Transport for Livable Cities." Worldwatch Paper 98 (October 1990). 49 pp. Also: "The Bicycle: Vehicle for a Small Planet." Worldwatch Paper 90 (September 1989). 62 pp. Washington, D.C.: Worldwatch Institute.

Good sources of general facts and statistics regarding the use of bicycles for transportation. Global in scope, with an emphasis on energy efficiency, pollution, comparative usage levels in different countries, and other social factors.

Macdonald, Stuart H. "Greenways: Preserving our Urban Environment." *Trilogy* (November-December 1991): 95-96.

A persuasive piece that makes a case for urban trails and greenways and urges the urban dweller to initiate

and guide trail development through citizen activism.

Mills, Judy. "Clearing the Paths for Us All Where Trains Once Ran." *Smithsonian* (April 1990): 132-41.

Provides a good overview of the rail-trail movement and discusses several rail-trails in states across the nation. Some statistics cited are now outdated.

Montange, Charles H. *Preserving Abandoned Railroad Rights-of-Way for Public Use: A Legal Manual*. Washington, D.C.: Rails-to-Trails Conservancy, 1989. 154 pp. plus appendices.

Examines the legal aspects of preserving abandoned railroad rights-of-way. Topics include an overview of the railroad abandonment process, sale for short line use, public-use conditions, reversionary interests, sources of funding and technical assistance, and legal liability and risk management. Fully footnoted with legal and other citations. Has not been updated to include important court decisions and changes in Interstate Commerce Commission procedures made after 1988.

National Park Service and the National Recreation and Park Association. *Trends—Recreational Trails and Greenways.* Vol. 28. Washington, D.C.: National Park Service and the National Recreation and Park Association, 1991. 48 pp.

Contains eleven essays on the growth and development of multiuse trails and greenways. Topics include greenways as transportation, corporate involvement in trail development, the role of government, and prospects for a nationwide trail system.

Nevel, Bonnie, and Peter Harnik. *Railroads Recycled: How Local Initiative and Federal Support Launched the Rails-to-Trails Movement 1965-1990.* Washington, D.C.: Rails-to-Trails Conservancy, 1990. 100 pp. Photos, maps.

Documents the tremendous success of a little known federal program to spur the development of rail-trails. The impact of $5 million of National Park Service funding assistance is described in 9 case studies. All 9 projects that received federal funding assistance were ultimately built. Of the 126 project applications that could not be funded with the small

congressional appropriation, 82 percent failed to become trails.

Rails-to-Trails Conservancy. *Converting Rails to Trails: A Citizen's Manual for Transforming Abandoned Rail Corridors into Multipurpose Public Paths.* Washington, D.C.: Rails-to-Trails Conservancy, 1990. 49 pp. Appendices.

This manual outlines the many steps involved in creating a rail-trail. Topics explored include assessing the feasibility of a conversion; building a coalition; working with the Interstate Commerce Commission and abandonment regulations; publicizing conversion efforts; working with government agencies; finding funds; working with corporations, elected officials, and railroads; dealing with trail opposition; and managing the trail. The guide contains appendices of relevant addresses, contacts, and resources.

———. "The Nine-Point Blueprint for a State Rails-to-Trails Program." Washington, D.C.: Rails-to-Trails Conservancy, 1990. Photocopy. 28 pp.

Outlines policy recommendations for rail-trail development and cites

state laws that promote trail growth. Useful for trail advocates working to create state policy that encourages trail development.

———. "The Economic Benefits of Rails-to-Trails Conversions to Local Economies." Washington, D.C.: Rails-to-Trails Conservancy, 1989. Photocopy. 20 pp.

A compendium of important facts, study findings, newspaper clippings, and letters from real estate agents and businesses that illustrate the local economic benefits of trails.

Rivers and Trails Conservation Assistance Program. *Economic Impacts of Protecting Rivers, Trails and Greenway Corridors: A Resource Book.* 2d ed. Washington, D.C.: National Park Service, 1991. 80+ pp. Illustrations, tables.

Examines the economic impacts of protecting rivers, trails, and greenway corridors in the following contexts: real property values, expenditures by residents and agencies, commercial uses, tourism, corporate relocation and retention, and public cost reduction. Includes a chapter on how to assess the benefits of projects, plus appendices that contain a sample survey. Also includes references.

Scenic Hudson. "Greenway Fact Sheets, 1-8." Poughkeepsie, N.Y.: Scenic Hudson, 1991. 8 pp. each.

This series of eight pamphlets provides information to assist with the creation and maintenance of local greenways: (1) Walkway Design Guidelines; (2) Trail Construction and Maintenance; (3) Volunteers: Getting the Greenway Underway; (4) Greenway Project Fund Raising; (5) Historic Preservation in Greenways; (6) Starting Your Own Land Trust; (7) Land Preservation Techniques; (8) Liability: Protecting Yourself and Others.

Siehl, George. *Trails Programs in Federal Agencies: A Data Compilation. A Congressional Research Service Report for Congress.* Washington, D.C.: Congressional Research Service, 1989. 81 pp. Tables, charts, maps.

Offers a summary of federal agency trail programs and the extent of future needs. Covers four agencies: the U.S. Forest Service, National Park Service, Fish and Wildlife Service, and Bureau of Land Management.

Stokes, Samuel N., et al. *Saving America's Countryside: A Guide to Rural Conservation.* Baltimore: Johns Hopkins University Press, 1989. 306 pp.

A comprehensive guide to rural conservation at both the public and private levels. Includes a list of federal and nonprofit assistance programs as well as an annotated bibliograpy and twenty-eight case studies.

Untermann, Richard K. *Accommodating the Pedestrian: Adapting Towns and Neighborhoods for Walking and Bicycling.* Seattle: Van Nostrand Reinhold, 1984.

Identifies the pedestrian pathway as the most important public right-of-way. Makes recommendations for improvement of the pedestrian pathway by looking at current American and European trends. Suggests that the American preoccupation with the automobile has blinded us to opportunities for other modes of travel. Behavior patterns of people on foot are discussed, as well as suggested remedies for communities, downtowns, and urban areas. Suggests that only when safe pedestrian access to and from daily activities is provided will there be relief from

air, noise, and energy problems. (Adapted from *Duffy, An Annotated Bibliography*; see "Additional Bibliographies.")

Wilburn, Gary. "Routes of History: Recreational Use and Preservation of Historic Transportation Corridors." Information Series 38. Washington, D.C.: National Trust for Historic Preservation, 1985. 16 pp.

In addition to providing several case studies—the Illinois and Michigan Canal National Heritage Corridor, the Patriot's Path in New Jersey, and the Columbia River Scenic Highway—this discussion of historic transportation corridors identifies sources of nonprofit and federal assistance and provides a selected reading list.

Chapter 1

Wisconsin Department of Natural Resources. "Representative Rails-to-Trails Feasibility Study." Washington, D.C.: Rails-to-Trails Conservancy. Photocopy. 12 pp.

This sample feasibility study illustrates the scope of analysis that the Wisconsin DNR applies to every railroad abandonment. It covers the corridor's location and its natural and built features as well as needs for a rail-trail and its potential usage, land ownership, costs, and operations.

Chapter 2

American Trails. *Trails on Electric Utility Lands: A Model of Public-Private Partnership.* Washington, D.C.: Edison Electric Institute, 1989. 50 pp.

Contains nine case studies of trails and projects across the United States. General discussion covers maintenance, cost, liability, and the impacts of electromagnetic fields on trail users.

Arizona Bicycle Task Force and Arizona State Committee on Trails. "Trail Use Policy." Phoenix: Arizona Department of State Parks, 1991. Photocopy. 5 pp.

Outlines policies for nonmotorized, recreational trail use. The discussion stresses the need for user involvement in the planning and management stages of trail development. Includes an appendix of organizations and agencies and their education programs for responsible trail use.

Bay Area Ridge Trail Council. "Landowner Options: Your Handbook on How Private Landowners Can Participate in the Bay Area Ridge Trail." San Francisco: Bay Area Ridge Trail Council, 1992. 28 pp.

Includes a discussion of easements, leases, and land sales or donations and their various benefits and considerations. Also contains a short list of references and resources and includes sample easements and leases. While it was written specifically for the Bay Area Ridge Trail, much of this handbook can be applied to other projects.

Bicycle Forum. "Bikeway Planning on Trial." Spring 1987: 8-15.

An interview with transportation engineer Alex Sorton, who discusses problematic planning and design issues that can lead to liability problems—many of which can be prevented through planning and design.

Florida Department of Transportation, Safety Office. *Florida Pedestrian Safety Program.* Tallahassee: Florida Department of Transportation, 1992. 75 pp. Photos, tables, appendices.

This strong plan, formed in response to rising pedestrian injuries and deaths in Florida, outlines steps for the planning, engineering, educational efforts, enforcement, and implementation of a pedestrian safety program. Valuable reading, especially for planners of pedestrian facilities that intersect or parallel streets.

Gobster, Paul H. *The Illinois State-wide Trail User Study.* Chicago: U.S. Forest Service, 1990. Available from Rails-to-Trails Conservancy, Illinois Chapter. 61 pp. Tables, photos.

This study's objectives were to determine trail-use patterns and reasons for use, identify perceptions of trail users, and create a demographic profile of users. It focuses on recreational rather than transportation uses (all the interviews were conducted on weekends). The study's major finding: That on urban and suburban trails a significant majority of users come from nearby neighborhoods and that nearly 50 percent of local users use the trail "virtually every week."

Harlem Valley Rails-to-Trails Association. "Harlem Valley Rail-Trail:

Proposal to the Columbia County Board of Supervisors." Copake, N.Y.: Harlem Valley Rails-to-Trails Association, October 1986. Photocopy available from Rails-to-Trails Conservancy. 10 pp.

A model trail proposal. Outlines a multi-use trail proposal prepared by a citizen group for the local government of Columbia County, New York. Briefly presents each key component of a rail-trail proposal—land acquisition, funding, trail use, trail development, operation and maintenance, enforcement, liability, and economic benefits.

Hoffman, Williams, Lafen & Fletcher. *Economic and Tax Implications of Rail-Trails*. A component of the *Illinois Railbanking Study* produced for the Illinois Department of Conservation. Silver Spring, Md.: Hoffman, Williams, Lafen & Fletcher, 1990. 60 pp. Tables.

A broad examination of the social benefits and economic impacts of rail-trails: stimulation of commercial activity, recreational and other social benefits, effect on property values, environmental benefits, fiscal impacts, and potential for revenue generation through right-of-way leasing by utilities.

———. *Illinois Rail-Trails: Landowner and Community Concerns*. A component of the *Illinois Railbanking Study* produced for the Illinois Department of Conservation. Silver Spring, Md.: Hoffman, Williams, Lafen & Fletcher, 1990. 34 pp.

An assessment of the concerns expressed by adjacent property owners and communities about plans to retain abandoned rail lines for use as greenways and recreational trails. Includes a short section on ways for trail proponents to address concerns.

———. *Public Involvement Plan for Illinois Rail-Trails*. A component of the Illinois Railbanking Study produced for the Illinois Department of Conservation. Silver Spring, Md.: Hoffman, Williams, Lafen & Fletcher, 1990. 73 pp. Appendices.

This handbook for property owners, conservationists, and government agencies focuses on how to involve the public in efforts to convert abandoned rail lines to use as greenways and recreational trails. It provides a comprehensive discussion of the public input process, including sections on conflict resolution, techniques for education and outreach, process models, and strategy. Bibliography is brief but helpful.

Howe, Linda. *Keeping Our Garden State Green: A Local Government Guide for Greenway and Open Space Planning*. Mendham, N.J.: Association of New Jersey Environmental Commissions, 1989. 57 pp. Illustrations.

While written for local government agencies and activists in New Jersey, this guide provides a widely applicable outline for planning trail projects. Includes some short case studies and sections on planning tools, implementation, and public relations issues.

Kozlowski, James C., and Brett A. Wright. "State Recreational Use Statutes and Their Applicability to Public Agencies: A Silver Lining or More Dark Clouds?" Photocopy available from Rails-to-Trails Conservancy. 4 pp.

This paper looks at the results of several court cases involving public entity liability for recreational injuries and the effectiveness of recreational-use statutes.

———. "The Supply of Recreational Lands and Landowner Liability: Recreational Use Statutes Revisited." Originally published in *Trends*. Photocopy available from Rails-to-Trails Conservancy. 3 pp.

Reviews the recreational-use statute in relation to the coverage it provides landowners who allow their properties to be used for recreational purposes.

Lawton, Kate. "The Economic Impact of Bike Trails: A Case Study of the Sugar River Trail." 1986. Photocopy available from Rails-to-Trails Conservancy. 16 pp.

An early study of trail users' expenditure levels. Findings support general notions that out-of-area visitors to the trail spend more than local users and that rail-trails are an important factor in drawing tourists to a state.

Macdonald, Stuart. "Building Support for Urban Trails." *Parks and Recreation* (November 1987): 26-33.

This article includes case studies of three urban trail projects in Colorado that vary in scope and success. Fourteen practical recommenda-

tions are drawn from these studies to help future trail proponents.

Maryland-National Capital Park and Planning Commission. "Countywide Trails Plan for Prince George's County, Md." Upper Marlboro, Md., 1975. 40 pp. Maps, photos.

A good example of an integrated, multi-use trail plan for a suburban/rural region. The trails were planned primarily in existing stream-valley parks and integrated with bikeways on the local road system.

Mazour, Leonard P. "Converted Railroad Trails: The Impact on Adjacent Property." Master's thesis, Kansas State University, 1988. 159 pp. Photographs, newspaper articles, maps, surveys.

This study of the adjacent landowners along two trails in Minnesota—the Root River and Luce Line trails—reveals that the concerns of landowners before the trail conversions were greater than the problems actually experienced once trail development had occurred.

Minnesota Department of Natural Resources. "Living Along Trails:

What People Expect and Find." St. Paul: Minnesota Department of Natural Resources, 1979. Photocopy, 1987 (revised), available from Rails-to-Trails Conservancy. 4 pp.

This 1979 study is based on surveys of landowners neighboring two proposed trails and two existing trails in Minnesota. Findings show that their negative expectations of trail impacts—crime, trespassing, weed control, and minimal usage by local people—were not borne out after the trails were established.

———. "Milwaukee Road Corridor Study, Technical Appendix C: Transcript of Telephone Survey with Law Enforcement Officials Along Select Recreational Trails on Former Railroad Grades." St. Paul: Minnesota Department of Natural Resources, 1979. Photocopy available from Rails-to-Trails Conservancy. 21 pp.

This study involved three rail-trails in Wisconsin. Six county sheriffs whose jurisdictions involved one of these three trails were surveyed about the trail's impacts—incidence of crime, landowners' reactions, seasonal usage—and about their general opinions of the trail. Few serious crimes were cited, and, on the whole, the sheriffs viewed the trails as beneficial.

Moore, Roger L., et al. *The Impacts of Rail-Trails: A Study of Users and Nearby Property Owners from Three Trails*. Washington, D.C.: National Park Service, 1992. 100+ pp. Charts, tables.

This study of trail users and neighboring property owners examined two rural trails (in Iowa and Florida) and one suburban trail (in California). The study had four objectives: (1) to explore social benefits and direct economic impact of the trails; (2) to examine the trails' effects on adjacent and nearby property values; (3) to determine the types and extent of problems experienced by trail neighbors; and (4) to develop a profile of users. The findings revealed that (1) trails bring many benefits to communities, including "new money" brought in by tourists; (2) trails either enhance or do not significantly affect property values; (3) problems are minor and, by and large, benefits far outweigh negative impacts; (4) trail users are representative of the local population. This is the first extensive study to examine both users and neighbors of the same trails.

National Park Service and National Parks and Conservation Association. *Toward a Regionwide Network of Trails for the Mid-Atlantic States*. Washington, D.C.: National Park Service and National Parks and Conservation Association, 1992. 25 pp. Appendices, map.

Reports on 147 potential trail and greenway corridors and provides a 27-point action agenda identified by trail interests in the Mid-Atlantic states: Delaware, Maryland, New Jersey, Pennsylvania, Virginia, and West Virginia.

Northern Virginia Regional Park Authority. *Manual on Policies and Procedures Governing Easements and Licenses and Non-Park Uses of Northern Virginia Regional Park Authority Property*. Fairfax, Va.: Northern Virginia Regional Park Authority, 1989. 75 pp.

This manual outlines a set of easements, license agreements, and fees developed to protect trails and parks in the rapidly developing suburbs of Washington, D.C.

Rails-to-Trails Conservancy. "Fiber Optics Leasing Along Rail-Trails and Active Railroad Rights-of-Way." Washington, D.C.: Rails-to-Trails Conservancy, 1990. Photocopy. 6 pp.

Describes ten examples of fiber-optic lease easements and provides contacts in agencies responsible for such agreements.

Rodale Press. "Louis Harris Poll: Pathways for People." Emmaus, Pa.: Rodale Press, 1992. Packet of three documents: Summary, Complete Survey Report, Success Stories.

Survey results show that 72 percent of Americans want safe and accessible "pathways" included in transportation planning and that 59 percent want more government funding devoted to trail development. Packet includes a six-page summary and eleven-page detail of survey results on these and related questions. A twenty-five-page booklet outlines sixteen success stories and includes tables and charts. Also available from Rodale Press: 1991 Harris Poll findings describing Americans' strong interest in bicycling to work when safe paths and lanes are provided.

Scenic Hudson and the National Park Service. *Building Greenways in the Hudson River Valley: A Guide for Action.* Poughkeepsie, N.Y.: Scenic Hudson, 1989. 56 pp.

Contains twelve case studies of different greenway projects in the Hudson River Valley, ranging from canal trails and rail-trails to scenic roads, cultural parks, and hiking trails. Underscores the importance of citizen participation in creating community greenways.

Seattle Engineering Department and Office for Planning. *Evaluation of the Burke-Gilman Trail's Effect on Property Values and Crime.* Seattle: Seattle Engineering Department, May 1987. 42 pp. Executive summary available from Rails-to-Trails Conservancy. 42 pp. Appendices.

Analyzing data gathered through interviews with residents near and adjacent to the trail, real estate agents, and police officers, this study concludes that property values are enhanced by the trail's proximity and that burglaries and incidents of vandalism along the trail are below the neighborhood average.

Toalson, Robert F., and Patricia Sims Hechenberger. *Developing Community Support for Parks and Recreation.* Champaign, Ill.: American Academy for Park and Recreation Administration, 1985. 33 pp. Illustrations.

Written to assist park and recreation agencies in their efforts to build support for local programs. Several chapters—"The Winning Image," "Community Involvement," and "Volunteers and Giving"—are helpful to both government agencies and grass-roots groups involved in trail projects. The book discusses advocacy, planning, coalition building, and construction of multi-use trails.

University of Wisconsin Cooperative Extension Service. *A Look at Visitors on Wisconsin's Elroy-Sparta Bike Trail.* Madison, Wis.: Recreation Resources Center, University of Wisconsin Extension, 1989. 45 pp. Appendices. Eleven-page summary available from Rails-to-Trails Conservancy.

Examines trip characteristics, trip-related expenditures, users' geographic origins, and other social and demographic factors. Findings reveal that (1) avoiding dangerous auto traffic was the top reason for using the trail; (2) Fifty thousand visitors in 1988 brought $1,257,000 to the local economy in the form of direct expenditures; and (3) over 50 percent of trail users came from out of state—20 percent from Illinois and 10 percent from Minnesota.

Chapter 3

American Association of State Highway Transportation Officials. *Guide for the Development of Bicycle Facilities.* Washington, D.C.: AASHTO, 1991. 44 pp. Photos, diagrams.

Many highway engineers and transportation officials consider this document the primary authority on bikeway design. It provides planning, design, and construction guidelines and makes operation and maintenance recommendations for all types of bicycle facilities, including those independent from roadways. Note: This 1991 edition updates the earlier version.

Arkansas Trails Council and Arkansas State Parks. *Construction and Maintenance of Horse Trails in Arkansas State Parks.* Little Rock: Arkansas State Parks, 1983. 32 pp. Diagrams.

Offers design specifications and guidelines for horse trails and their amenities.

BRW. *The Jefferson County Open Space Master Plan.* Golden, Colo.: Jefferson County Open Space Program, 1989. 43 pp. Maps, color photos.

Provides extensive analysis of the trail corridor as part of the overall open space plan. Also details design guidelines for paved and unpaved multi-use trails and considers both recreational and transportation usage of the trail system.

Continental Bridge. *How to Buy a Bridge.* Alexandria, Minn.: Continental Bridge, 1991. 24 pp. Illustrations, photos, charts.

A helpful guide for purchasing prefabricated bridges.

Gay Mackintosh, ed. *Preserving Communities and Corridors.* Washington, D.C.: Defenders of Wildlife, 1989. 96 pp. Illustrations.

Includes five articles that advocate preservation of migration corridors as a practical and necessary approach to maintaining biological diversity. Illustrates how greenways and linear parks are key to environmental preservation.

Duffy, Hugh. *Surface Materials for Multiple-Use Pathways.* Lakewood, Colo.: National Park Service, Rocky Mountain Region, 1992. 4 pp.

Provides a framework and establishes criteria for evaluating what surface types should be considered for a multi-use path. Outlines design requirements, guidelines, and standards for surface materials. A useful introduction to an important aspect of trail design.

EDAW. *Trail Construction Guidelines.* Denver: Colorado Division of Parks and Outdoor Recreation, 1981. 33 pp. Illustrations, appendix.

A concise introduction to basic trail design—alignment, surface materials, and the trail's relationship to surrounding environments and structures.

Facilities Planning Committee of the Arizona Bicycle Task Force. *Arizona Bicycle Facilities Planning and Design Guidelines.* Arizona Department of Transportation, Engineering Records Section, 1988. 122 pp. Illustrations, diagrams, appendices.

A comprehensive document with useful diagrams and text on designing bicycle and multi-use paths.

General Services Administration. *Uniform Federal Accessibility Standards.* Government Printing Office, 1988. 89 pp.

Describes the minimum standards for designing and constructing facilities accessible to users with a wide range of physical disabilities. While the document does not address trails, the sections on historic buildings, restroom facilities, ramps, parking, and loading facilities will be essential in ensuring adequate design and construction of trail-related facilities.

Jarrell, Temple R. *Bikeways: Design—Construction—Programs.* Arlington, Va.: National Recreation and Park Association, 1974. 180 pp.

A thorough examination of the design and construction of bikeways. Some sections of the book are out dated (for example, funding programs that no longer exist are cited), but much of the book is relevant and valuable for planners of bicycle facilities. Provides design diagrams, case studies, and specifics of design such as drainage, bridges, and surface choice.

Keller, Kit, and Bicycle Federation of America. *Mountain Bikes on Public Lands: A Manager's Guide to the State of the Practice.* **Washington, D.C.: Bicycle Federation of America, 1990. 68 pp.**

Though written with backcountry trails in mind, this guide contains sections on "multiple-use management," "balancing user concerns," and other topics that are valuable to planners of multi-use trails.

Merriman, Kristin. "Multiple-Use Trails: A Question of Courtesy." *Outdoor Ethics.* **Vol. 7 (Summer 1988).**

Discusses some of the ethics of multiple-use rail-trails. The article's most important suggestion: Resolve multiple-use conflicts early in the planning process. Merriman notes that other forms of transportation, such as automobiles, boats, and airplanes, have laws regulating their use, but laws on how trails should be used are poor or lacking. (Adapted from *Duffy, An Annotated Bibliography*; see "Additional Bibliographies.")

McCoy, Michael, and Mary Alice Stoner. *Mountain Bike Trails: Techniques for Design, Construction and Maintenance.* **Missoula, Mont.: Bikecentennial, 1992. 18 pp. Photos, diagrams.**

A well-written, concise guide intended to assist trail managers in designing and maintaining trails for mountain bike use.

National Park Service and National Recreation and Park Association. *Design* **(Winter 1989, Spring 1989, Summer 1989, Fall 1989). 64 pp. each.**

Making recreational areas accessible to people of all abilities was the subject of all four issues of Design in 1989. Design is a quarterly publication of the Park Practice Program, a cooperative effort of the National Park Service and the National Recreation and Park Association.

National Wildlife Federation. *A Citizen's Guide to Protecting Wetlands.* **Washington, D.C.: National Wildlife Federation, 1989. 64 pp. Photos, government-agency contact lists.**

Outlines the strategies and processes citizens can use to protect wetlands.

Includes guides to federal and state laws that protect these areas.

Olson, Jana. *A Trail Manual.* **Oakland, Calif.: East Bay Regional Park Authority, 1976. 75 pp.**

An excellent set of guidelines created for the development of multiuse trails in the East Bay region near San Francisco. Discusses a range of trail users including bicyclists, hikers, and equestrians.

Pugh, Ben. "A Bicycle Parking Cookbook." Excerpted from the 2010 Sacramento City/County Bikeway Master Plan. North Highlands, Calif.: Ben Pugh, 1991. Photocopy. 32 pp. Diagrams.

Provides good information on bicycle racks (organized by security level) and includes a comprehensive set of drawings that highlight positive and negative aspects of bicycle-parking facilities. Contains a partial list of equipment suppliers.

Project for Public Spaces. *User Analysis: An Approach to Park Planning and Management.* **Washington, D.C.: American Society of Landscape Architects, 1982. 54 pp. Photographs.**

Describes the process of analyzing how people use parks; includes case studies using analysis techniques and discusses the whys, whens, and hows of such evaluations. Methods presented can help identify user needs and suggest solutions for meeting needs and avoiding conflicts.

Seier, David. "Urban Trails." *Grist* (Summer 1990): 25-28.
Discusses the design and maintenance of urban trails; also provides information on signs. *Grist* is a quarterly publication of the Park Practice Program, a cooperative effort of the National Park Service and the National Recreation and Park Association.

Seyried, Robert K. "Bicycle Facility Design and Legal Liability." *Bicycle Forum* 8 (Winter 1981-2): 18-21.
Provides solid information on the factors involved in lawsuits stemming from accidents on bicycle facilities. Good discussion of what constitutes negligence coupled with facts from a settled case to highlight each point.

Ski Industries America. *Cross-Country USA Operations Manual.* McLean, Va.: Ski Industries America, 1984. 335 pp. Diagrams.
A detailed workbook on the design, construction, maintenance, and operation of cross-country skiing trails and facilities. An executive summary providing an overview of the subject is also available.

Trapp, Suzanne, et al. *Signs, Trails, and Wayside Exhibits.* Stevens Points, Wis.: University of Wisconsin — Stevens Point Foundation Press, 1992. 108 pp. Diagrams, color photos.
An excellent source for developing a wide range of trail signs, this book includes information on materials and colors. The emphasis is on how to make a visual impact and effectively convey a message through the use of signs. The 100-plus color photos offer inspiring ideas.

United Ski Industries Association. *Cross Country Close to Home: A Ski Area Development Manual.* McLean, Va.: United Ski Industries Association, 1989. 190 pp.
A comprehensive workbook on the design and operations of cross-country skiing facilities. Focuses on development of ski areas and includes chapters on history and future trends, trail design, marketing and promotions, and developing partnerships.

U.S. Department of Transportation. *Manual on Uniform Traffic Control Devices (MUTCD), Bicycle Facilities.* Washington, D.C.: U.S. Superintendent of Documents, 1988. Approx. 200 pp. Diagrams, color graphics.
This book is the accepted standard for all road and bikeway signs. Part IX, "Traffic Controls for Bicycle Facilities," includes twenty-four pages on bikeway signs. A number of sections discuss signs and signal systems for trails used by both bicyclists and pedestrians. Many color graphics show standard sign shapes, designs, and dimensions.

U.S. Equal Employment Opportunity Commission and U.S. Department of Justice. *The Americans with Disabilities Act Questions and Answers.* Washington, D.C.: Government Printing Office, July 1991. 19 pp.
Provides answers to a series of questions relating to implementation of the Americans with Disabilities Act,

including public spaces such as parks.

U.S. Forest Service. *Standard Specifications for Construction of Trails.* Publication no. EM 7720-102. Washington D.C.: U.S. Forest Service, 1984.

"This is an excellent reference document for trail specifications for all trail designers. . . . General specifications, earthwork, drainage, structures, surfacing, incidental construction, and materials are included." (Annotation from *Duffy, An Annotated Bibliography*; see "Additional Bibliographies.")

U.S. Forest Service and National Park Service. *Design Guide for Accessible Outdoor Recreation.* Washington, D.C.: Government Printing Office. Forthcoming, 1993.

Will offer a comprehensive set of guidelines to make recreational facilities (including trails) accessible to people of all abilities.

Velo Quebec. *Technical Handbook of Bikeway Design: Planning, Design, Implementation.* Montreal: Velo Quebec, 1992. 169 pp. Photos, diagrams.

A thorough handbook and reference manual for those planning bicycle facilities. Discusses many types of facilities and a detailed range of planning considerations, including grades, curves, intersections, and bicycle parking. The many photos and diagrams provide excellent visual examples of bicycle facilities. While the "Bicycle and the Law" section applies only to Canada, most information is useful to all designers and engineers.

White, John. "Why Bother to Protect Prairies Along Railroads?" Arlington, Va.: The Nature Conservancy, 1987. Photocopy.

In this speech presented at the Ninth American Prairie Conference, the author describes why it is important to save prairie along abandoned railroad tracks: in some midwestern states, it is the only native prairie remaining.

Chapter 4

Adams, Christopher. *A Trails Study: Neighbor and User Viewpoints, Maintenance Summary.* Oakland, Calif.: East Bay Regional Park District, 1978. 58 pp.

Examines two urban trails in the San Francisco Bay Area: impacts of the trails on neighboring residents, characteristics of trail users, and maintenance issues.

Gold, Seymour M. "A Basic Risk Management Library." *Trends* 26, no. 4 (1989): 45-48.

Reviews public agency responsibility for safety in recreational areas and provides a comprehensive list of publications that should be part of the public agency library. Each book cited also contains a bibliography of additional references.

Hahn, Tom, and David Eubanks. "An Analysis of Five Existing Trails Converted from Abandoned Railroad Tracks." Chicago: Open Lands Project, 1985. Photocopy available from Rails-to-Trails Conservancy. 17 pp.

Examines the physical and cultural aspects of five midwestern rail-trails. Discussion covers usage levels and economic impacts of tourist spending in communities adjacent to the trail.

Minnesota Department of Natural Resources. *Interpretive Plan for State*

Trails. St. Paul: Minnesota Department of Natural Resources, Trail Planning Section, Trails and Waterways Unit, 1987. 62 pp. Charts.

While this plan was designed specifically for Minnesota, much of the text is valuable to those elsewhere who may be considering an interpretive component for a trail. The plan identifies the educational benefits of historical and geological interpretation and describes some projects in Minnesota. Includes recommendations for choosing an appropriate type of interpretative program and a step-by-step guide for its design and execution.

National Park Service and National Recreation and Park Association. *Design for Maintenance: A Park Management Aid.* Washington, D.C.: Government Printing Office, 1983. 75 pp.

Discusses maintenance requirements and the importance of considering maintenance when designing and planning park and recreation facilities. Diverse projects such as traffic islands are cited in case studies, but many of the guide's recommendations for upkeep and safety may be applied to multi-use trails.

National Recreation and Park Association. "Risk Management: The Defensive Game Plan." *Parks and Recreation* (September 1988): 53-55.

An effective article describing basic but often-overlooked ways to reduce the risk of liability problems.

Northern Virginia Regional Park Authority. *Manual on Policies and Procedures Governing Easements and Licenses and Non-Park Uses of Northern Virginia Regional Park Authority Property.* Fairfax, Va.: Northern Virginia Regional Park Authority, 1989. 75 pp.

This manual outlines a set of easements, license agreements, and fees developed to protect trails and parks in the rapidly developing suburbs of Washington, D.C.

U.S. Forest Service. *Trails Management Handbook.* FSH 2309.18. Washington, D.C.: U.S. Forest Service, 1985.

"Discussions cover trail planning, development, preconstruction and construction activities, and trail operations and maintenance. Numerous exhibits showing forms used, and suggested construction details are included." (Annotation from

Duffy, An Annotated Bibliography; see "Additional Bibliographies.")

Volunteers for the Outdoors. *Adopt-a-Trail Handbook: A Guide to Volunteer Trail Maintenance in the Southwest.* Albuquerque: New Mexico Natural Resources Department, 1984. 52 pp. Illustrations.

This description of the "Adopt a Trail" program in New Mexico illustrates how volunteers can help assume responsibility for trail maintenance. While much of this guide pertains to backcountry hiking trails, it raises relevant points for multi-use trails on such topics as safety, the responsibilities of trail managers and groups that adopt trails, and the merits of "Adopt a Trail" programs.

Chapter 5

Association of Bay Area Governments. "Financing and Implementing the Bay Trail: Tools and Strategies." Bay Area Technical Report no. 1. Oakland, Calif.: Association of Bay Area Governments, 1989. 30 pp.

While many of the potential funding sources are specific to California, this document provides a valuable compendium of potential funding sources and strategies, especially for trails and trail networks in multi-jurisdictional areas.

Carver, John. *Boards That Make a Difference.* San Francisco: Jossey-Bass, 1990. 242 pp.
Includes guidelines for bylaws. Chapter 10, "Focusing on Results: Clarifying and Sustaining the Organization's Mission," is especially useful.

Flanagan, Joan. *The Grass Roots Fundraising Book: How to Raise Money in Your Community.* Chicago: Contemporary Books, 1982.
A comprehensive compilation of the why, how, and who in raising money for grass-roots initiatives.

Ingram, Richard T. *Ten Basic Responsibilities for Nonprofit Boards.* Washington, D.C.: National Center for Nonprofit Boards, 1988. 22 pp.
Discusses responsibilities of boards and individual board members. Charts the evolution of governance structure as organizations change over time.

Kunofsky, Judith, and M. Thomas Jacobson. *Tools for the Greenbelt: A Citizen's Guide to Protecting Open Space.*

San Francisco: People for Open Space, 1985. 70 pp.
A well-organized handbook for activists seeking to create greenways in their communities. Provides detailed information on zoning and other techniques for protecting land use. Funding techniques popular at the date of publication are outlined. Includes case studies of two California counties, Marin and Solano.

Lord, James Gregory. *The Raising of Money.* Cleveland: Third Sector Press, 1988. 135 pp.
Focuses on the up-front planning and preparation essential for effective fundraising. Its themes are that an organization doesn't have needs—it has solutions and opportunities—and that funds are not handouts or charity but an investment. Easy-to-read book.

Maryland Department of Natural Resources. *Guide to the Northern Central Railroad Trail.* Silver Spring, Md.: Howling Wolf Publications, 32 pp. Maps, photos.
This colorful booklet is a good prototype for a visitor's guide. It combines general trail information with detailed maps that depict historic sites,

points of interest, restrooms, stores, and boating access.

Minnesota Department of Natural Resources. *Along the Trail: A Guide to Nature on the Heartland Trail.* St Paul: Department of Natural Resources. 24 pp. Illustrations.
A model trail nature guide that lists regional plants and animals, harmful plants to avoid, and wildflowers arranged by color.

Moore, Roger L., Vicki LaFarge, and Thomas Martorelli. *Organizing Outdoor Volunteers.* Boston: Appalachian Mountain Club, 1987. 86 pp. Photos.
A manual for partnerships between volunteer organizations and government land managers. Documents the "hands-on" approach of the Appalachian Mountain Club's volunteer project and provides guidelines for beginning a volunteer program, recruiting volunteers, and developing a volunteer organization. Includes a reading list divided topically (for example, board development and fundraising) and lists contacts for volunteer projects.

National Park Service. *National Recreation Trails: Information and*

Application Procedures for Designation. Washington, D.C.: Government Printing Office, 1983. 13 pp.

Outlines the procedures and criteria for requesting that a trail be designated a "National Recreation Trail." (A National Recreation Trail is one of the four types of trails in the National Trails System. Almost any trail will qualify. It may be owned and operated by the federal government, a state or local government, a nonprofit organization, or the private sector.)

————. *1991 Annual Report and Program Brochure—Rivers, Trails & Conservation Programs.* 16 pp. Photos.

Provides an introduction to the various technical assistance programs that the National Park Service offers to conserve rivers and establish trails on land outside the NPS system. Includes regional contacts for the Rivers, Trails and Conservation Assistance program and lists the FY 91 funded projects and partners, which include many rail-trails and greenways.

O'Connell, Brian. *The Board Member's Book: Making a Difference in Voluntary*

Organizations. New York: The Foundation Center, 1985. 208 pp.

Using the American Heart Association as an example, Chapter 13, "Fundraising," outlines procedures for raising funds and describes thirteen types of fundraising initiatives.

Panas, Jerold. *Mega Gifts.* Chicago: Pluribus Press, 1984. 231 pp.

An easy-to-read book on what motivates people to give large gifts. Documented from the author's research and twenty years of experience in the fundraising field.

Rails-to-Trails Conservancy. "ISTEA Action Plan." Washington, D.C.: Rails-to-Trails Conservancy, 1992. Photocopy. 8 pp. Appendices.

Written to help familiarize citizen activists—particularly those working on rail-trail projects—with the basics of the 1991 Intermodal Surface Transportation Efficiency Act (ISTEA) and to outline the act's potential as a funding source. Appendices include Federal Highway Administration memoranda regarding transportation enhancements and simplified procedures for bicycle and pedestrian projects, an RTC fact sheet about the enhancements

program, and a fact sheet about the National Recreational Trails Act.

Turner, Helen. *A Guide to the Illinois Prairie Path.* Wheaton, Ill.: The Illinois Prairie Path, 1991. 32 pp. Illustrations.

An innovative guide to one of the nation's oldest rail-trails. This booklet, which includes information on geology, trees, flowers, birds, and animals, can serve as a model for trail managers.

ADDITIONAL BIBLIOGRAPHIES

Duffy, Hugh. *An Annotated Bibliography of Non-Motorized Trails Literature.* Denver: National Park Service, December 1989. 28 pp.

A functional bibliography with detailed annotations. Topical sections cover building citizen support; trail planning; types of trails; and trail construction, maintenance, and management.

————. *Pathways Bibliography.* Denver: National Park Service, April 1992. 2 pp.

A short, well-chosen list of important sources for trail planning. Not annotated.

Harvey, Thomas R. *Directory of Technical Assistance Materials for Trails Development and Maintenance.* Washington, D.C.: American Hiking Society, 1989. 42 pp.

This bibliography of annotated and nonannotated sources is divided into two sections: the "Technical Assistance Materials Directory," which cites publications, and the "Technical Expertise Directory," which lists resource groups by state.

Hoffman, Williams, Lafen & Fletcher. *Illinois Rail-Trails: A Selected Bibliography. A component of the Illinois Rail-banking Study* produced for the Illinois Department of Conservation. Silver Spring, Md.: Hoffman, Williams, Lafen & Fletcher, 1990. 18 pp.

Lists current references that address issues involved in the creation of rail-trails and greenways. Categories include economic impacts, legal issues, planning and assessments, studies of existing trails, and physical development of trails. This bibliography is not annotated.

Contributors and Supporters

Trails for the Twenty-first Century would not have been possible without the cooperation of the National Park Service, Recreation Resources Assistance Division.

Rails-to-Trails Conservancy also received generous support from the American Conservation Association, the National Endowment for the Arts, the Andy Warhol Foundation, the United States Department of Transportation, Federal Highway Administration, and the New-Land Foundation.

Acknowledgments

I would like to offer special recognition to several contributing authors. First, Elizabeth Porter of the National Park Service deserves my heartfelt appreciation for her overall involvement with the manual and also for writing the "Public Involvement" and "Trail Protection" sections of the book and researching the "Meeting the Needs of Adjacent Landowners" section.

Thanks also to three other contributing writers: Peter Harnik of the Rails-to-Trails Conservancy, who wrote the "Tunnels" and "'Friends of the Trail' Groups" sections; Anne Lusk of Stowe, Vermont, author of the "Promoting and Marketing Your Trail" section; and Dan Cupper of Harrisburg, Pennsylvania, author of the "Historic Preservation" section.

A warm thank you to Bob Patten of the Rails-to-Trails Conservancy for his extensive work on the annotated resource directory. Thanks also to Susan Bloomfield of the National Park Service for her research on trail user etiquette and to Bernie Dahl of Purdue University's School of Horticulture and Landscape Architecture for his input on using university resources for trail planning and design. In addition, April Moore deserves special recognition for her skillful copyedit of the draft text.

In January 1991, a dedicated group of individuals participated in the Rails-to-Trails Conservancy/National Park Service Design and Management Symposium. Their expertise and thoughtful insights developed the foundation for this manual. Each of them deserves special recognition:

Mark Ackelson
Iowa Natural Heritage Foundation,
Des Moines, Iowa

Stan Bales
Bureau of Land Management,
Susanville, California

Diana Balmori
Balmori Associates,
New Haven, Connecticut

Ardon Belcher
Minnesota Department
of Natural Resources,
Bemidji, Minnesota

David Burwell
Rails-to-Trails Conservancy,
Washington, D.C.

Mary Austin Crofts
Blaine County Recreation Department,
Hailey, Idaho

Bob Doyle
East Bay Regional Park District,
Oakland, California

Hugh Duffy
National Park Service,
Denver, Colorado

Steve Elkinton
National Park Service,
Washington, D.C.

Steve Fiala
East Bay Regional Park District,
Oakland, California

Charles A. Flink
Greenways, Inc.,
Cary, North Carolina

Eric DeLony
National Park Service,
Washington, D.C.

Chuck Frayer
U.S. Forest Service,
Portland, Oregon

Peter Harnik
Rails-to-Trails Conservancy,
Washington, D.C.

Susan Henley
American Hiking Society,
Washington, D.C.

David Hobson
Northern Virginia Regional
Park Authority,
Fairfax, Virginia

Peggy Johnson
Paint Creek Trailway Commission,
Rochester, Michigan

Jack Keene
Anne Arundel County Department
of Parks and Recreation,
Annapolis, Maryland

Peter Lagerwey
Seattle Engineering Department,
Seattle, Washington

Roger Lohr
Ski Industries America,
McLean, Virginia

Anne Lusk
American Trails,
Stowe, Vermont

Roger Moore
North Carolina State University,
Raleigh, North Carolina

Elizabeth Porter
National Park Service,
Washington, D.C.

Tom Ross
National Park Service,
Washington, D.C.

Robert M. Searns
Urban Edges,
Denver, Colorado

William T. Spitzer
National Park Service,
Washington, D.C.

Merle Van Horne
National Park Service,
Washington D.C.

Susan Wood
Rails-to-Trails Conservancy
of Pennsylvania,
Paoli, Pennsylvania

Karen-Lee Ryan
September 1993

Index